It's <u>Your</u>

Charles G. Bird, MBA

This Product uses O*NET-TM Career Exploration Tools, version as of August 2015. The trademark logo or icon for the

O*NET-TM IN IT bug is:

This book may include material used by:
O*NET Interest ProfilerTM
O*NET Work Importance LocatorTM
O*NET Computerized Interest ProfilerTM
O*NET Work Importance ProfilerTM (computerized)
O*NET Ability ProfilerTM.

About the Author: Charles G. Bird, MBA

I earned a BA in Psychology and and MBA at Wayne State University in Detroit, Michigan. I completed training at the University of Wisconsin-Stout in Vocational Evaluation and Work Adjustment. I also studied Guidance & Counseling at Oakland University.

I am a past member of the American Personnel & Guidance Association, and the Vocational Evaluation & Work Adjustment Association.

My work experiences include: Vocational Evaluator, Rehabilitation Counselor, and careers as a State Energy Project Coordinator, Material Handling Business Manager, and Information Systems Manager. He has worked in the private sector, the public sector, been self-employed and had business partners.

I recently co-designed and delivered a series of 8 workshops specifically designed for short-term and long-term unemployed, including the never employed, and those seeking their first jobs. Topics covered included Coping & Dealing with Long Term Unemployment, Motivation, Job Loss Grief, Using O*NET, Using My Next Move, Networking for Beginners, Job Keeping Skills, "What Do Employers Want?", Informational Interviewing, Problem Solving, Goal Attainment, "Finding Your Most Rewarding Job", and more.

I have completed this book and it's companion, "It's Your Life Workbook". I am producing a documentary about the Great Storm of 1913 and any such other projects as catch my interest.

This book is dedicated to my wife, Linda.

I hope that you find the material interesting, motivating, and useful to you in getting your most rewarding jobs and careers.

Table of Contents

Part 1: Preparation (Being prepared is not just for scouts).

Once upon a time, a group of ants spent a summer's day collecting grain. As they toiled and struggled to bring it back to their home, the anthill, a grasshopper happened by.

"What are you doing?" the grasshopper asked. "We're collecting grain to store for the winter" they replied. "That's silly" said the grasshopper, "there's food everywhere and in abundance." And he hopped away.

That fall, the grasshopper came upon the ants once again and asked "what are you doing?" "We're drying the grain we collected, so that it will last all winter" they answered. "That's silly, there's food everywhere about us" he retorted, and hopped away.

Many weeks later, on a cold, and snowy day, the grasshopper approached the anthill and called out "help me, I've no food to eat and you're so <u>lucky</u> you have plenty, surely you can spare a bite for me." "Sorry" replied the ants, "we've stored up enough for us for the entire winter it is true, but it wasn't luck, we prepared, as you should have. Now go and find your own food, maybe you will be as lucky."

With a hat's off to Aesop and a slight fracturing of one of his tales, the moral remains the same, you must "prepare for success." That is the surest path to being "lucky."

What does it mean to "be prepared" when it comes to your next and most rewarding job and career?

Do you recognize opportunities? Suppose you came across someone seated across from you at a wedding, would you know to add them to your network? Would you find out if they had any good job leads or just dismiss them since you didn't know them? The next time you are in a restaurant or waiting in line somewhere, imagine this: "what if the guy next to you was a CEO or a vice-president and who could see to it you were hired. Would you discover it? How would you find out?

How much do you really know about work and jobs? Have you really explored your own, yes, your own options?

While you are out traveling about your daily life, look around at the buildings you see. Ever wonder what goes on inside this building or that? Does it look like someplace you might like to work? What do they do? What could you do there?

Suppose you had a magic key that permitted you to walk into anyone's office and leave your resume, would you know whose office to walk into?

What if you saw a sign for a Job Fair as you were driving, would you have a resume with you to hand to one of the employers there? If you did drop in, would you know which employers you were interested in meeting? Would you know how to get them interested in you?

Do you know your top three, four or five best, most rewarding jobs? Do you know where to find them or jobs like them, near you?

All of this and more is what "being prepared" is. Being ready! Ready for what? Ready for whatever comes your way. It is being "lucky" by being prepared when opportunity comes your way.

"Ability is of little account without opportunity." — Napoleon (1769-1821) Emperor of France and general.

The entire career process and job hunt process is a set of defined steps that you take. The less you know, the less prepared you are, the less you get. The less pay, the less benefits, the less rewards, intrinsic and extrinsic you receive. The less you know, the fewer options you have and the narrower your options are.

The less you know the less fulfilled your life and career will be. The more you will drift. The less control over your own life and destiny you will have. Less opportunity.

This would be a terrible waste.

The less prepared you are, the more others will determine what will happen to you. They will be able to intimidate you into taking less than you are worth. They will be able to force you to do things you don't want to do, work hours you don't want to work. They'll be able to tell you whether you can continue to work for them. They will be able to outsource your job or send it offshore, along with hundreds and thousands of others.

They are in charge and they do not let you forget it. Got a bad boss, too bad. Got bad working conditions, too bad. Want time off? You can have it ... if they say so.

Not all jobs are for "bad companies." Not all bosses are "bad." Even good companies have a way of taking charge of you and your career. You need to be careful when you have a good job in a good company. Bad things can happen to them as well.

They can be taken over by a bigger company or put out of business by an unforeseen change in business conditions, by a competitor and even economic catastrophes. When businesses merge, the rule of thumb is, "somebody has to go". Which somebody will it be? You?

Stress, anxiety, financial worries, stability, depression, tension, pressure, hopelessness, all accompany us in modern life. For many of us, we do the best we can working in these conditions not by choice but by default, we see or have no other options. If we feel we have no other options, we will see no way out.

This is not the way our lives should be. We need to see all of our choices and to understand which ones would be best for us and therefore for our communities.

Instead of being fearful about what will befall us, we should be, you should be, prepared to take charge of your life.

This is not to say that you will be able to get your "dream" job or that everyone's idea of a "dream" job is even the same. They are not. Money isn't the big motivator for everyone. It is nice. It is a form of power, the power to make things be like you want them to be. It is not all there is. Alone, it is not what makes work rewarding even though it is a very measurable reward.

Do you want to be in charge? Make the decisions? Do you want to conquer? Do you want to explore new territory? Do you want excitement? Do you want comfort and joy in your family and your community? Do you want to help those less fortunate. Do you want to help animals? Do you want to see tangible results for your efforts? Perhaps you want to make a difference, one that you may never see, know or otherwise experience? Do you crave adventure? Security? Glamour and fame? Obscurity and anonymity? A rich social life with many friends and non-stop action and activity? Or maybe a few, good friends and a quieter, more peaceful life. Indoors or outdoors or a mix, what would you choose? City, suburbs or country life? Mountains, seashores, prairies? Variable weather or more temperate.

The more you understand yourself and the things you want in your life, the more likely you are to have them.

This isn't the "positive thinking." There is a place in this world for that but thinking alone won't do it. It takes action. But actions can be misguided, ill-timed , erroneous and come to naught, especially if you lack proper and sufficient information.

Evaluation:

The purpose of this book is to help you evaluate. Evaluate yourself from the career and job perspective. What is evaluation?

Definition: Evaluation is the process of placing, or determining, relative values.

Evaluation provides a basis for making comparisons. This book, and the accompanying workbook, will give you tools to evaluate yourself and the work world, to help lead you to success. Of course, there is no guarantee you will be successful and I'd suggest you not trust anyone who says their book will guarantee results, at least not too much. But the tools you will work with in the these books have worked for others and they can work for you.

This book will give you direction, tools, guidance and encourage you to take action, actions that can lead to your success.

Success Defined:

Success is finding and obtaining your most rewarding job and career.

It will take both thought (thinking) and action (effort) on your part but it will be easy for you to see the value of each and every step that we take.

For example, we spend a lot of time on helping you to investigate the many ways work is rewarding, and then direct *you* to determine which of those rewards *you* want. If you want a stable career helping others, you will be able to see it as what you want compared to all the other things there are and that *you* don't want. You'll know why you want that. You will find resources for you to determine potential jobs and careers that offer those rewards. You will be able to identify the possible jobs you can get now, and later, with or without additional training or education. In other words you will see your own potential career path(s).

Since life presents many obstacles to us on our career and life path, we add in tools that help us deal with them. Problem solving, goal attainment, stress and stress reduction, and motivational resources and how to tap into yours.

Sometimes life is stressful, on the job or when out of work. Sometimes, the loss of a job impacts us so much that we can scarcely overcome our feelings about it, let alone move on. There are tools and techniques to help you with these too.

When you do have a solid feel for your own career path you can then take the steps that will help you get that next most rewarding job. We spend time going through each step of the process and give you insights into what works best at each stage. We show you ways to beat your competition or eliminate it entirely, by being the only one considered for a job that was created just for you.

You have the right to as rewarding a career as you possibly can obtain. You have the right to choose your rewards and to obtain them. With this book and your effort you can achieve them. It will not be a matter of luck, it will be a matter of knowing more than you did and using your new found knowledge to succeed. You will because of the five "P's", Proper Preparation Prevents Poor Performance and they lead to success.

When I set out to write this book, I set a goal of writing 250 pages, as this first draft is written, it is 262 pages in length. It will be re-written, edited and revised prior to publication.

It was my goal to write a book designed to help people like *you*, get their next and most rewarding job and career. I achieved my goal, to write this book, and I believe you can achieve yours too!

Directions: Take your time and work through the material because it is your future and you are worth it. Putting in time here can make you money, lead you to better jobs and more rewarding career. It can save you the grief that goes with bad jobs. Work on your future!

"The past is written in ink, the future in pencil." - Author

Chapter 1: The Beginning

"And suddenly you know: It's time to start something new and trust the magic of beginnings." — Meister Eckhart (1259 - 1327) German theologian and philosopher)

Where do we begin?

The basic job hunt sequence is deceptively simple: 1) need a job, 2) apply for a job, 3) interview, 4) get hired.

It should be so easy, right? Of course, that's an over-simplification. Even the first step, "need a job", isn't as straight-forward as it sounds.

How do you come to realize you need a job? Someone, your parents or a friend for example, may say to you, "you need a job." Maybe you look around and want things and figured out that for you, the only way to get them was to earn them. Maybe you tried stealing them, got caught, paid for your crime and now want a legitimate, acceptable way to earn a living. Maybe you are the son or daughter in a wealthy family and they're cutting you off, so now you have to earn your own way, or you reject their wealth and want to earn your own.

Maybe you are a twenty or thirty something who has sponged off, ermm lived with, their family, a "failure to launch" and one day you just woke up and wanted your independence. Speaking of independence, maybe you are a second or third generation welfare recipient and don't want to be enslaved by the "free money, food, healthcare and housing" that extended welfare offers. The enslavement that robs you of your self-respect and your motivation. Maybe the politicians in your state have changed the rules and you will no longer get lifetime welfare benefits, and so now you have to think in terms of "get a job."

Perhaps you're one of the many, many people who have simply lost their job.

Outsourcing, down-sizing, right-sizing, globalized, screwed-up-and-got-canned, take-this-job-and-shove-it quit and lots of other reasons for "lost-my-job and now I need a new one" realization. What does that mean anyway, "lost my job,"? Did you misplace it, like your car keys? Or a rental car in a huge parking lot in Orlando? Or that $20 bill you could of sworn was in your pocket (or purse) last night?

In that "realization" of the need for a job, how did it relate to your career? Did you see it as a step in the development of your entire career?

Where are you on your life-career path? Are you young, like really young, under 18? Or young like under 25. Or maybe you are older, over 55, over 50, over 40? Or somewhere in-between 25 and 40. What does that mean along with your realization that you might need a job?

Did you get divorce or lose a spouse and now have to get a job never having had one before? Or maybe you had one but it was a long, long time ago? Or you want to go to college or go through a job training program that will take money and you want or need to be self-supporting to get that knowledge and credential?

And what other options to the realization that you might need a job are open to you.

So, if that was the easy step, what about the others? What if there is more to it than that simple little 4-step sequence at the beginning of this chapter? That's right, more things than those four steps?

So, what else? Think about it.

Give up?

Well, if your parents are rich and ridiculously supporting or you inherit a big chunk of money or invent the next "latest and greatest" thing no one can live without and get rich maybe you don't need a job or a career. Or if you have a parent or relative who owns a business, and you can just join the family business, maybe it's a "no-brainer" for you.

For the rest of us though, giving up isn't an option. Whenever that realization occurs, and for whatever reason it occurs, there are lots of things you can do to get a job. Even better, much better is the fact that with some effort on your part, your next job can be the right job for you or at least closer to it.

Hmmm, what's that mean "the right job"? Glad you asked, that is the subject of the next chapter. The chapters that follow are filled with information and insights, practical suggestions, advice and exercises to will guide you to your "Personal Success." Along the way, words of wisdom and encouragement with helpful hints will be given to you for your personal gratification.

I think you are a Very Important Person. You are a VIP in your life. You have the starring role in your life. You are the lead character in the story of your life. And you either bought this book, or borrowed it, and are at least reading it, which makes you a VIP in my world. Thank you for that much at least.

Chapter 2: The Right Job

"A good job is more than just a paycheck. A good job fosters independence and discipline, and contributes to the health of the community. A good job is a means to provide for the health and welfare of your family, to own a home, and save for retirement." — James H. Douglas, Jr (1899-1988) Former Assistant Secretary of the Treasury and Deputy Secretary of the Defense.

So what's the right job? More importantly, and accurately, what is the right job for you?

The easy answer is "it depends" but that is not much of an answer or a very satisfying answer, is it? How about this: "*The right job is the most rewarding job for you,* now and in the future."

That's accurate but still a bit vague because we need to define some terms and discuss this simple question, "what's the right job?" from several different points of view.

Let's start with some dictionary definitions; job, work, employment and career. According to Merriam Webster[1], (www.merriam-webster.com) a job is "the work that a person does regularly in order to earn money," work is "a job or activity that you do regularly especially in order to earn money," employment is "activity in which one engages or is employed" and a career is "a job or profession that someone does for a long time."

For our purposes, and to keep things simple, let's think of a "job" as simply "paid work." Let's think of "employment" as the fancy word for "job." Keeping it simple and to add some variety to this book, I'll use any of those words, or phrases, depending on which seems to fit the sentence better and make for better or easier reading.

Notice though that I said, "paid work" as being the same as "job" and that "job" is not the same as "work." We all do many kinds of work that we do not get paid for. We do yard work, cutting grass, pulling weeds, planting flowers. We do housework, washing dishes, vacuuming, making dinner, doing the laundry. We do homework, too. That all seems like stuff we do, don't get paid money for it and isn't "play."

There are other kinds of work we don't get paid for. Some of these are short, one time bursts, others are routine. This is the world of volunteer work. We might volunteer and help a neighbor cut up and remove a fallen tree, or offer our services at a church function, like a fund raiser. These are less formal examples of short-duration volunteer efforts or work. We could offer to help on a regular, scheduled basis, like volunteering at a food kitchen or pantry, working at a VA hospital, or as a Big Brother or Sister. We'll talk more about "volunteer work" throughout this book. Right now let's just say there is a world or work that needs to be done and you should be a volunteer, but you won't get paid so it's not a job. But it is okay if you say, "I've got a volunteer job," because you don't get paid with money, you get paid other ways.

Confused? Don't worry about it. Doesn't really make much difference in the grand scheme of things if you use job and work and employment as all meaning things you do for money or as a volunteer. The bigger difference is what follows.

Notice that according to Merriam-Webster, a job, or "paid work" is not a career until you do it for a long time.

So, what's the difference and does the difference matter? Let's take a look at some ways you can get paid for something you do but don't quite qualify as jobs. You can sell your blood, or to get personal, your sperm or your eggs. Not much work in the effort, and you can only do it every so often. You can also get paid to do a task, like distribute fliers for a local business. These paid tasks also aren't quite up to the level of a job.

There is another dimension to "job", "paid work" and "employment," the time dimension. We expect a job to last over a period of time. Is there any easy time period to use as a cutoff? Not really. We could say though, that a job is paid work that is expected to last awhile. That is closer to our typical expectations. We get hired for a job that is going to last awhile. It might be a summer job, lasting from June to September, or a temporary job, "temp job" lasting a few weeks, or maybe even a long term "rest-of-your-work-life" job.

---

1 www.merriam-webster.com, an Encyclopedia Britannica Company

We can't really say that a "job" has regular hours; some don't. We can't say that it has particular days or is done on a regular schedule, some don't. But we can say that we expect the job to last, even though some don't last as long as we might want (and some last too long).

This "time dimension" of a job fits into a discussion about careers. We tend to think of a career as something long term, occurring over years and not days or weeks or months. We think of it as something that involves stages, levels of preparation, like education or training or apprenticeships. We tend to think of it as something more than "just a job." We see it as something that you get better at over time and that it will take time to master the craft or skills involved in the "job" aspects of a career.

That is not always true. Some folks look back at the one job they've had all their lives and realize they made a career of it. Maybe they got lucky (more about that pesky guy - "Lucky" later) and got a job in a factory and stayed with it their entire work-life.

Earlier we used the term "work-life" let's talk about it and what it means. Maybe you've heard the phrase "some people work to live, others live to work"? Either way, there is a distinction being made between "living" or "life" and "work." There is more to life than working. There really is.

There is family, friends, community, country, society. There is play, rest, relaxation. There are vacations, and travel. There is volunteering and yard work and house work.

However, most of us will experience a work-life. Yours will be different than mine but we will share some common experiences. The most basic of these is that our work-life is what we do, have done and will do, for pay in a job setting, over our lifetime. This is not to say that those who have a "calling" in life and don't work for money don't get paid, the rewards are different.

Returning to the discussion of careers, we said some people got "lucky", got a job and stayed in it their entire work-life. There are more examples than the person who got a factory job "for-life." There are salespersons who got a job selling a product for a company and were lucky enough to stay with the same employer their entire work life. In most cases their skills evolved through training and experience and they became better at their job. Some civil servants have been hired in and dedicated themselves to a job they fit and loved and stayed with it for their entire career. There was a shoe shiner who retired a few years ago, who had spent his life shining shoes in the court building in Macomb County, Michigan. I spoke recently to a waiter at a popular Detroit restaurant, the Roma, who had spent his entire work life as a waiter there, and supported and raised a large family of successful children based on his job.

For these and many others, a career can be as "simple" as "got a job and kept it" their entire work life. They found rewarding, satisfying work and kept it. You can too.

We still haven't differentiated or distinguished between "job" and "career" though. Perhaps the thing that makes a career different from a job is the time dimension: jobs ordinarily being short and careers being long. Often a series of jobs, each requiring a "higher" level of skills, education, experience, knowledge or capability, leads to a long term career. Each lower level of job being a platform for the next level to be built on.

A medical career as a specialist doctor requires undergraduate training, typically in "pre-med," then medical school education, followed by work experience as an intern. The internship is followed by residency, which in turn leads to specialization. This is an over-simplification as there is so much more to becoming a medical doctor specialist than this but it is indicative of an upward path in a career.

There are countless examples of careers like this. *You* should take a few minutes and think of other examples. I'll name a few here: Fire Chief, College Professor, Master Carpenter, Master Electrician, Master Plumber, Airline Pilot, Airline Flight Attendant, Registered Nurse, Ship Captain, Army General, and Navy SEAL. All of these require experience, and personal growth and development.

Still, others of us never quite find a path that is so clear-cut. We don't land the "job-for-life." We don't find entry into a career work-life path that leads from "the bottom" to "the top." Does that mean we don't have careers? Of course not.

There are many factors that may prevent us from having a clear-cut career path. We change jobs, in our quest to find "something better." Employers come and go, taking jobs with them. Career fields disappear.

Life happens, we get married have children and "make sacrifices" on their behalf and give up our dream careers. Other things in life happen and we are prevented from following our planned path.

Sometimes it is our own lack of knowledge and insight that kept us from finding our path.

Still, we end up working over our lifetime, and that work-life becomes our career with all that insight and hindsight can reveal. You look back and see how one job led to another. Sometimes it is clear. Sometimes there seems to be no plan, no growth and no development. Sometimes that is true. Sometimes it is not.

What is more evident now than ever before is that most of us, the overwhelming majority of us, will have more than one job in our lifetime. Most of us will have more than one employer. Many of us will have more than one career. More than one career? Yes.

Let's talk about that aspect of career, that all the work done in one field of endeavor is a career. Huh? Okay, how about it is all the work done in one Standard Occupational Classification?

According to the United States Department of Labor, Bureau of Labor, Standard Occupational Classifications are defined this way: "The 2010 Standard Occupational Classification (SOC) system is used by Federal statistical agencies to classify workers into occupational categories for the purpose of collecting, calculating, or disseminating data. All workers are classified into one of 840 detailed occupations according to their occupational definition. To facilitate classification, detailed occupations are combined to form 461 broad occupations, 97 minor groups, and 23 major groups. Detailed occupations in the SOC with similar job duties, and in some cases skills, education, and/or training, are grouped together."

Huh? More simply it is all the work you do in the same field. Doctors and nurses work in medicine, pilots fly airplanes (or helicopters), waiters work in restaurants. None of them works as a butcher, a baker, or candlestick maker as part of their career. (They could temporarily get jobs doing one of these, and in the most broadest sense it would be part of their career-life but none of these jobs would really contribute to their career, now would they?).

So, in a nutshell, careers are one job or a series of jobs, within one field and generally long term. However, when we talk about your career specifically, we are talking about the jobs you hold over your lifetime, or all the jobs you hold in one field, so that your career might consist of several shorter careers in different industries.

That brings up an important aspect of what "the right job" is, that is that it is rewarding, which we'll go into more detail in Chapter 6 - What is a Rewarding Job. And we mean rewarding to you, not me, the next person or anyone else. That's what you want, right, *your* most rewarding job?

Chapter 3: Where Are You?

"Life isn't about finding yourself. Life is about creating yourself." — George Bernard Shaw (1856-1950) Irish playwright, co-founder London School of Economics.

Background:

That is the question, where are you? Where are you in life? What are you looking for? A job? A career? A job leading to a career?

How will you evaluate yourself? How will you evaluate jobs, careers and workplaces? It will start by you asking questions. This book is filled with questions, the right ones you should ask about yourself, job hunting, career building, jobs, careers and workplaces.

Where exactly are you in the hunt for your next job or your career? Are you currently working or unemployed? Does that make a difference? Yes and no, and what difference does it make?

Are you young with little or no experience? Older than young but still with little or no experience? Young or older than young with some experience already? Are you further along in life, what some would call middle-aged, or an older worker? Are you even older than that, like in your 50's, 60's or even 70's?

How about your education? Have you had training? What skills do you possess?How knowledgeable are you? About what? What kind of worker are you? What are your traits as a worker?

Do you want or need to change fields? Do you know what your next job could or should be? Do you know what kinds of jobs you could get being exactly who you are now? Or what kinds of jobs you could get with a little training, education or experience?

Where do you live? In a big city, a little one, or near one? In a small town, a village, or somewhere out in the "country," the boonies? Are you willing to move to get the job or career of your dreams? Are you willing to move to get a job to just get by? Is that what you want, "to just get by?" Just how far are you willing to travel each day, one way, to get the next, right job? Five miles? Ten? 50?

Where is that right job located? What if it is 500 miles away? Could there be one closer?

How long have you been looking for work? One week? Ten weeks? A year or more? What's that experience been like? Do you have a resume? How many did you send out with a cover letter? How many did you hand carry to potential employers? How many applications have you completed in person and how many on line? How many interviews have you had? Did you send every one of them a thank you letter? How many jobs have you turned down?

Speaking of potential employers, who are they? Who have you identified as a potential employer? Who have you identified as a potential employer within just five miles of your home? How many are there?

Did you answer all of those questions? Why not? Go back and see if you can answer all of them. Get out a sheet of paper (Or take the "Where Are You?" survey in the "It's Your Future" Workbook) and write down each question and then give your best answer to it.

Okay, okay, I know there are a lot of questions. So what? It's *your* life and *your* career we're talking about. You should plan on investing time and effort on developing your career, or job series because of the payoffs to *you*. Do you have to answer all these questions? No, of course not. You should be able to answer them all, especially those that are important to you or potential employers. You don't even have to formally write out the answers, though it well be helpful to you if you do. You should at least think about each question and see what answers you come up with, even if only in your mind.

There will be benefits to others that are important to you like your family, your friends, your community, your country and everyone else. Your success is important to and good for all of them. It is certainly worth putting the time in on your career, If you don't, who will? No one will do it for you and even if they did, they wouldn't and couldn't do it as well as you.

If you are a typical American worker, you will spend 40 or more years working. Did you know that if you were to average just $12.50 an hour over your lifetime you would earn more than *one million dollars*, that's $1,000,000.

That's just if you average $12.50 an hour. You could work 10 years at $8/hour, 10 more years at $10/hour, then 10 years at $15/hour and finally 10 years at $17/hour and average $12.50/hour for your lifetime.

With serious effort you can double that and more. Why shouldn't you be able to average $25.00 an hour? Lots of people do and so can you. Later, we'll show you how you can find your most rewarding job and a career where you can make that kind of money and more!

So really now what's stopping you from answering the questions? You don't have to do them all at once. Try answering them one at a time and do as many as you want in one sitting. It's an investment in yourself. But answer those questions to your own satisfaction, it's that important.

I can tell you that by taking the time to develop your future now, you will save time in the long run. You will avoid getting lost in life. Avoid getting bad jobs, wrong jobs or minimize the time you're stuck in one of them. So make the investment in yourself. Save yourself time in the future. Make more money. What's a little work now to give yourself a better future?

We will come back to your answers to these questions as we go along. Ask yourself these questions: How can I get somewhere without knowing where I am? How do I know which way to go even if I know where I want to end up, if I don't know where I'm starting from?"

If you wanted to go to the North Pole, it would be easy, just go north from wherever you are until you can't go any further "north." It wouldn't matter where you started.

How easy would it be for you to walk out the front door and get to Omaha, Nebraska, or Saginaw, Michigan, or San Antonio, Texas, especially if you didn't know where you were starting from, let alone where they are? It would be difficult, very difficult. You would probably have to look at map to find them, more specifically where they are in reference to your starting point. Then you could work out a path to get from where you are to where they are. You would still have problems to solve, little things like how were you going to get there and how long you wanted the trip to take. Still, you would be able to work out a plan to get from here, where you are, to there, where you want to be.

Your approach to jobs, job hunting, careers, career growth and development, should be as well planned, even better planned than a road trip. You are worth more to you if your approach to job hunting and career development is well defined. You will increase your chance for success if it is. You will increase your lifetime value, to yourself and to others, if it is.

If you haven't done this already, get out that sheet of paper and begin to answer the questions. Keep it up until you have answered them all.

Some of them will be really easy. Here's an example: Question: How far are am I willing to travel one way to work, if it is the right job? Answer: 10 miles (or whatever your right answer is).

That seemed pretty simple didn't it? Think again. Being willing to travel 10 mile one way means you are willing to spend about 25 minutes going to work each day, for a daily total of about one hour. If you earn only $10/hour that is a "cost" to you of $10. No biggie, eh? It's just your time after all and you have to spend it doing something and "everyone" has to go to work, right?

Well, no, everyone doesn't. Some people work at home or from home and have no commute.

Here's another way to look at: that 20 miles day in a car you drive might cost you one gallon of gas or about $4.00 per day, as this is written in July, 2014. Again, if you are earning just $10/hour and work 8 hours each day, you need to subtract that $4 from the $80 you make (before taxes). This may still be no biggie.

What if you have to pay a childcare worker or center, $8 for an hour of childcare. That's a cost of $8 (before income taxes) for that commute. So you're paying $12 a day or $60 per week for the privilege of working at that job. What if you could got a job closer to you and you could cut that in half. That means you could accept a job that paid $.75 an hour less and still end up with the same disposable income ($30/40 hours - $.75 an hour). Suppose you said you were willing to travel 25 miles one way? The cost for that grows right along with it. Which means you have to earn even more money to cover the cost.

Scientists, business people, and others also talk about something called an "opportunity cost." This represents what else you could have done during that time. In other words, if you are spending one hour a day traveling to and form work, what else could you do with that one hour each day, or five hours each week (five-day job)?

Spend more time playing? More time with your kids or spouse? More time on your hobbies? More time relaxing? Reading? Studying? Sleeping? Whatever.

If you obtain the right job and only travel 15 minutes to work, and 15 minutes to get home, instead of 30 minutes each way, you will save ½ hour per day, 2 ½ hours per week. Many people commute one hour each way or ten hours per week. If they could cut that to 2 ½ hours per week, they would save 7 ½ hours per week. That's an astonishing savings to them of one 7 ½ hour work day every week! For the rest of their lives. Plus there are additional savings in fuel, wear and tear on their car and on themselves. But maybe you like long commutes in heavy traffic, do you?

It is better to take the right job close to home, than to take the right job further away. It is a matter of economics. If the only criteria you applied to your definition of the "right" job was the one that paid the most, or financially benefitted you the most, you need to think in terms of "net income" that part of what you earn that you get to keep and spend. The cost of working should be in your calculations.

So, even the simple things are a bit more complex when you get into them. As we work on your jobs and career, your future, we will examine the things worth considering each step of the way so that you are as completely and fully informed as you can, and need to be when it comes to work.

Chapter 4: Things Change

"Everyone thinks of changing the world, but no one thinks of changing himself."
— Leo Tolstoy (1828-1910) Russian author.

"It is not necessary to change. Survival is not mandatory." — W. Edwards Deming (1900-1993) American engineer, statistician, professor, author, lecturer, and management consultant.

"Everything changes and nothing stands still," said Heraclitus of Ephesus (535 BC - 475 BC) a Greek philosopher.

"We live in a state of perpetual transition." - author

For over 2,500 years people have been noticing that things change. Times change, people change. Countries come and go. Buildings come and go. Jobs come and go. Change is constant. The rate of change isn't.

The difference between how things were at some point in the past and how they are subsequently, is a measure of change. How much they've changed between two points in time, as compared to two other points in time, is the rate of change. The rate of change appears to be accelerating, dramatically.

It took hundreds of years for formal religious music in Christian churches to leave Gregorian chants in favor of Cantatas. It took years to musically grow from the first operas of the early 1,600's to the development of concerts and symphonies. Just listen to the music of the 20th century, from Ragtime and Tin Pan Alley to Big Bands in the 20s, 30s and 40s, to Folk Music and Rock 'n' Roll. In Rock 'n' Roll from Elvis and Ricky Nelson to the Beatles, the Rolling Stones, the Who to Bruce Springsteen to Taylor Swift to, well whomever you'd like to add. It is always about the new band and the new sound.

Even the technology of music, from literally just remembering the music and how it was supposed to sound, to the act of creating written musical scores. Then to go from a handful of basic instruments, to the array of instruments invented in the baroque period of the 1700's, and then on to electric and electronic music of today.

We go from the early beginnings to modern techniques of sound recording. Initially the first recordings were made by an analog process (like singing into a large cone that directly and mechanically etched the sound onto a recording cylinder and then later a flat disk). Then microphones and magnetics became part of the process. Technology pushed for more accuracy in the recording. From monophonic to stereophonic. Tape recording on reel-to-reels, then onto cassettes, 8 track, to small cartridges. Then to digital recordings on disks, then MP3 players and "iPods."

One more realm to think about before we talk about how this impacts on jobs and your future. Let's look at business and industry, specifically about the distribution of goods. For hundreds, even thousands of years, goods were carried by boats and ships or on horse and ox drawn carts or on people's backs. Although these methods are still used, it was through the mid-1800s that goods were shipped on sailing ships and when the first steam ships began moving freight around the world.

Before those steam ships were invented, ships were at the mercy of the weather and could not be counted upon to deliver goods by a particular date. Technology, like the compass (invented in China, about 206 BC, adapted by the Chinese for maritime use around 1,100 AD, and around 1,200 AD by Western Europeans) improved their capacity to get from point A to point B. The sextant was invented around 1757 and along with the compass made their location known to sailors which improved navigation and made sailing more predictable. Still, until the mid-1800s, ships depended on wind for motion.

In little time, less than 100 years, shipping was completely revolutionized. Wooden hulls were displaced by steam-powered, iron and then steel-hulled craft. In even less time, steamships were displaced by diesel driven ships.

So, faster and faster goes the world. From calculating on your fingers or with an abacus, to early mechanical calculators to electronic calculators to computers. From large big-as-a-building computers to desktop then laptop to iPads, notebooks and Kindle. From oil lights to candles. Candles to gas lamps. Gas lamps to the electric light. From incandescent to LED. Faster and faster. Less time between big changes.

So, how does this apply to you? O, so what?

Once upon a time, you entered a field of work and you stayed there. You were born to be a king, a carpenter, a priest, a farmer or a soldier and stayed there for life.

Times changed, more jobs developed. Sheriffs (once called the "shire reeve") and policemen. Firemen and clerks. Merchants, doctors, lawyers, even politicians. Then with the industrial revolution, factory work and workers and foremen, salespersons and more.

Still, once you got in, into a job, you might stay in that job or profession all of your work life. By the early 20th century, companies like Ford, General Motors, Caterpillar, John Deere, Armour, Swift, Stroh's, Budweiser, Phillip Morris, Coca-cola and more were absorbing much of the workforce into career opportunities. Opportunities that not only never before existed but paid well and offered benefits (fought for by union activists) and growingly, life time employment for ordinary people like you and me.

Then change being as it always is, more workforce changes began to emerge. Calamities befell companies. Hudson and Packard, motor car companies, disappeared in the 1950s as did many of their early competitors during the Depression of 1929. Suburban malls opened up, causing city centers, and their businesses, with limited parking to decline. Cities declined as people moved to suburbs. Ever faster the times change.

Computers and robots began to displace workers. A robot here on an assembly line, a robot there, welding cars on the moving assembly adapted by Henry Ford at the Highland Park plant. Computers replacing people in accounting departments, that once used hundreds and thousands of people to keep current the accounts receivable in companies. People who kept track of goods and raw materials were supplanted by computers able to do more, more accurately.

Still faster the rate of change accelerates. Even in the computer world, keypunch operators came and went as that work was eliminated by direct data entry.

Jobs come and go. Businesses come and go. People come and go. What was once considered to be a special relationship, the worker and the employer, one that fostered trust and loyalty bent to the unrelenting demands of the times. The cost of rewarding loyal employees could not always be carried by well-meaning employers, let alone the nefarious among them. Competition. Greed. Self-centeredness versus social-centeredness. Then the modern scourge, globalization. All of these have made the work place less supportive of individual employees over an entire work life.

No longer can you, as a worker, count on your employer to take care of you for your entire work life. You are more likely to have as many as five different employers during your work life than just one. You may even change fields several times.

That's some of the most pessimistic material we'll talk about. Let's talk about the positives now.

Even with globalization, even with competitive pressures to operate a business or a governmental department or program efficiently, there are opportunities. With more changes comes new jobs and new fields. To be sure, some of these make it difficult for you as a worker to be able to depend on this or that employer to "take care" of you for life. That burden has been transferred to you.

You must prepare for change. The good news, no better yet, the *best* news is that you can. Your survival may depend upon it. Your life today and in the future will depend upon your actions and effort. Does this not put a lot of power in your hands? You are no longer dependent on the "generosity" of an employer to build the future you want for you and your family.

All these changes and the rate of change are creating opportunity, opportunity for you.

As new fields come into existence, workers with new skills are required for new jobs. Those who go out and get those skills have the opportunity to step forward, step up and step into those new jobs. As new companies come into existence in these new, exciting and emerging fields, new jobs are created in more traditional business roles. People with those more traditional skills are needed too. Accounting, sales, warehousing are just a few of the traditional work areas that are needed in new companies as well as old.

The rapidly changing world is filled with problems – problems that need solutions and solving.

Is the earth undergoing climate change? I don't know, but I do know that whether it is or isn't, there are opportunities for people to find or create jobs related to climate change.

Are we running out of food or water? Will oil and gas reserves be depleted? Are more people moving into cities or out of them?

What about support for the aging population of the United States and other countries? Problems or opportunities? The answer may be yes to most of those questions, but that means there will be new industries developing and emerging to deal with these problems and new jobs to fill.

Still another consideration to keep in mind is that with all the other kinds of change in our world, the people in jobs at the moment you read this, will not all be in those jobs in one day, one week, one month, one year or even in ten years.

It is a well-known axiom that "people come and people go." That is the nature of life, people, and of people in jobs. It is one of the fundamentals of the changing world around us.

One day you go to work and look around. You see one hundred people in the workplace. A short time later someone is gone. Maybe they quit or got fired. Maybe they retired, went on extended sick leave and were unable to return to work. Maybe they passed away. Perhaps they were promoted or transferred to another department or branch in another area.

Even in a stable business, there is a regular change of personnel in jobs.

Ultimately, these facts, that nothing stays the same, that change is inevitable, that problems exist, work to your advantage as a job and career seeker.

One more thing that has changed – and you benefit from it – is the way the United States Department of Labor collects, disseminates, and makes accessible to you their vast occupational information.

Bureau of Labor Statistics and the Occupational Information Network (O*NET) replaced their publication, the Dictionary of Occupational Titles. For over 75 years, the Dept. of Labor, Bureau of Labor Statistics and the Employment and Training Division have worked to make excellent, detailed, occupational information available to workers and employers. We will spend considerable time using those resources in the following chapters. Turn to "Appendix A: The O*NET Content Model". This appendix will introduce you to the most current model of relating workers to occupations and occupations to workers.

Chapter 5: Where Are You? - Part 2

"We come fresh to the different stages of life, and in each of them we are quite inexperienced, no matter how old we are" — François de la Rochefoucauld (1613-1680) French classical author.

"He who knows others is wise; he who knows himself is enlightened." — Lao Tzu (lived during the Zhou dynasty (c. 1046–256 BC)in China, philosopher, poet and author.

"'Know Thyself' was written over the portal of the antique world. Over the portal of the new world, 'Be Thyself' shall be written." — Oscar Wilde, 1854-1900, Irish author, playwright and poet.

"The first thing you have to know is yourself. A man who knows himself can step outside himself and watch his own reactions like an observer." — Adam Smith (1723-1790) philosopher and pioneer political economist.

The most straightforward job and career path is the one where you know exactly what you want to do, have the prerequisite skills, knowledge, experience, and qualifications to obtain that job and career and have a clear plan and process in place to move into that job and career path. You have a resume that matches the job applications that you complete. Your interview skills match your application and your resume and are likely to land you that job. You are prepared and have a plan.

Did I say, straightforward? Actually I said, "most straightforward" and even then, how clearcut was the rest of that to you?

There are a few key elements in finding your most rewarding job and developing a career plan. These four key elements are: 1) Self-knowledge, 2) Career and Job Knowledge, 3) Job Seeking Preparation and 4) Job Seeking Action.

These key elements consist of certain very specific components. These are:
- Self-knowledge
  - Skills
  - Knowledge
  - Education
  - Experience
  - Training
  - Abilities
  - Interests
  - Values
  - Styles
- Career and Job Knowledge
  - Job Information
  - Industry Information
  - Jobs within Industries
  - Jobs in Companies in Industries
  - Requisite knowledge, skill, abilities, experience, education for Jobs
  - Job and Career Path requirements
- Job Seeking Preparation
  - Employer Information
  - Resumes
  - Application
  - Interview Packaging

- Appearance
- Behavior
- Job Seeking Action
  - Organized (Marketing) Plan
  - Contact
  - Follow-up

If you spend time on these key elements and their components, you can put that knowledge to work for you to obtain your most rewarding job and use it to guide you on your career plan.

Do you know which one job or career path is "best" for you? Do you have other job or career alternatives in mind. How many options do you have?

What did you base your decision making on? How do you know what jobs or careers you would find rewarding? Is you career or job choice based on a childhood dream? "I always wanted to be a dentist" or "I always wanted to be a sanitation engineer" or "teacher," "insurance salesperson" or whatever.

How do your skills line up with your chosen career or job, if you've got one in mind? How about your education? Or your knowledge? Does your experience line up with the job you're targeting, whether entry level or advanced?

Are you sure you would like the environment of the that job or career? How about the types of organizations that you could work in? Have you given them much thought?

How do your values match to the work you are seeking? Or your preferred style of working.

There are tools available to help you see yourself in the work context, from the employment point of view. We will introduce you to these as we work along. So one step is the process of self-discovery while another is exploration of the World of Work.

The more you know about yourself and your potential, even if you are in your 30's, 40's or older still, the more options you have available. More options is a good thing! Whoever you are, you have potential and you can have even more! More good news is that there are more resources and new tools available to help you see yourself in a new light, and all the possibilities you have.

Knowing more about you is not enough. You need as much information about potential jobs and careers as you can learn about.

Suppose that there is some magical, mystical resource you could go to and ask three questions. First question, "How many different jobs could I do?" Second question, "How many different companies have these jobs?" Third and final question, "How many jobs is that altogether?" If you could ask those questions and have a "genie" give you the answers, they could do no more for you than you can for yourself! That's right, the potential number of jobs you could have can be discovered by you! You don't need a genie!

If you know you can do one job, and you only know of one employer who hires people to do that job, then your potential is one job. If they are not hiring, you have zero chance of getting a job, and less chance of a career.

If you search and find that 500 employers who hire people to do that one job, your odds just improved of getting hired. Now you only have to keep applying until you get that job with one of them and you are likely too!

That is a simplistic way to look at it. Most of us can do more than one job, there may in fact be several or many that we can do. The key to that is knowing about occupations and about ourselves. One of the areas most of us have little knowledge about is meaningful occupational information that can make you an informed job seeker and career developer, specializing in _you_!

You will directly benefit from knowing more about yourself and about occupations. This knowledge will provide you with a range of potential jobs and careers from which you can choose.

Your choice of jobs and careers will form a basis for a plan that you can put into effect to find your future and develop it.

You probably already have a good idea about potential jobs and careers that you seek. Something has drawn you to them, something feels right about them. At least until you get the job and work in it awhile, then you may find yourself thinking you've made a mistake.

For example, you chose to be a teacher. You got through the college work including being a student teacher, and then after 4 -5 years, you wake up one day and realize you don't want to do it anymore. Sometimes we call it burnout. The "I just can't do it anymore" awakening!

But maybe the job and career you've picked out is perfect for you.

Let's suppose you know a great deal about you. You think you know a lot about the skills you possess. You know how much education you have and what classes you were best at or enjoyed the most. You even have a reasonably accurate sense of what knowledge you possess.

Do you know how those skills, that knowledge and education, and educational experience, relate to potential job and career opportunities for you? Put another way, how many jobs or careers can you identify that need those skills or knowledge or education, or all three? How many? One? Two? 1,147 of them? If I said to you, "name them, write them down, I want to see it in writing" could you do that, put them in writing?

In the workbook there is a place for you to write down your job options called, "Name Them," and it is my challenge to you. I urge you to turn to that page now and write them down, and put a date next to them. Later, after you work with this book and other resources, go back and add more options, more job possibilities, more career options and put the dates you add them in as well. It will give you visual evidence of your own growth in understanding about your potential.

We will spend more time on those terms, skills, knowledge and education and many others with which you should become familiar. They are part of the language of jobs, job seekers, interviewers and employers! You should understand how they relate to work.

It is important for you to realize that even seeing that you have one more skill than you ever gave thought to, could open up many more job opportunities for you. The same holds true for knowledge, ability, and other characteristics of us as workers.

Having more career and job options is one of the ways you can develop a more rewarding and secure future for yourself. This is especially true if you are stuck between jobs or have been dissatisfied in the jobs you have had. Perhaps you like using the skills you have but really didn't like the environment or perhaps the work "went away," being out-sourced or off-shored.

Once you have thoroughly explored yourself as a worker, and occupations in the work place, there is still more to do. It is especially important to find work that is "rewarding" to you. We will spend time on that concept and help you see what kinds of work are your most rewarding jobs.

We will spend time on the more straight-forward sequence involved in finding and getting that most rewarding job. We give you tools to help you along the way, to make it easier for you, to help give you support through the tough times you might experience during the job hunt if you are unemployed. You can do this, build a better future for yourself, you really can!

Chapter 6: What is a rewarding job?

"There are two things people want more than sex and money – recognition and praise." – Mary Kay Ash (1918-2001) American businesswoman and founder of Mary Kay Cosmetics.

We will receive not what we idly wish for but what we justly earn. Our rewards will always be in exact proportion to our service. – Earl Nightingale (1929-1989) American motivational speaker and author.

"Far and away the best prize that life offers is the chance to work hard at work worth doing." – Theodore Roosevelt (1858-1920) American President.

Background:

If you think the answer to "what is a rewarding job?" is "the one that pays the most money" you're only right if that's it, "money," and nothing else. If that is it for you, you probably won't find a truly rewarding job. Even if you stretch your definition a little and say "the one that let's me buy all the things that money can buy and that I want." You are still missing the much bigger picture of what constitutes or makes up, "a rewarding job." Money isn't everything.

Okay, okay, money is important. "Money changes everything," and lots of other sayings exist because on the whole, it is better to have money than not. We do work for money! But is that what makes work rewarding?

Some of the best paid "workers," top athletes and top entertainers make lots of money but they do what they like doing. They enjoy using their skills, abilities and all the rest, along with the money. Some of them would do it even if it wasn't as monetarily rewarding. Ever hear of a "starving artist"? There are legions of entertainers and athletes, who never make the big bucks, but still they perform.

Let's assume that you expect to get paid to work when you take a job. That's fine but there are jobs people take where they don't get paid! Yes there are! Ever hear about volunteer work? People do volunteer work because it is <u>rewarding</u>. We will say more about volunteer work but first let's talk about why we work.

We work (the verb, in the sense of action or doing something) because we are motivated to do something. Something needs to be done and we are ready, willing and able to do it *and* motivated to do it.

Did you notice we didn't even mention "money"? That's because some of the work you and I do is work we don't get paid to do. Don't believe me? Did you ever cut grass, wash dishes, shovel snow, do laundry, make a bed? Housework, yard work, homework are all examples of things we do, that aren't necessarily "fun" but are work and we don't get paid to do them. They are rewarding though. Don't you get some satisfaction from looking at these tasks when they're done and being pleased with the results? They were all things that needed to be done and you were motivated to do them. Not to mention, who else was going to do it anyway?

If we are going to talk about "work" and "rewards," we need to talk about "motivation" too.

What is motivation? It is the "why" that explains what we do, what our "motives" are.

Definitions of the word "motivation" suggest its meaning as "to move" or literally what moves you. Different things move you than move me. At times, different things move you.

If you are hungry, you will do things to get food and satisfy your hunger. Needs are all basic expressions of motives. We need to breathe, to eat, to drink, sleep and to relieve ourselves. These are the most basic needs we have. In fact, failing to do these things can bring death fairly quickly. Have one of these needs interfered with and we act quickly to resolve the problem. Did you ever find yourself underwater and needing air to breathe, found yourself struggling, and maybe even panicking? In that situation, you act because survival, your survival depended on it, that was your motivation, your survival.

How about while on a long drive and you need to use a restroom? Have you found yourself thinking "Can I make it to the next rest stop?" Then as your urgency mounts, thinking, "maybe I should hop off at the next gas or restaurant exit?" Then "I can't wait, I'm just going to pull over and go in the ditch by the roadside!" If that wasn't you, maybe your child, spouse or another person with you?

These basic needs cannot be frustrated long. How long do you go between meals? Hours most probably, a day if you are fasting or are trying to lose weight, or if you're really short of money and food. How about going without a drink of water or something similar? Most of us drink something everyday, not even going hours without drinking something.

Let's distinguish "needs" and "wants." Needs are the true necessities of life; without them we die. Period. Wants on the other hand are under our control and are expressions of physical, psychological, social, spiritual and emotional desires.

If you want a particular thing to eat, a steak say or a salad, that is a personal expression of how you want a basic need satisfied. That personal expression can be refined to a particular item, as for example, "I want a 16-ounce Porterhouse Steak, cooked medium-rare." Or even more specifically, "I want a juicy, 16-ounce Porterhouse Steak, cooked medium-rare from the (name your favorite) Steakhouse."

There are more needs than the basic survival, the "stay alive", needs. Abraham Maslow's first proposed in 1943 in his book, "A Theory of Human Motivation," that we have several set of needs, a "Hierarchy of Needs,". Maslow believed that you needed to resolve your "lower order" needs before you could go on to work on "higher" level needs. Needs at the bottom of the pyramid would need to be satisfied before higher level needs would or could become motivating. He modified his thinking over time to allow for simultaneously working on multiple needs.

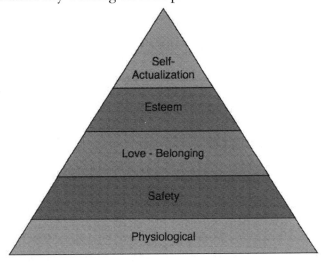

Figure 5-1: Maslow's Hierarchy of Needs

From the bottom up, these needs are:
- Physiological
  - Breath
  - Water
  - Food
  - Sleep
  - Excretion
  - Reproduction
- Safety and Security of
  - Body
  - Family
  - Resources
  - Employment

- Property
- Love and Belonging
  - Friendship
  - Family
  - Intimacy
  - Membership
- Esteem
  - Self-Esteem
  - Confidence
  - Achievement
  - Respect of and by others
- Self-Actualization
  - Morality
  - Creativity
  - Spontaneity
  - Problem Solving
  - Lack of Prejudice
  - Acceptance of facts

This is an over-simplification. How these needs are grouped, whether other "needs" should be included is certainly open to debate and discussion. It is entirely possible to be doing something about a higher level need while engaged in a "lower level" one. Whether any of the needs outside of the "stay alive needs" at the any of the levels are absolutely correctly identified as "needs" is even debatable. Not everyone seems to need sex, or any of the "higher" level needs. They do seem to be common desires but not everyone needs "family" or "employment." Not everyone seeks "friendship" or "property."

There are other theories of motivation, such as William James descriptions of human instincts, like attachment, play, shame, anger, fear etc. Theories like Incentive Theory, Drive Theories, Humanistic Theories, Psychoanalytic Theories like those of Freud and Jung. All of these are attempts to explain "what moves us."

In particular the work of clinical psychologist Frederick Herzberg, a pioneer of "job enrichment" in his book, "The Motivation to Work" attempts to explain why we work. His work speaks to much of what makes us satisfied in our work and what makes us dissatisfied. In fact, his works suggest that the things that satisfy us about a job are different from the things that make us dissatisfied. He said, "that the job satisfiers deal with the factors involved in doing the job, whereas the job dis-satisfiers deal with the factors which define the job context."

So, what's that got to do with you? Unless you are someone who likes to study theory maybe not so much. On the other hand we can use this and other material to help you understand what moves *you* to work and that is very important.

There are sections in the Workbook for this manual that will help guide you to discover more about what moves you. I suggest that you wait until you finish this chapter before you turn to it but if you can't wait, feel free to set this book down and do the exercises now.

The reason I suggested that you wait is there is more good stuff to read and think about before you do the exercises.

You should understand that what moves *you* is unique to <u>you</u> even though others will share those motives too. Without being judgmental, there is nothing wrong with your motivations, they are yours.[2] What moves you is what moves you. Those things are not subjectively "better" or "worse" than someone else's. It is more important to spend time on identifying *what* moves you than *why*, or where it comes from, at least in

---

2 Unless your motivations are seriously illegal, immoral, or otherwise not socially acceptable. In other words if you have no problem with stealing or committing other crimes, or treat other people with disdain and contempt, then perhaps there is something wrong with your motivations. Still, even then they are your motivations and you should be able to "own them" as yours.

the context of a book about jobs and careers. It is very important to self-understanding to spend time on why those things move and where that comes from, but again that is not the purpose of the book. If you are interested in knowing those things about yourself, you should consider reading books on the subject of motivation or consider taking classes in psychology or even consider therapy (if you think you need some form of "adjustment" or for your mental health).

Returning to the subject of "what is rewarding work?", we can summarize the motivational theories in this context as those things that satisfy our needs and that they are unique to each of us. We get something as a result of our effort to satisfy our need(s), that something is the _reward_.

Earlier we mentioned that there is one whole world of work that doesn't involve "getting paid", i.e. volunteer work. Why do people do it? If you are someone who volunteers, why do you do it? Certainly not to get rich because you don't get paid for it.

Recently, the "National Council of Voluntary Organisations" (a British organization) gave the following summary as to why people volunteer.

Reason	Percentage
I wanted to improve things or help people	62%
The cause was really important to me	40%
I had spare time to do it	33%
I wanted to meet people or make friends	33%
I thought it would give me a chance to use my existing skills	32%
I felt there was a need in my community	28%
It was connected with the needs of my family or friends	25%
It's part of my philosophy of life to help people	25%
I thought it would give me a chance to learn new skills	20%
My friends or family did it	19%
It's part of my religious belief to help people	17%
I felt there was no one else to do it	12%
It helps me get on in my career	9%
I had received voluntary help	4%
It gave me the chance to get recognized in a qualification	3%

Figure 6 - 1: Why people volunteer

Study that table, look at it carefully, think about each of those answers. If you have volunteered, which ones appealed to you, resonated with you? Perhaps it's part of your philosophy of life that you should help others. Maybe it's something your friends and family did and so you chose to as well.

If you have never volunteered, take a look at the reasons why others do. Would those be some reasons you would or might volunteer?

Volunteering is rewarding work as is easily seen by the responses people gave in that survey. In the United Kingdom over 22.7 million people volunteer. How about closer to home? How many volunteer in the United States? How about 62.6 million people volunteered between Sept 2012 and Sept 2013.[3]

Some other reasons people volunteer: 1) connects you with others, 2) make new friends and contacts, 3) increases social and relationship skills, 4) increases self-confidence, 5) combats depression, 6) stay physically healthy, 7) makes you happy, 8) can provide career experience, 9) can learn valuable job skills, 10) it's fun, 11) it's fulfilling.[4]

Still more reasons: 1) to build up your resume, 2) try new things, 3) learn about different cultures, 4) feel and be needed, 5) because you can! [5]

There are even more reasons. How about to make yourself useful, especially while you are unemployed. Think about this, the contacts you make may lead to a most fulfilling career. Did you know that many people are sent by their employers to be volunteers? Many high level executives, people with the power to hire and fire people, volunteer, often for personal reasons. It is entirely possible that the volunteer standing next to you is someone who could hire you! They could be someone with clout in a company and can send you to someone who will feel compelled to hire because of the referral.

Former President Jimmy Carter is famous for his work for Habitat for Humanity. Wouldn't it be great to work next to him and have him refer you to someone for a job?

Business persons, leaders, executives often volunteer for personal reasons. They may have a child with disabilities, or a sibling, and so they are motivated to volunteer. Perhaps they needed assistance when they were young. For all of the reasons given, powerful, influential people give generously of their time and talent. If you impress them while working next to them as a volunteer, it could be your way of landing your next, best job.

There is even more benefit to you though. Sometimes it happens that volunteers become the next person hired in the organization they volunteer in. You can get in the "next-hired" line in some organizations simply by volunteering to work for them.

If that wasn't enough, for many unemployed people, the excess time on their hands, the non-productive use of their time and talent begins to drain and depress them. Volunteering by its very nature is an antidote. It uses some of your time productively. It will make you feel good.

It is also a fact that many organizations depend on volunteers to stay in existence, especially as donor funds and government funds have been reduced. They always need people, and they need you. It is nice to be needed and almost no one doesn't get the job when they apply for a volunteer position. Nearly guaranteed success.

In the workbook, there are several exercises designed to help you identify those hidden reasons for why you work. One of them is based on the notion of why people work for no money at all. Why would they do that?

Why is it important for you to consider? If you examine some of the reasons you would be willing to work for no money, or why you already volunteer, those reasons could be incorporated into a paid position. Wouldn't that automatically be more rewarding than a job you did just for the money. Of course it would.

We turn now to other reasons people work, this time looking at paid positions.

So, why do we work? Because it is rewarding.

These is so much to this concept. Of course it is your livelihood and provides you and your family with your basic needs, fuel, food, clothing, shelter.

3 Department of Labor, Bureau of Labor Statistics, Economic News Release, "Volunteering in the United States, Feb 25, 2014.

4 www.Helpguide.org

5 svee.hubpages.com/hub/10-Reasons-People-Volunteer

Work rewards you in other ways. It provides the basis for many of our human relationships, opportunity for personal development. Elements of personal satisfaction like being of service or security or success and happiness are intertwined.

There are always the basic reasons: Compensation, like wages, Benefits, like healthcare, pension, Affiliation, like belonging to an organization, team or group membership, Work Content, like the job duties, challenge, autonomy, meaningful work, or Career reasons, like advancement opportunities, training, growth.

Herzberg suggested these: achievement, recognition, the work itself, responsibility, advancement, salary, growth, positional role in interpersonal relationships, such as your relationship with subordinate or superiors and peers, status, technical supervision, company policies and administration, working conditions, personal life and job security.

What is important though, is for you to identify what you will find rewarding in the workplace. Turn now to the workbook and work through the "Why I Work" exercises.

Part 2: Pre-search

This section is labeled "Pre-search" because it deals with what you do *before* you start your job search. It contains material you can use to figure out what occupations and jobs match up well for you as a potential worker. Before you start a job or career search, you need to know what you are looking for, so "pre-search" is the research you do *before* you engage in the job search. Investing your time on this step can help you avoid spending years of your life in the wrong career for you. Why work at a job that you find unsatisfying, that just doesn't suit you or isn't right for *you?*

We'll explore knowledge, skills and abilities in general, and yours in particular in the following chapters. Looking ahead, "knowledge" is literally what you've learned. "Skills" are things you can do. "Abilities" are capacities to do particular things well, or your natural talents or gifts.

Much of the material in the next few chapters comes from the United States Department of Labor, Bureau of Labor Statistics and the Occupational Information Network (O*NET) which replaced their publication, the Dictionary of Occupational Titles.

In 1939, the U.S. Department of Labor first published its landmark work, "The Dictionary of Occupational Titles" (DOT) as part of its effort to collect and disseminate comprehensive occupational data.

The goal of the DOT, was to make useful information available for "job placement, occupational research, career guidance, labor-market information, curriculum development, and long-range job planning"[6].

The last complete edition of the DOT was published in 1991. During the 1990s, work was started to make the information it contained accessible through the means of an online database system. During this period, different approaches to making the information available were developed. One of these approaches converted the content of the DOT to webpages and the developers[7] of the website (www.occupationalinfo.org) still provide that information.

The other major project was a re-thinking of the structure and accessibility of the content of the Dictionary of Occupational Titles, this resulted in the Occupational Information Network or O*NET. For more about the world of O*NET, visit the O*NET Resource Center at its website: www.onetcenter.org. At that website you can learn about the resources of O*NET, its content, means of data collection, developer information, plans, products and more. There is information on career exploration tools, ways and means of accessing these tools (physical places you can go to be able to use them, and as well as others, all available on line). See Appendix A for an overview of the O*NET Content Model.

---

6 Robert A Schaerfl, Director, U.S. Employment Service, Dictionary Of Occupational Titles (4th Ed., Rev. 1991) – Foreword

7 1 Photius Coutsoukis and Information Technology Associates (1995-2011)

Chapter 7: What is Knowledge?

"I did then what I knew how to do. Now that I know better, I do better." — Maya Angelou (1928-2014), American author, poet, dancer, actress, singer.

The next best thing to knowing something is knowing where to find it." — Samuel Johnson (1709-1784) British author.

"Knowledge is of no value unless you put it into practice." — Anton Chekhov (1860-1904), Russian author, playwright and physician.

"Knowing is not enough; we must apply. Willing is not enough; we must do." — Johann Wolfgang von Goethe (1749-1832) German playwright, poet, novelist and dramatist.

Background:

What is knowledge? The short answer is, "knowledge what you know", you're "know-how".

You have all kinds of knowledge stored up in that human being we call "you." Bits of data and information you've accumulated over the years, like "who starred in the Brady Bunch?", "whose batting average was highest in 1989? (Kirby Puckett)", "who's buried in Grant's tomb?", and "there are 5,280 feet in a mile". All of that kind of stuff is knowledge.

Memories. Memories of places you've been, people you've known, books you've read, games you've played, schools you attended. That's more knowledge.

Information about things and how things work are another kind of knowledge. Rules about things and how they operate. Rules about getting along, rules about society, rules about school and work. Rules about interacting with other people or conduct. Rules about relationships.

Knowledge is stored inside us in collections of related material, organized with sets of principles that help us use that knowledge. Sometimes we get things wrong but still we take all that stuff we know and apply it to the world, our world, in ways that make sense to us.

Why this talk about knowledge in a book about jobs and careers? It's one aspect, and an important one, of jobs. What you "know how" to do.

When it comes to work, the Department of Labor and O*NET suggest that there are 33 "organized set of principles and facts applied in general domains."

The domains and the organized sets of principles and facts are[8]:

1) Administration and Management — Knowledge of business and management principles involved in strategic planning, resource allocation, human resources modeling, leadership technique, production methods, and coordination of people and resources.

2) Biology — Knowledge of plant and animal organisms, their tissues, cells, functions, interdependencies, and interactions with each other and the environment.

3) Building and Construction — Knowledge of materials, methods, and the tools involved in the construction or repair of houses, buildings, or other structures such as highways and roads.

4) Chemistry — Knowledge of the chemical composition, structure, and properties of substances and of the chemical processes and transformations that they undergo. This includes uses of chemicals and their interactions, danger signs, production techniques, and disposal methods.

---

8 All of the following material is from O*NET Online. I strongly, repeatedly urge you to visit their website: www.onetonline.org.

5) Clerical — Knowledge of administrative and clerical procedures and systems such as word processing, managing files and records, stenography and transcription, designing forms, and other office procedures and terminology.

6) Communications and Media — Knowledge of media production, communication, and dissemination techniques and methods. This includes alternative ways to inform and entertain via written, oral, and visual media.

7) Computers and Electronics — Knowledge of circuit boards, processors, chips, electronic equipment, and computer hardware and software, including applications and programming.

8) Customer and Personal Service — Knowledge of principles and processes for providing customer and personal services. This includes customer needs assessment, meeting quality standards for services, and evaluation of customer satisfaction.

9) Design — Knowledge of design techniques, tools, and principles involved in production of precision technical plans, blueprints, drawings, and models.

10) Economics and Accounting — Knowledge of economic and accounting principles and practices, the financial markets, banking and the analysis and reporting of financial data.

11) Education and Training — Knowledge of principles and methods for curriculum and training design, teaching and instruction for individuals and groups, and the measurement of training effects.

12) Engineering and Technology — Knowledge of the practical application of engineering science and technology. This includes applying principles, techniques, procedures, and equipment to the design and production of various goods and services.

13) English Language — Knowledge of the structure and content of the English language including the meaning and spelling of words, rules of composition, and grammar.

14) Fine Arts — Knowledge of the theory and techniques required to compose, produce, and perform works of music, dance, visual arts, drama, and sculpture.

15) Food Production — Knowledge of techniques and equipment for planting, growing, and harvesting food products (both plant and animal) for consumption, including storage/handling techniques.

16) Foreign Language — Knowledge of the structure and content of a foreign (non-English) language including the meaning and spelling of words, rules of composition and grammar, and pronunciation.

17) Geography — Knowledge of principles and methods for describing the features of land, sea, and air masses, including their physical characteristics, locations, interrelationships, and distribution of plant, animal, and human life.

18) History and Archeology — Knowledge of historical events and their causes, indicators, and effects on civilizations and cultures.

19) Law and Government — Knowledge of laws, legal codes, court procedures, precedents, government regulations, executive orders, agency rules, and the democratic political process.

20) Mathematics — Knowledge of arithmetic, algebra, geometry, calculus, statistics, and their applications.

21) Mechanical — Knowledge of machines and tools, including their designs, uses, repair, and maintenance.

22) Medicine and Dentistry — Knowledge of the information and techniques needed to diagnose and treat human injuries, diseases, and deformities. This includes symptoms, treatment alternatives, drug properties and interactions, and preventive health-care measures.

23) Personnel and Human Resources — Knowledge of principles and procedures for personnel recruitment, selection, training, compensation and benefits, labor relations and negotiation, and personnel information systems.

24) Philosophy and Theology — Knowledge of different philosophical systems and religions. This includes their basic principles, values, ethics, ways of thinking, customs, practices, and their impact on human culture.

25) Physics — Knowledge and prediction of physical principles, laws, their interrelationships, and applications to understanding fluid, material, and atmospheric dynamics, and mechanical, electrical, atomic and sub-atomic structures and processes.

26) Production and Processing — Knowledge of raw materials, production processes, quality control, costs, and other techniques for maximizing the effective manufacture and distribution of goods.

27) Psychology — Knowledge of human behavior and performance; individual differences in ability, personality, and interests; learning and motivation; psychological research methods; and the assessment and treatment of behavioral and affective disorders.

28) Public Safety and Security — Knowledge of relevant equipment, policies, procedures, and strategies to promote effective local, state, or national security operations for the protection of people, data, property, and institutions.

29) Sales and Marketing — Knowledge of principles and methods for showing, promoting, and selling products or services. This includes marketing strategy and tactics, product demonstration, sales techniques, and sales control systems.

30) Sociology and Anthropology — Knowledge of group behavior and dynamics, societal trends and influences, human migrations, ethnicity, cultures and their history and origins.

31) Telecommunications — Knowledge of transmission, broadcasting, switching, control, and operation of telecommunications systems.

32) Therapy and Counseling — Knowledge of principles, methods, and procedures for diagnosis, treatment, and rehabilitation of physical and mental dysfunctions, and for career counseling and guidance.

33) Transportation — Knowledge of principles and methods for moving people or goods by air, rail, sea, or road, including the relative costs and benefits.

That is quite a wide range of fields of knowledge isn't it? Let's take a moment to talk about "work" knowledge. It boils down to occupational know-how. You acquire the know-how in schools, in training programs, and on-the-job. The areas listed above all seem like they are very formal and it is somewhat difficult to see how many jobs fit into these neat categories.

So let's take a moment and look into O*NET, some jobs and how knowledge applies to them. We're going to go to http://www.onetonline.org/find/descriptor/browse/Knowledge/ and try a few things. If you have access to a computer, why not go online and work through these things while you continue reading?

If you go to that webpage, you will notice something called the "occupation quick search" box in the upper right hand corner. It looks like this:

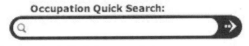

Figure 7 -1 Quick search box.

If you type in "bartender", the page will change and present a list of jobs that match "bartender." Selecting "bartenders" will take you to a summary report on "bartenders." On that page look a few lines down for a section that looks like this (in part):

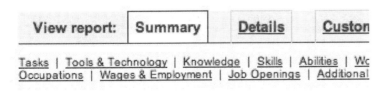

Figure 7 -2 Summary report tabs section

If you were to click on "Knowledge", or if you scroll down the page a little, you would find the category of "Knowledge" and learn that a "bartender" has knowledge in: 1) Customer and Personal Service, 2) Sales and Marketing, 3) Administration and Management, 4) English Language and 5) Psychology. Perhaps this is not what you thought a bartender's practical work knowledge is but then when you think about it, you can see it.

Let's try another. Type in "machinist." When you follow the path and get to "Knowledge" you find it consists of these areas: 1) mathematics 2) mechanical 3) production and processing 4) English language and 5) design. Some of those you may have guessed, some you may not have.

What you should begin to see is that many jobs, most jobs in fact, draw on more than one type or kind of knowledge. As someone who is seeking a career or job path, how does that help you? Even if you knew all the possible jobs that existed and out of all of them, which ones interested you, or which ones you had the skills to do, would you enter them one at a time and see what knowledge was needed for them? Seems unlikely.

There is something you can do though. Let's try another approach. Suppose you knew that you happened to have some knowledge in one of the categories, like "Mechanical." If you go to the website at the http://www.onetonline.org/find/descriptor/browse/Knowledge/ page and scrolled down to reveal "Mechanical" and clicked on it, you would get a list of jobs that required mechanical knowledge.

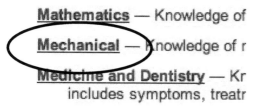

Figure 7 -3 Knowledge:

So do it, click on "mechanical.

Knowledge — Mechanical Save Table (XLS/CSV)

Knowledge of machines and tools, including their designs, uses, repair, and maintenance.

Sort by: Importance ▲	Level	Code	Occupation
96	92	49-3042.00	Mobile Heavy Equipment Mechanics, Except Engines
95	83	53-5031.00	Ship Engineers
93	98	49-3011.00	Aircraft Mechanics and Service Technicians
93	80	49-9021.02	Refrigeration Mechanics and Installers ☼ Bright Outlook ✦ Green
92	93	49-9044.00	Millwrights ✦
92	88	49-9043.00	Maintenance Workers, Machinery
91	85	47-4021.00	Elevator Installers and Repairers ☼

Figure 7 - 4 Jobs requiring Mechanical Knowledge

The page changes to a listing of jobs where Mechanical Knowledge is important; in fact it shows them in order of importance to each job and starts by showing you the top 30. But if you click on "Show All Occupations" you will find hundreds and hundreds of jobs that require less and less mechanical knowledge.

Knowledge — Mechanical Save Table (XLS/CSV)

Knowledge of machines and tools, including their designs, uses, repair, and maintenance.

Sort by:	Importance	Level ▼	Code	Occupation
	14	5	35-9011.00	Dining Room and Cafeteria Attendants and Bartender Helpers ☼ Bright Outlook
	8	6	31-1013.00	Psychiatric Aides
	4	7	15-2091.00	Mathematical Technicians
	9	7	25-2012.00	Kindergarten Teachers, Except Special Education
	10	7	39-3011.00	Gaming Dealers
	16	7	43-5021.00	Couriers and Messengers

Figure 7 - 5. Jobs requiring little or no mechanical knowledge.

Notice too, that not only are they listed by how important mechanical knowledge is to that job but that it lists what level of knowledge is required, where "a lot" is represented by a number in the "90s" and "a little" would be anything below 10.

Let's take a moment and think about these two aspects, "Importance" and "Level." The "Level" referred to here is how knowledgeable you need to be to do this job. "Importance" refers to how much the job is composed of this type of knowledge.

Knowledge

Customer and Personal Service — Knowledge of principles and processes for providing customer and personal services. This includes customer needs assessment, meeting quality standards for services, and evaluation of customer satisfaction.

Figure 7 - 6. Customer and personal service

These two categories are "sortable" so if you click on either of them, the list re-sorts by reversing from highest to lowest or lowest to highest. Try it and you should find that "dining room and cafeteria attendants and bartender assistants" require a low level of mechanical knowledge to do their jobs.

If you clicked on that job title group, you would get the summary report for those jobs and then scrolling down to Knowledge would reveal that the main type of knowledge needed is "Customer and Personal Service" knowledge and nothing else is listed. That is because so little of the knowledge required is mechanical that what little is needed is easily acquired on the job and not prerequisite knowledge ("prerequisite knowledge" is knowledge you must have before you can even be hired. (Note: when it comes to getting jobs, "prerequisites" like knowledge are more like guidelines that are often thrown out the window by an employer so they can hire the person they want whether they have the "prerequisites" or not.)

This information provides you with an introduction to the "Knowledge" aspect of jobs as opposed to the "Skills" or anything else you bring to the job search. In the workbook, the job knowledge categories are listed, and it is suggested that you investigate these categories to improve your understanding of them. You may recognize that you have more knowledge than you realized!

You are encouraged to explore O*NET. Poke around on the O*NET Knowledge page, see what kind of jobs are in each category. Skim over the lists and write down any jobs that seem to appeal to you based on your current knowledge or knowledge you can get. Go to the workbook and highlight or circle the ones that seem to best fit you.

Chapter 8: What are Abilities?

"I am only one, but I am one. I cannot do everything, but I can do something. And because I cannot do everything, I will not refuse to do the something that I can do." — Edward Everett Hale (1822-1909) American author, historian, and minister.

"Believe in yourself! Have faith in your abilities! Without a humble but reasonable confidence in your own powers you cannot be successful or happy." — Norman Vincent Peale (1898-1983) minister and author.

Background:

What are abilities, especially if they are not skills or knowledge? Abilities are mental and physical attributes, characteristics, things about you that, in part, determine your performance in the world .

According to the Department of Labor O*NET, there are four major clusters of these attributes:
* Cognitive (abilities to acquire and use knowledge to solve problems)
* Physical (abilities that use strength, coordination, flexibility, balance and stamina)
* Psychomotor (abilities that involve manipulating and controlling things and objects)
* Sensory (using your senses, vision, hearing, speech perception, tactile or touch and olfactory or smell).

Abilities

Enduring attributes of the individual that influence performance.

▶ ▢ **Cognitive Abilities** (21 elements) — Abilities that influence the acquisition and application of knowledge in problem solving

▶ ▢ **Physical Abilities** (9 elements) — Abilities that influence strength, endurance, flexibility, balance and coordination

▶ ▢ **Psychomotor Abilities** (10 elements) — Abilities that influence the capacity to manipulate and control objects

▶ ▢ **Sensory Abilities** (12 elements) — Abilities that influence visual, auditory and speech perception

Figure 8 - 1: O*NET Abilities groups

Together these four clusters, or groupings, are broken down into 52 elements, types or categories, of the major clusters. These are all in a table the workbook, so that you can keep track of your abilities.

By Ability cluster they are:

Sensory:
* Auditory Attention — The ability to focus on a single source of sound in the presence of other distracting sounds.
* Depth Perception — The ability to judge which of several objects is closer or farther away from you, or to judge the distance between you and an object.
* Far Vision — The ability to see details at a distance.
* Glare Sensitivity — The ability to see objects in the presence of glare or bright lighting.
* Hearing Sensitivity — The ability to detect or tell the differences between sounds that vary in pitch and loudness.
* Near Vision — The ability to see details at close range (within a few feet of the observer).
* Night Vision — The ability to see under low light conditions.
* Peripheral Vision — The ability to see objects or movement of objects to one's side when the eyes are looking ahead.
* Sound Localization — The ability to tell the direction from which a sound originated.
* Speech Clarity — The ability to speak clearly so others can understand you.
* Speech Recognition — The ability to identify and understand the speech of another person.

- Visual Color Discrimination — The ability to match or detect differences between colors, including shades of color and brightness.

Physical:
- Dynamic Flexibility — The ability to quickly and repeatedly bend, stretch, twist, or reach out with your body, arms, and/or legs.
- Dynamic Strength — The ability to exert muscle force repeatedly or continuously over time. This involves muscular endurance and resistance to muscle fatigue.
- Explosive Strength — The ability to use short bursts of muscle force to propel oneself (as in jumping or sprinting), or to throw an object.
- Extent Flexibility — The ability to bend, stretch, twist, or reach with your body, arms, and/or legs.
- Gross Body Coordination — The ability to coordinate the movement of your arms, legs, and torso together when the whole body is in motion.
- Gross Body Equilibrium — The ability to keep or regain your body balance or stay upright when in an unstable position.
- Stamina — The ability to exert yourself physically over long periods of time without getting winded or out of breath.
- Static Strength — The ability to exert maximum muscle force to lift, push, pull, or carry objects.
- Trunk Strength — The ability to use your abdominal and lower back muscles to support part of the body repeatedly or continuously over time without 'giving out' or fatiguing.

Psychomotor:
- Arm-Hand Steadiness — The ability to keep your hand and arm steady while moving your arm or while holding your arm and hand in one position.
- Control Precision — The ability to quickly and repeatedly adjust the controls of a machine or a vehicle to exact positions.
- Finger Dexterity — The ability to make precisely coordinated movements of the fingers of one or both hands to grasp, manipulate, or assemble very small objects.
- Manual Dexterity — The ability to quickly move your hand, your hand together with your arm, or your two hands to grasp, manipulate, or assemble objects.
- Multi-limb Coordination — The ability to coordinate two or more limbs (for example, two arms, two legs, or one leg and one arm) while sitting, standing, or lying down. It does not involve performing the activities while the whole body is in motion.
- Rate Control — The ability to time your movements or the movement of a piece of equipment in anticipation of changes in the speed and/or direction of a moving object or scene.
- Reaction Time — The ability to quickly respond (with the hand, finger or foot) to a signal (sound, light, picture) when it appears.
- Response Orientation — The ability to choose quickly between two or more movements in response to two or more different signals (lights, sounds, pictures). It includes the speed with which the correct response is started with the hand, foot, or other body part.
- Speed of Limb Movement — The ability to quickly move the arms and legs.
- Wrist-Finger Speed — The ability to make fast, simple, repeated movements of the fingers, hands, and wrists.

Cognitive:
- Category Flexibility — The ability to generate or use different sets of rules for combining or grouping things in different ways.
- Deductive Reasoning — The ability to apply general rules to specific problems to produce answers that make sense.

- Flexibility of Closure — The ability to identify or detect a known pattern (a figure, object, word, or sound) that is hidden in other distracting material.
- Fluency of Ideas — The ability to come up with a number of ideas about a topic (the number of ideas is important, not their quality, correctness, or creativity).
- Inductive Reasoning — The ability to combine pieces of information to form general rules or conclusions (includes finding a relationship among seemingly unrelated events).
- Information Ordering — The ability to arrange things or actions in a certain order or pattern according to a specific rule or set of rules (e.g., patterns of numbers, letters, words, pictures, mathematical operations).
- Mathematical Reasoning — The ability to choose the right mathematical methods or formulas to solve a problem.
- Memorization — The ability to remember information such as words, numbers, pictures, and procedures.
- Number Facility — The ability to add, subtract, multiply, or divide quickly and correctly.
- Oral Comprehension — The ability to listen to and understand information and ideas presented through spoken words and sentences.
- Oral Expression — The ability to communicate information and ideas in speaking so others will understand.
- Originality — The ability to come up with unusual or clever ideas about a given topic or situation, or to develop creative ways to solve a problem.
- Perceptual Speed — The ability to quickly and accurately compare similarities and differences among sets of letters, numbers, objects, pictures, or patterns. The things to be compared may be presented at the same time or one after the other. This ability also includes comparing a presented object with a remembered object.
- Problem Sensitivity — The ability to tell when something is wrong or is likely to go wrong. It does not involve solving the problem, only recognizing there is a problem.
- Selective Attention — The ability to concentrate on a task over a period of time without being distracted.
- Spatial Orientation — The ability to know your location in relation to the environment or to know where other objects are in relation to you.
- Speed of Closure — The ability to quickly make sense of, combine, and organize information into meaningful patterns.
- Time Sharing — The ability to shift back and forth between two or more activities or sources of information (such as speech, sounds, touch, or other sources).
- Visualization — The ability to imagine how something will look after it is moved around or when its parts are moved or rearranged.
- Written Comprehension — The ability to read and understand information and ideas presented in writing.
- Written Expression — The ability to communicate information and ideas in writing so others will understand.

One thing you may have noticed, especially in the "Sensory Abilities" categories, is that smell and touch are over-looked by the Department of Labor and O*NET. Yet, they are required in some jobs, and are a significant contributor to success in that job. Chefs and cooks use their sense of smell, as do doctors, and quality control people in the coffee and wine industries. The ability to feel is significant in many other jobs, especially in the garment industry where a feel for the cloth is very important and in medicine. Doctors are very much "hands on" people as they learn much by their sense of touch. I cannot say why these capacities are ignored but just be aware of it.

In the workbook, you will find an exercise that lists the categories within the four major Abilities Clusters. Before you turn to the exercises, why not go to the O*NET website and investigate each category, looking for jobs where the item is important. This will help to give you a better "feel" for what each item is.

Let's take a look at just one physical ability, "Extent Flexibility." What is it? Figure 8-2, Physical Abilities, can be found on O*NET at "http://www.onetonline.org/find/descriptor/browse/Abilities/:"

On that web page, click on "Physical Abilities". On that page, click on "Extent Flexibility" to see what jobs require various degrees of that physical ability.

At the top of the list are "Dancers" (importance rating of 88), followed by "Automotive Specialty Technicians" (importance rating of 75). "Automotive Specialty Technicians" (which has notes behind it that indicate it has a "Bright Outlook" for job growth in the

Abilities — Physical Abilities

Abilities that influence strength, endurance, flexibility, balance and coordination

Dynamic Flexibility — The ability to quickly and repeatedly bend, stretch, twist, or reach out with your body, arms, and/or legs.

Dynamic Strength — The ability to exert muscle force repeatedly or continuously over time. This involves muscular endurance and resistance to muscle fatigue.

Explosive Strength — The ability to use short bursts of muscle force to propel oneself (as in jumping or sprinting), or to throw an object.

Extent Flexibility — The ability to bend, stretch, twist, or reach with your body, arms, and/or legs.

Gross Body Coordination — The ability to coordinate the movement of your arms, legs, and torso together when the whole body is in motion.

Gross Body Equilibrium — The ability to keep or regain your body balance or stay upright when in an unstable position.

Stamina — The ability to exert yourself physically over long periods of time without getting winded or out of breath.

Static Strength — The ability to exert maximum muscle force to lift, push, pull, or carry objects.

Trunk Strength — The ability to use your abdominal and lower back muscles to support part of the body repeatedly or continuously over time without 'giving out' or fatiguing.

Figure 8 - 2: Physical abilities

and it is a "green" occupation meaning the work is strongly related to the growth of the energy and conservation industry). That seems to be a very good job to look into further. So click on it.

Abilities — Extent Flexibility Save Table (XLS/CSV)

The ability to bend, stretch, twist, or reach with your body, arms, and/or legs.

Sort by: Importance ▲	Level	Code	Occupation
88	71	27-2031.00	Dancers
75	Not available	49-3023.02	Automotive Specialty Technicians ☺ Bright Outlook ✎ Green
72	57	47-2131.00	Insulation Workers, Floor, Ceiling, and Wall ☺ ✎
69	61	47-5061.00	Roof Bolters, Mining
69	57	37-3013.00	Tree Trimmers and Pruners
69	55	47-2171.00	Reinforcing Iron and Rebar Workers ☺
69	52	47-2021.00	Brickmasons and Blockmasons ☺
66	64	49-3042.00	Mobile Heavy Equipment Mechanics, Except Engines
66	61	47-2152.02	Plumbers ☺ ✎
66	59	47-5011.00	Derrick Operators, Oil and Gas
66	57	27-2032.00	Choreographers ☺
66	57	49-9092.00	Commercial Divers ☺
66	57	39-9031.00	Fitness Trainers and Aerobics Instructors
66	55	47-2041.00	Carpet Installers

Figure 8 - 3: Jobs requiring "extent" physical abilities.

When you do, you will see a summary report that gives you an excellent description of many aspects of this job. Tasks, Tools & Technology, Knowledge, Skills, Abilities, Work Activities, Work Context, Job Zone, Education, Credentials, Interests, Work Styles, Work Values, and Related Occupations are all reviewed.

Summary Report for:
49-3023.02 - Automotive Specialty Technicians

Updated 2011
Bright Outlook
green

Repair only one system or component on a vehicle, such as brakes, suspension, or radiator.

Sample of reported job titles: Automotive Technician (Auto Technician), Technician, Mechanic, Air Conditioning Technician (A/C Technician), Trim Technician, Alignment Specialist, Automobile Mechanic (Auto Mechanic), Automotive Worker, Brake Technician, Drivability Technician

View report: **Summary** Details Custom

Tasks | Tools & Technology | Knowledge | Skills | Abilities | Work Activities | Work Context | Job Zone | Education | Credentials | Interests | Work Styles | Work Values | Related Occupations | Wages & Employment | Job Openings | Additional Information

Tasks

- Examine vehicles, compile estimates of repair costs, and secure customers' approval to perform repairs.
- Repair, overhaul, or adjust automobile brake systems.
- Troubleshoot fuel, ignition, and emissions control systems, using electronic testing equipment.
- Repair or replace defective ball joint suspensions, brake shoes, or wheel bearings.
- Inspect and test new vehicles for damage and record findings so that necessary repairs can be made.
- Test electronic computer components in automobiles to ensure proper operation.
- Tune automobile engines to ensure proper and efficient functioning.
- Install or repair air conditioners and service components, such as compressors, condensers, and controls.
- Repair, replace, or adjust defective fuel injectors, carburetor parts, and gasoline filters.
- Remove and replace defective mufflers and tailpipes.

Figure 8 - 4: Upper portion of O*NET Summary report of Automotive Specialty Technicians.

Toward the bottom of the summary, is something called the "job Zone". Let's look at that Job Zone category as it is important to you, the job seeker. The website breaks all jobs down into one of five categories of Job Zones based on the levels of education, experience, and training necessary to perform the occupation.

Job Zone

Title	Job Zone Three: Medium Preparation Needed
Education	Most occupations in this zone require training in vocational schools, related on-the-job experience, or an associate's degree.
Related Experience	Previous work-related skill, knowledge, or experience is required for these occupations. For example, an electrician must have completed three or four years of apprenticeship or several years of vocational training, and often must have passed a licensing exam, in order to perform the job.
Job Training	Employees in these occupations usually need one or two years of training involving both on-the-job experience and informal training with experienced workers. A recognized apprenticeship program may be associated with these occupations.
Job Zone Examples	These occupations usually involve using communication and organizational skills to coordinate, supervise, manage, or train others to accomplish goals. Examples include food service managers, electricians, agricultural technicians, legal secretaries, interviewers, and insurance sales agents.

Figure 8 - 5: Job Zone for Automotive Specialty Technician.

The five levels Job Zones are categorized into are: 1) Little or No Preparation Needed, (say, wouldn't that be useful to you if you have little or no experience, or little or no experience in a new field, or are looking for a new field to go into?), 2) Some Preparation Needed, 3) Medium Preparation Needed, 4) Considerable Preparation Needed, and 5) Extensive Preparation Needed.

✓ **One: Little or No Preparation Needed**
Two: Some Preparation Needed
Three: Medium Preparation Needed
Four: Considerable Preparation Needed
Five: Extensive Preparation Needed
All Job Zones

Figure 8 - 6: Job zone options on drop-down menu.

A click on category 1) Little or No Preparation Needed lists 48 occupations that require little or no preparation to get. Are they all the kinds of jobs you can or want to base a career, and your life, on? No! But some are. You can make a career of being a "Cook", a "Farmworker, a "Meat Cutter' , a "Model", a "Stock Clerk" or a "Waiter" for example.

Still, I would suggest that you take a look at all the five Job Zone levels to familiarize yourself with the types of jobs within each. Click on the jobs of initial interest to you and learn more about them.

Returning to the "Abilities - Extent Flexibility" page. You can click on the "Importance" heading and it will re-sort the list bottom to top. Now jobs where that ability is unnecessary are listed first. Why is this important to you? Suppose you have little or none of this particular ability, wouldn't it be useful for you to see some jobs that don't require it?

If you instead choose to sort the list by "level" or how much of it is used on the job, you might be surprised to see this skill, "Extent Flexibility" is needed even more by "Automotive Master Technicians" than by "Dancers." Who knew? The Department of Labor and O*NET did, now so do you!

Chapter 9: What are Skills?

"Man often becomes what he believes himself to be. If I keep on saying to myself that I cannot do a certain thing, it is possible that I may end by really becoming incapable of doing it. On the contrary, if I have the belief that I can do it, I shall surely acquire the capacity to do it even if I may not have it at the beginning." — Mahatma Mohandas Gandhi (1869-1948), civil rights leader in India

"Every artist was first an amateur." — Ralph Waldo Emerson (1803-1882) essayist, lecturer, poet.

"I didn't list listening as one of my skills, probably because I didn't hear what the interviewer asked." — Jarod Kintz (1982 -) author "This Book Title is Invisible" and others.

Background:

A skill is an ability to do something. We usually think of a skill as being possessed by a person if they have that ability, in other words they have learned, practiced and developed that skill enough to say "I have that skill." You can think of skills as those things for which you have a talent. Do you have a gift for writing or getting along with people? The "gift of gab"? You just seem to understand machines? These are examples of skills.

Skills broadly fall into two groups, job specific and transferable. Transferable skills are the sort of skills you use in many jobs and they don't belong to just one. Transferable skills allow you to take what you learned in one place and re-apply it in another setting. If you are a good public speaker, you can do this in many different settings. If you have good math skills, you can use these in many different jobs.

Job-specific skills are those that you develop your gift or talent in one specific job, through experience, education and training. You may have a talent for constructing things but you develop that skill from apprentice to journeyman to master of that job.

A skill set is a range of skills or talents required for a task or job.

Some jobs require a few skills, some many. The Department of Labor, Bureau of Labor Statistics groups skills into the following classifications: 1) Basic 2) Complex Problems Solving 3) Resource Management 4) Social 5) Systems and 6)Technical Skills.

If you go to www.onetonline.org, you will find that Basic Skills are developed capacities that facilitate learning or the more rapid acquisition of knowledge. In other words these are skills that help you acquire other skills.

Basic Skills include: learning, listening, thinking, learning strategies, math, reading, writing, speaking, and problem solving.

Complex Problem Solving Skills are those used when facing new, hard to define problems in the complex real-world setting. It involves reviewing related information, developing and evaluating alternatives and options, and implementing solutions. Creativity and "thinking outside the box" and critical thinking are part of this set of skills.

Resource Management Skills are the ability to allocate resources efficiently. They include managing finances (money), materials, personnel and time.The management of these resources include you as well as others as resources. Financial resource management is determining how money will be spent to get the work done and accounting for it. Materials management involves equipment, facilities and material to get the work done., Personnel management involves motivating, developing and directing people as they work and identifying the best people for jobs. Time management pertains to managing your time and others time to get work done.

Social Skills are those involving with others to achieve goals. They involve activities that may include: coordination, instruction, negotiation, persuasion, providing or being of service, or being aware of how and why others react as they do.

Systems skills are those involved in understanding, monitoring and improving socio-technical systems. Primary skills in this area are: judgment and decision making, systems analysis and systems evaluation. Judgment and decision making is examining the costs and benefits between potential action to take and choosing the most appropriate one based on the information available at the time. Systems analysis examines how a system works or could work if changes are made in conditions, operations, and the environment and predicting the outcomes if changes are made. Systems evaluation identifies measures (indicators) of system performance and determines actions needed to improve or correct performance in line with the system goals.

Technical Skills are those used to design, set-up, operate and correct malfunctions involving things like machines or technological systems. Primary skills in this area are: equipment maintenance, equipment selection, installation, operation and control, operations monitoring, operations analysis, programming, quality control analysis, repair, technology design, and troubleshooting.

Equipment maintenance is determining when, what kind of routine maintenance is required and performing it. Equipment selection involves what tools and equipment are needed to do a job. Installation of equipment, machines, wiring or program to specifications are the skills in installation. Operating and control refers to controlling equipment and systems. Operations monitoring are skills necessary to watch gauges, dial or other types of indicators to be certain a machine is working properly. Operation analysis involves examining the needs and product requirements necessary to create a design.

Programming specifically refers to writing computer programs for whatever purpose may exist. Quality Control Analysis involves inspecting and testing products, services or processes to evaluate their performance or quality. Repairing is the skills related to fixing machines or systems using tools and ingenuity. Technology Design means generating or adapting equipment and technology to serve user needs. Troubleshooting is the term applied to figuring out the cause when things go wrong and what to do about it.

That is an overall explanation of what "skills" means in the context of jobs and careers, especially as broadly defined by the U.S. Department of Labor and the O*NET website. I strongly urge you, as someone who is seeking their next job and is pursuing a career plan, to visit the O*NET website.

Before we proceed, there are some areas of skills that aren't easily categorized by the O*NET approach. Where, for example, do the skills of professional athletes fall into these definitions of skills? How about highly successful rock and roll musicians? Or something many of us dream of being, entrepreneurs, people who start and develop their own businesses, large and small and everything in between? Especially since it would be nearly impossible to predict what new businesses may come into existence to solve a problem that no one knew existed until the product and the business came to be. Who imagined the entire electrical industry, and light bulbs, before Thomas Edison? Personal Computers before Stephen Jobs and Bill Gates? Who didn't know we needed cell phones a hundred years ago or even thirty?

Aren't a Major League pitcher, outfielder, infielder, batter or an NFL linebacker or quarterback, or an NBA center or guard or an NHL goalie or center, wing or defenseman or world class soccer player skilled? How about a rock and roll superstar? You can criticize them but still need to acknowledge their skills exist even if you don't like them.

The more technical side of the skills involved in these areas are captured by the Department of Labor and O*Net but they do not really capture the flavor of the skills involved because they are atypical jobs and career. There is something more to them, skill-wise, that is hard to capture and express.

For example, instrumental musicians skills are listed as "Active Listening, Coordination (with others), Social Perceptiveness, and Speaking." Athletes possess these same skills plus "Speaking, Critical Thinking, Monitoring and Judgment and Decision Making." Really? Those don't seem like the skills my friends and I, and perhaps you and your friends, argue, ermm I mean, discuss when we're comparing our favorite quarterbacks or pitchers. Yah, I really like the active listening skills of Brett Favre but they do have to listen, there is no denying.

And there is no "occupation" listed under "entrepreneur." The closest are "General and Operations Managers." Again, really? This is not a criticism of the U.S. Department of Labor nor the O*Net project. In fact I am an avid supporter of it and will not only urge you to use it but will spend more time on it here and elsewhere in this book.

Why? Why recommend it to you if there are exceptions? If you are one of those people endowed with unusual athletic physical ability, or musical drive, ambition and talent (questionable as it may be others), or are dedicated to starting, owning and operating your own business, you are an exceptional person. Not only are you exceptional, it is very hard, if it is even possible, to define exactly what skills you will need to possess to make a career out of your gifts. Those skills are quite probably unique to you. You could even be the person who creates an entirely new job, like "UX Designer" or "App Developer" were just a short time ago.

The O*NET system is really designed for everyone else and is the most comprehensive way you can get at useful, work-related information that you can use to design and implement your career-work-life plan. In other chapters we discuss some of the other aspects of jobs that you can find on their website a few of these are: Knowledge, Abilities, and Work Activities and Context.

According to O*NET and Labor Department, skills are "Developed capacities that facilitate learning or the more rapid acquisition of knowledge." In the accompanying workbook, these are arranged for you to help identify your skills, and arrange them in meaningful and rewarding ways.

There are six broad categorical types of skills:
• Basic Skills (10 elements) — Developed capacities that facilitate learning or the more rapid acquisition of knowledge
• Complex Problem Solving Skills (1 element) — Developed capacities used to solve novel, ill-defined problems in complex, real-world settings
• Resource Management Skills (4 elements) — Developed capacities used to allocate resources efficiently
• Social Skills (6 elements) — Developed capacities used to work with people to achieve goals
• Systems Skills (3 elements) — Developed capacities used to understand, monitor, and improve socio-technical systems
• Technical Skills (11 elements) — Developed capacities used to design, set-up, operate, and correct malfunctions involving application of machines or technological systems.

The 10 Basic Skills - Developed capacities that facilitate learning or the more rapid acquisition of knowledge) are:
• Active Learning — Understanding the implications of new information for both current and future problem-solving and decision-making.
• Active Listening — Giving full attention to what other people are saying, taking time to understand the points being made, asking questions as appropriate, and not interrupting at inappropriate times.
• Critical Thinking — Using logic and reasoning to identify the strengths and weaknesses of alternative solutions, conclusions or approaches to problems.
• Learning Strategies — Selecting and using training/instructional methods and procedures appropriate for the situation when learning or teaching new things.
• Mathematics — Using mathematics to solve problems.
• Monitoring — Monitoring/Assessing performance of yourself, other individuals, or organizations to make improvements or take corrective action.
• Reading Comprehension — Understanding written sentences and paragraphs in work related documents.
• Science — Using scientific rules and methods to solve problems.
• Speaking — Talking to others to convey information effectively.
• Writing — Communicating effectively in writing as appropriate for the needs of the audience.
The single Complex Problem Solving Skill (Developed capacities used to solve novel, ill-defined problems in complex, real-world settings) is:
• Complex Problem Solving — Identifying complex problems and reviewing related information to develop and evaluate options and implement solutions.

The 4 Resource Management Skills (Developed capacities used to allocate resources efficiently) are:

• Management of Financial Resources — Determining how money will be spent to get the work done, and accounting for these expenditures.

• Management of Material Resources — Obtaining and seeing to the appropriate use of equipment, facilities, and materials needed to do certain work.

• Management of Personnel Resources — Motivating, developing, and directing people as they work, identifying the best people for the job.

• Time Management — Managing one's own time and the time of others.

The six Social Skills (Developed capacities used to work with people to achieve goals) are:

• Coordination — Adjusting actions in relation to others' actions.

• Instructing — Teaching others how to do something.

• Negotiation — Bringing others together and trying to reconcile differences.

• Persuasion — Persuading others to change their minds or behavior.

• Service Orientation — Actively looking for ways to help people.

• Social Perceptiveness — Being aware of others' reactions and understanding why they react as they do.

The three Systems Skills (Developed capacities used to understand, monitor, and improve socio-technical systems) are:

• Judgment and Decision Making — Considering the relative costs and benefits of potential actions to choose the most appropriate one.

• Systems Analysis — Determining how a system should work and how changes in conditions, operations, and the environment will affect outcomes.

• Systems Evaluation — Identifying measures or indicators of system performance and the actions needed to improve or correct performance, relative to the goals of the system.

The 11 Technical Skills (Developed capacities used to design, set-up, operate, and correct malfunctions involving application of machines or technological systems) are:

• Equipment Maintenance — Performing routine maintenance on equipment and determining when and what kind of maintenance is needed.

• Equipment Selection — Determining the kind of tools and equipment needed to do a job.

• Installation — Installing equipment, machines, wiring, or programs to meet specifications.

• Operation and Control — Controlling operations of equipment or systems.

• Operation Monitoring — Watching gauges, dials, or other indicators to make sure a machine is working properly.

• Operations Analysis — Analyzing needs and product requirements to create a design.

• Programming — Writing computer programs for various purposes.

• Quality Control Analysis — Conducting tests and inspections of products, services, or processes to evaluate quality or performance.

• Repairing — Repairing machines or systems using the needed tools.

• Technology Design — Generating or adapting equipment and technology to serve user needs.

• Troubleshooting — Determining causes of operating errors and deciding what to do about it.

The following examples of Skills and Jobs to illustrate the jobs where the skill is very important. It is not meant to suggest that only one skill is important to a job but rather to show you some jobs where that skill is very important *along with other skills*. The occupations listed are only a small subset of the jobs listed within each category. They are not necessarily "representative" in that you should only consider jobs like those listed, there are many diverse jobs in these groups, as you can see by those included in this section, and others may use these skills as well.

Jobs that rely on the Basic Skills examples by category:
Active Learning
• Molecular and Cellular Biologists

- Astronomers
- Physicians and Surgeons
- Physics Teachers, Postsecondary
- Psychiatrists
- Neuropsychologists and Clinical Neuropsychologists
- Judges, Magistrate Judges, and Magistrates
- Chief Executives
- Nursing Instructors and Teachers, Postsecondary
- Anthropology and Archeology Teachers, Postsecondary
- Clinical Psychologists
- Political Science Teachers, Postsecondary
- Art, Drama, and Music Teachers, Postsecondary
- Clinical Nurse Specialists
- Counseling Psychologists
- Education Teachers, Postsecondary
- Instructional Coordinators
- Program Directors
- Surgeon

Active Listening
- Mental Health Counselors
- Marriage and Family Therapists
- Social Workers
- Psychiatrists
- Arbitrators, Mediators, and Conciliators
- Counseling Psychologists
- Clergy
- Neuropsychologists and Clinical Neuropsychologists
- Lawyers
- Reporters and Correspondents
- Air Traffic Controllers
- Farm and Home Management Advisors
- Travel Agents
- Equal Opportunity Representatives and Officers
- Allergists and Immunologists
- Education Administrators, Elementary and Secondary School
- Educational, Guidance, School, and Vocational Counselors
- First-Line Supervisors of Police and Detectives
- Eligibility Interviewers, Government Programs
- Financial Managers, Branch or Department
- Sports Medicine Physicians
- First-Line Supervisors of Office and Administrative Support Workers
- Patient Representatives
- Order Clerks

Critical Thinking
- Mathematical Technicians
- Neuropsychologists and Clinical Neuropsychologists   Bright Outlook
- Anesthesiologists
- Administrative Law Judges, Adjudicators, and Hearing Officers

- Lawyers
- Molecular and Cellular Biologists
- Ophthalmologists
- Chief Executives
- Obstetricians and Gynecologists
- Dentists, General
- Family and General Practitioners
- Physicists
- Actuaries
- Biostatisticians
- Physicians
- Forest Fire Fighting and Prevention Supervisors
- Pediatricians, General
- Allergists and Immunologists
- Education Administrators, Elementary and Secondary School
- Psychiatrists
- Program Directors
- Biomedical Engineers
- Biochemists and Biophysicists
- Political Scientists

Learning Strategies
- Training and Development Managers & Specialists
- Teachers
- Education Administrators, Elementary and Secondary School
- Instructional Coordinators
- Coaches and Scouts
- Farm and Home Management Advisors
- Instructional Designers and Technologists

Mathematics
- Mathematicians and Mathematical Technicians
- Statisticians and Statistical Assistants
- Biostatisticians
- Physicists
- Mathematical Science Teachers, Postsecondary
- Actuaries
- Operations Research Analysts
- Geodetic Surveyors
- Engineers
- Astronomers
- Economists
- Chemists
- Cost Estimators
- Treasurers and Controllers
- Accountants
- Gaming Cage Workers
- Biochemists and Biophysicists
- Mapping Technicians
- Surveyors

Monitoring

- Gaming Supervisors
- Gaming Surveillance Officers and Gaming Investigators
- Coaches and Scouts
- Foresters
- Air Traffic Controllers
- Allergists and Immunologists
- Anesthesiologists
- Critical Care Nurses
- Psychiatrists
- Sports Medicine Physicians
- Industrial Production Managers
- Technical Directors/Managers
- Education Administrators
- First-Line Supervisors of Police and Detectives
- Producers
- Financial Managers, Branch or Department
- First-Line Supervisors of Non-Retail Sales Workers
- Lodging Managers
- Airline Pilots, Copilots, and Flight Engineers
- First-Line Supervisors of Correctional Officers
- First-Line Supervisors of Mechanics, Installers, and Repairers
- Instructional Coordinators
- Nurse Practitioners
- Spa Managers
- Dentists, General
- Environmental Science Teachers, Postsecondary

Reading Comprehension

- English Language and Literature Teachers, Postsecondary
- Historians
- Neuropsychologists and Clinical Neuropsychologists
- Editors
- Molecular and Cellular Biologists
- Allergists and Immunologists
- Sports Medicine Physicians
- Law Teachers, Postsecondary
- Sociology Teachers, Postsecondary
- Clergy
- Political Scientists
- Social Work Teachers, Postsecondary
- Instructional Coordinators
- Judicial Law Clerks
- Lawyers
- Education Administrators, Elementary and Secondary School
- Instructional Designers and Technologists
- Mathematical Technicians
- Preventive Medicine Physicians
- Agricultural Sciences Teachers, Postsecondary

- Sociologists
- Atmospheric, Earth, Marine, and Space Sciences Teachers, Postsecondary
- Epidemiologists
- Geneticists
- Urologists

Science
- Molecular and Cellular Biologists
- Physicists
- Biologists
- Epidemiologists
- Internists, General
- Chemical Engineers
- Chemists
- Astronomers
- Veterinarians
- Animal Scientists
- Biomedical Engineers
- Atmospheric and Space Scientists
- Materials Scientists
- Environmental Science Teachers, Postsecondary
- Nurse Practitioners
- Geoscientists, Except Hydrologists and Geographers
- Atmospheric, Earth, Marine, and Space Sciences Teachers, Postsecondary
- Biostatisticians
- Natural Sciences Managers
- Soil and Plant Scientists
- Anthropologists
- Chemistry Teachers, Postsecondary
- Neuropsychologists and Clinical Neuropsychologists
- Physics Teachers, Postsecondary
- Pediatricians, General

Speaking
- Social Work Teachers, Postsecondary
- Education Teachers, Postsecondary
- Radio and Television Announcers
- Clinical Psychologists
- Sociology Teachers, Postsecondary
- Art, Drama, and Music Teachers, Postsecondary
- Child, Family, and School Social Workers
- Lawyers
- Clergy
- History Teachers, Postsecondary
- Sales Representatives, Wholesale and Manufacturing, Technical and Scientific Products
- Eligibility Interviewers, Government Programs
- Public Address System and Other Announcers
- Business Teachers, Postsecondary
- Foreign Language and Literature Teachers, Postsecondary
- Health Specialties Teachers, Postsecondary

- Training and Development Managers
- English Language and Literature Teachers, Postsecondary
- Public Relations and Fundraising Managers
- Reporters and Correspondents
- Education Administrators, Elementary and Secondary School

Writing
- Poets, Lyricists and Creative Writers
- Technical Writers
- Historians
- Reporters and Correspondents
- English Language and Literature Teachers, Postsecondary
- Editors
- Archeologists
- Radiologists
- Copy Writers
- Government Property Inspectors and Investigators
- Environmental Science Teachers, Postsecondary
- Forestry and Conservation Science Teachers, Postsecondary
- Biological Science Teachers, Postsecondary
- Sociology Teachers, Postsecondary
- Education Teachers, Postsecondary
- Mathematical Science Teachers, Postsecondary
- Sociologists
- Geographers
- Lawyers
- Neuropsychologists and Clinical Neuropsychologists
- Nuclear Medicine Physicians
- Chief Executives
- Public Relations and Fundraising Managers

The single Complex Problem Solving Skill (Developed capacities used to solve novel, ill-defined problems in complex, real-world settings) is:

Complex Problem Solving
- Chief Executives
- Air Traffic Controllers
- Operations Research Analysts
- Judges, Magistrate Judges, and Magistrates
- Physicists
- Surgeons
- Oral and Maxillofacial Surgeons
- Administrative Law Judges, Adjudicators, and Hearing Officers
- Internists, General
- Clinical Psychologists
- Industrial-Organizational Psychologists
- Emergency Management Directors
- Biomedical Engineers
- Mathematicians

- Water/Wastewater Engineers
- Actuaries
- Mechanical Engineers
- Mining and Geological Engineers, Including Mining Safety Engineers
- Allergists and Immunologists
- Foresters
- Agricultural Engineers

Jobs associated with the four Resource Management Skill Areas include:

Management of Financial Resources
- Chief Executives
- Treasurers and Controllers
- Purchasing Agents, Except Wholesale, Retail, and Farm Products
- Training and Development Managers
- Cost Estimators
- Purchasing Managers
- Lodging Managers
- Biomass Power Plant Managers
- Construction Managers
- Medical and Health Services Managers
- Brownfield Redevelopment Specialists and Site Managers
- Social and Community Service Managers
- Industrial Production Managers
- Information Technology Project Managers
- Geothermal Production Managers
- Actuaries
- Compensation and Benefits Managers
- Storage and Distribution Managers
- Personal Financial Advisors
- Education Administrators, Elementary and Secondary School
- Public Relations and Fundraising Managers
- Spa Managers
- First-Line Supervisors of Animal Husbandry and Animal Care Workers
- Logistics Managers
- Education Administrators, Postsecondary
- Environmental Economists
- Producers
- Clergy
- Transportation Engineers
- Curators

Management of Material Resources
- Chief Executives
- Supply Chain Managers
- Industrial Production Managers
- Lodging Managers
- Construction Managers
- Cooks, Private Household
- Logistics Managers

- Purchasing Managers
- Curators
- Biomass Power Plant Managers
- First-Line Supervisors of Mechanics, Installers, and Repairers
- Mining and Geological Engineers, Including Mining Safety Engineers
- Brownfield Redevelopment Specialists and Site Managers
- Chefs and Head Cooks
- General and Operations Managers
- Geothermal Production Managers
- First-Line Supervisors of Animal Husbandry and Animal Care Workers
- Nursery and Greenhouse Managers
- Purchasing Agents, Except Wholesale, Retail, and Farm Products
- Manufacturing Engineers
- Information Technology Project Managers
- Medical and Health Services Managers
- Spa Managers
- Civil Engineers
- First-Line Supervisors of Aqua-cultural Workers
- Architects, Except Landscape and Naval
- Social and Community Service Managers
- Clergy
- First-Line Supervisors of Agricultural Crop and Horticultural Workers
- Program Directors

Management of Personnel Resources
- Coaches and Scouts
- Lodging Managers
- Human Resources Managers
- Social and Community Service Managers
- Education Administrators
- First-Line Supervisors
- Program Directors
- Gaming Managers
- Nursery and Greenhouse Managers
- First-Line Supervisors of Aqua-cultural Workers
- Medical and Health Services Managers
- Financial Examiners
- Spa Managers
- Training and Development Managers
- Purchasing Managers
- Sales Managers
- Biomass Power Plant Managers
- Construction Managers
- Financial Managers, Branch or Department
- Municipal Fire Fighting and Prevention Supervisors

Time Management
- Social and Community Service Managers
- Gaming Managers
- Logistics Managers

- Art, Drama, and Music Teachers, Postsecondary
- Coaches and Scouts
- First-Line Supervisors
- Operators
- Lodging Managers
- Program Directors
- Licensed Practical and Licensed Vocational Nurses
- Education Administrators, Postsecondary
- Industrial Production Managers
- Medical and Health Services Managers
- Advertising and Promotions Managers
- Financial Managers, Branch or Department
- Information Technology Project Managers
- Art Directors
- Education Administrators, Preschool and Childcare Center/Program
- Forest Fire Fighting and Prevention Supervisors
- Loss Prevention Managers
- Transportation Managers
- Meeting, Convention, and Event Planners
- Choreographers
- Secretaries and Administrative Assistants, Except Legal, Medical, and Executive
- Reporters and Correspondents

Jobs within the six Social Skills clusters include:

Coordination
- Lodging Managers
- Ship and Boat Captains
- Foresters
- Emergency Management Directors
- Social and Community Service Managers
- Technical Directors/Managers
- Clinical Research Coordinators
- Purchasing Managers
- First-Line Supervisors of Police and Detectives
- Training and Development Managers
- Coaches and Scouts
- First-Line Supervisors of Correctional Officers
- Spa Managers
- First-Line Supervisors of Office and Administrative Support Workers
- Licensed Practical and Licensed Vocational Nurses
- Choreographers
- Clinical Nurse Specialists
- Producers
- Brownfield Redevelopment Specialists and Site Managers
- Industrial Production Managers
- Clergy
- Forest Fire Fighting and Prevention Supervisors
- Medical and Health Services Managers
- Sales Managers

- Human Resources Managers
- Information Technology Project Managers

Instructing
- Coaches and Scouts
- Teachers, all levels, any subjects
    - Adult Basic and Secondary Education and Literacy Teachers and Instructors
    - Communications Teachers, Postsecondary
    - Vocational Education Teachers, Postsecondary
    - Career/Technical Education Teachers, Secondary School
    - Secondary School Teachers, Except Special and Career/Technical Education
    - Elementary School Teachers, Except Special Education
    - Forestry and Conservation Science Teachers, Postsecondary
    - Recreation and Fitness Studies Teachers, Postsecondary
- Music Directors
- Training and Development Managers

Negotiation
- Arbitrators, Mediators, and Conciliators
- Chief Executives
- Agents and Business Managers of Artists, Performers, and Athletes
- Lawyers
- Real Estate Sales Agents
- Sheriffs and Deputy Sheriffs
- Purchasing Managers
- Human Resources Managers
- Sales Engineers
- Counseling Psychologists
- Marriage and Family Therapists
- Wholesale and Retail Buyers, Except Farm Products
- Insurance Adjusters, Examiners, and Investigators
- First-Line Supervisors of Office and Administrative Support Workers
- School Psychologists
- First-Line Supervisors of Correctional Officers
- Residential Advisors
- Construction Managers
- Sales Managers
- Sales Representatives, Wholesale and Manufacturing,
- Brownfield Redevelopment Specialists and Site Managers
- Education Administrators, Postsecondary
- Lodging Managers
- Logistics Managers
- Property, Real Estate, and Community Association Managers
- Claims Examiners, Property and Casualty Insurance

Persuasion

- Sales Representatives, Wholesale and Manufacturing, Technical and Scientific Products
- Sales Engineers
- Chief Executives

- Clergy
- Arbitrators, Mediators, and Conciliators
- Sales Agents, Financial Services
- Agents and Business Managers of Artists, Performers, and Athletes
- Telemarketers
- Sales Agents, Securities and Commodities
- Sales Managers
- Lawyers
- Advertising Sales Agents
- Door-To-Door Sales Workers, News and Street Vendors, and Related Workers
- Real Estate Sales Agents
- Coaches and Scouts
- Counseling Psychologists
- Marriage and Family Therapists
- Sales Representatives, Wholesale and Manufacturing, Except Technical and Scientific Products
- Public Relations and Fundraising Managers
- Purchasing Managers
- Marketing Managers
- Financial Managers, Branch or Department
- Wholesale and Retail Buyers, Except Farm Products
- First-Line Supervisors of Non-Retail Sales Workers
- Loss Prevention Managers
- Retail Salespersons
- Sheriffs and Deputy Sheriffs
- Spa Managers
- Mental Health Counselors
- Human Resources Managers

Service Orientation

- Clergy
- Emergency Management Directors
- Counseling Psychologists
- Marriage and Family Therapists
- Concierges
- Licensed Practical and Licensed Vocational Nurses
- Mental Health Counselors
- Adapted Physical Education Specialists
- Parts Salespersons
- Child, Family, and School Social Workers
- Travel Agents
- Clinical Psychologists
- Morticians, Undertakers, and Funeral Directors
- Patient Representatives
- Clinical Nurse Specialists
- Lodging Managers
- Nurses
- Social and Human Service Assistants
- Reservation and Transportation Ticket Agents and Travel Clerks
- Food Service Managers

- Nursing Assistants
- Transportation Attendants, Except Flight Attendants
- Healthcare Social Workers
- Psychiatrists
- Mental Health and Substance Abuse Social Workers
- Naturopathic Physicians
- Nurse Practitioners

Social Perceptiveness

- Psychologists and Psychiatrists
- Mental Health Counselors
- Clergy
- Marriage and Family Therapists
- Neuropsychologists and Clinical Neuropsychologists
- Social Workers
- Substance Abuse and Behavioral Disorder Counselors
- Educational, Guidance, School, and Vocational Counselors
- Healthcare Social Workers
- Naturopathic Physicians
- Neurologists
- Morticians, Undertakers, and Funeral Directors
- Registered Nurses
- Community Health Workers
- Sales Managers
- Education Administrators, Elementary and Secondary School
- Public Relations and Fundraising Managers
- Nannies
- Rehabilitation Counselors
- Social and Community Service Managers
- Physical Medicine and Rehabilitation Physicians
- Probation Officers and Correctional Treatment Specialists

The three Systems Skills (and some of the occupations within them) are:

Judgment and Decision Making

- Chief Executives
- Judges, Magistrate Judges, and Magistrates
- Air Traffic Controllers
- Actuaries
- Doctors and Surgeons
- Mathematical Technicians
- Treasurers and Controllers
- Lawyers
- Dentists, General
- Education Administrators, Elementary and Secondary School
- Coaches and Scouts
- Oral and Maxillofacial Surgeons
- Forest Fire Fighting and Prevention Supervisors

- Government Property Inspectors and Investigators
- Industrial-Organizational Psychologists
- Marriage and Family Therapists
- Program Directors
- Biomedical Engineers
- Foresters
- Mining and Geological Engineers, Including Mining Safety Engineers

Systems Analysis

- Chief Executives
- Logistics Engineers
- Industrial-Organizational Psychologists
- Foresters
- Actuaries
- Chemical Engineers
- Sales Agents, Securities and Commodities
- Operations Research Analysts
- Water Resource Specialists
- Nuclear Engineers
- Clergy
- Manufacturing Engineers
- Computer and Information Research Scientists
- Risk Management Specialists
- Software Developers, Applications
- Mining and Geological Engineers, Including Mining Safety Engineers
- Business Continuity Planners
- Farm and Home Management Advisors
- Network and Computer Systems Administrators
- Social and Community Service Managers
- Electronics Engineers, Except Computer
- Financial Examiners
- Fire-Prevention and Protection Engineers
- Industrial Safety and Health Engineers
- Medical and Health Services Managers
- Regulatory Affairs Specialists
- Computer Network Architects
- Emergency Management Directors
- Informatics Nurse Specialists

Systems Evaluation

- Chief Executives
- Operations Research Analysts
- Industrial-Organizational Psychologists
- Engineers
- Actuaries
- Coaches and Scouts
- Computer and Information Research Scientists
- Computer Systems Engineers/Architects

- Transportation Planners
- Water Resource Specialists
- Medical and Health Services Managers
- Occupational Health and Safety Specialists
- Software Developers, Applications
- Human Resources Managers
- Network and Computer Systems Administrators
- Social and Community Service Managers
- Clergy
- Farm and Home Management Advisors
- Foresters
- Loss Prevention Managers
- Education Administrators, Elementary and Secondary School

Finally occupations within the 11 Technical Skills areas are:

Equipment Maintenance

- Aircraft Mechanics and Service Technicians
- Industrial Machinery Mechanics
- Signal and Track Switch Repairers
- Farm Equipment Mechanics and Service Technicians
- Medical Equipment Repairers
- Maintenance and Repair Workers, General
- Refrigeration Mechanics and Installers
- Avionics Technicians
- Automotive Master Mechanics
- Mobile Heavy Equipment Mechanics, Except Engines
- Robotics Technicians
- Elevator Installers and Repairers
- Maintenance Workers, Machinery
- Millwrights
- Heating and Air Conditioning Mechanics and Installers
- Ship Engineers
- Home Appliance Repairers
- Bicycle Repairers
- Electric Motor, Power Tool, and Related Repairers
- Outdoor Power Equipment and Other Small Engine Mechanics
- Wind Turbine Service Technicians
- Electronic Equipment Installers and Repairers, Motor Vehicles
- Robotics Engineers
- Electrical and Electronics Repairers, Powerhouse, Substation, and Relay
- Electrical and Electronics Repairers, Commercial and Industrial Equipment
- Electronics Engineering Technologists

Equipment Selection

- Mathematical Technicians
- Automotive Master Mechanics
- Elevator Installers and Repairers

- Signal and Track Switch Repairers
- Refrigeration Mechanics and Installers
- Electric Motor, Power Tool, and Related Repairers
- Robotics Engineers
- Farm Equipment Mechanics and Service Technicians
- Bicycle Repairers
- Manufacturing Engineering Technologists
- Electrical and Electronics Repairers, Commercial and Industrial Equipment
- Robotics Technicians
- Cabinetmakers and Bench Carpenters
- Industrial Machinery Mechanics
- Home Appliance Repairers
- Camera and Photographic Equipment Repairers
- Mobile Heavy Equipment Mechanics, Except Engines
- Aircraft Mechanics and Service Technicians
- Avionics Technicians
- Tool Grinders, Filers, and Sharpeners
- Electronic Equipment Installers and Repairers, Motor Vehicles
- Grinding and Polishing Workers, Hand

Installation

- Millwrights
- Heating and Air Conditioning Mechanics and Installers
- Refrigeration Mechanics and Installers
- Solar Photovoltaic Installers
- Electronic Equipment Installers and Repairers, Motor Vehicles
- Electro-Mechanical Technicians
- Elevator Installers and Repairers
- Electricians
- Radio, Cellular, and Tower Equipment Installers and Repairers
- Signal and Track Switch Repairers
- Mechanical Door Repairers
- Electronic Home Entertainment Equipment Installers and Repairers
- Security and Fire Alarm Systems Installers
- Automotive Master Mechanics
- Robotics Technicians
- Maintenance and Repair Workers, General
- Automotive Glass Installers and Repairers
- Electrical and Electronics Repairers, Commercial and Industrial Equipment
- Aircraft Structure, Surfaces, Rigging, and Systems Assemblers
- Weatherization Installers and Technicians
- Home Appliance Repairers
- Electric Motor, Power Tool, and Related Repairers

Operation and Control

- Airline Pilots, Copilots, and Flight Engineers
- Commercial Pilots
- Pilots, Ship

- Subway and Streetcar Operators
- Excavating and Loading Machine and Dragline Operators
- Mine Shuttle Car Operators
- Ship and Boat Captains
- Chemical Plant and System Operators   Green
- Locomotive Engineers
- Continuous Mining Machine Operators
- Logging Equipment Operators
- Earth Drillers, Except Oil and Gas
- Grinding, Lapping, Polishing, and Buffing Machine Tool Setters, Operators, and Tenders, Metal and Plastic
- Rolling Machine Setters, Operators, and Tenders, Metal and Plastic
- Heavy and Tractor-Trailer Truck Drivers   Bright Outlook
- Nuclear Power Reactor Operators
- Operating Engineers and Other Construction Equipment Operators
- Pile-Driver Operators
- Crushing, Grinding, and Polishing Machine Setters, Operators, and Tenders
- Nuclear Equipment Operation Technicians
- Agricultural Equipment Operators

Operation Monitoring

- Airline Pilots, Copilots, and Flight Engineers
- Gas Plant Operators
- Nuclear Equipment Operation Technicians
- Pilots, Ship
- Chemical Plant and System Operators
- Petroleum Pump System Operators, Refinery Operators, and Gaugers
- Commercial Pilots
- Aircraft Mechanics and Service Technicians
- Furnace, Kiln, Oven, Drier, and Kettle Operators and Tenders
- Grinding, Lapping, Polishing, and Buffing Machine Tool Setters, Operators, and Tenders, Metal and Plastic
- Nuclear Power Reactor Operators
- Wellhead Pumpers
- Crushing, Grinding, and Polishing Machine Setters, Operators, and Tenders
- Electro-Mechanical Technicians
- Computer-Controlled Machine Tool Operators, Metal and Plastic
- Industrial Machinery Mechanics
- Rolling Machine Setters, Operators, and Tenders, Metal and Plastic
- Derrick Operators, Oil and Gas
- Locomotive Engineers
- Subway and Streetcar Operators
- Earth Drillers, Except Oil and Gas
- Cooling and Freezing Equipment Operators and Tenders
- Locomotive Firers
- Manufacturing Production Technicians
- Pile-Driver Operators
- Power Plant Operators
- Service Unit Operators, Oil, Gas, and Mining

- Ship and Boat Captains

Operations Analysis

- Nuclear Engineers
- Aerospace Engineers
- Biomedical Engineers
- Civil Engineers
- Computer Systems Engineers/Architects
- Operations Research Analysts
- Marine Architects
- Natural Sciences Managers
- Computer Network Architects
- Medical and Health Services Managers
- Web Developers
- Landscape Architects
- Set and Exhibit Designers
- Marine Engineers
- Mechanical Engineers
- Architects, Except Landscape and Naval
- Energy Engineers
- Product Safety Engineers
- Chief Executives
- Fire-Prevention and Protection Engineers
- Marketing Managers
- Psychiatrists
- Remote Sensing Scientists and Technologists

Programming (Interesting to realize this technical skill area is less than 80 years old)

- Computer Programmers
- Computer Numerically Controlled Machine Tool Programmers, Metal and Plastic
- Web Developers
- Video Game Designers
- Software Developers, Applications
- Network and Computer Systems Administrators
- Biostatisticians
- Computer and Information Research Scientists
- Physicists
- Software Quality Assurance Engineers and Testers
- Computer Systems Analysts
- Statisticians
- Statistical Assistants
- Computer Systems Engineers/Architects
- Web Administrators
- Mathematical Technicians
- Biomedical Engineers
- Database Administrators
- Robotics Engineers
- Social Science Research Assistants

- Clinical Data Managers
- Computer Network Architects

Quality Control Analysis

- Agricultural Inspectors
- Quality Control Analysts
- Quality Control Systems Managers
- Signal and Track Switch Repairers
- Aviation Inspectors
- Musical Instrument Repairers and Tuners
- Fire Inspectors
- Aircraft Mechanics and Service Technicians
- Electro-Mechanical Technicians
- Robotics Engineers
- Electrical and Electronics Repairers, Commercial and Industrial Equipment
- Grinding, Lapping, Polishing, and Buffing Machine Tool Setters, Operators, and Tenders, Metal and Plastic
- Rolling Machine Setters, Operators, and Tenders, Metal and Plastic
- Electric Motor, Power Tool, and Related Repairers
- Manufactured Building and Mobile Home Installers
- Automotive Master Mechanics
- Farm Equipment Mechanics and Service Technicians
- Manufacturing Engineering Technologists
- Avionics Technicians
- Computer-Controlled Machine Tool Operators, Metal and Plastic
- Environmental Compliance Inspectors

Repairing

- Bicycle Repairers
- Aircraft Mechanics and Service Technicians
- Farm Equipment Mechanics and Service Technicians
- Industrial Machinery Mechanics
- Electric Motor, Power Tool, and Related Repairers
- Maintenance and Repair Workers, General
- Refrigeration Mechanics and Installers
- Avionics Technicians
- Medical Equipment Repairers
- Signal and Track Switch Repairers
- Electrical and Electronics Repairers, Commercial and Industrial Equipment
- Motorcycle Mechanics
- Elevator Installers and Repairers
- Home Appliance Repairers
- Automotive Master Mechanics
- Camera and Photographic Equipment Repairers
- Heating and Air Conditioning Mechanics and Installers
- Mobile Heavy Equipment Mechanics, Except Engines
- Robotics Technicians
- Wind Turbine Service Technicians

- Automotive Specialty Technicians
- Electronic Equipment Installers and Repairers, Motor Vehicles
- Outdoor Power Equipment and Other Small Engine Mechanics

Technology Design

- Manufacturing Engineers
- Human Factors Engineers and Ergonomists
- Biomedical Engineers
- Mechanical Engineers
- Robotics Engineers
- Software Developers, Applications
- Computer Systems Analysts
- Computer Network Architects
- Aerospace Engineers
- Photonics Engineers
- Water/Wastewater Engineers
- Industrial Engineering Technicians
- Informatics Nurse Specialists
- Commercial and Industrial Designers
- Manufacturing Engineering Technologists
- Mechatronics Engineers
- Physicists
- Fire-Prevention and Protection Engineers
- Electrical Engineering Technicians
- Orthotists and Prosthetists
- Agricultural Engineers
- Computer and Information Research Scientists
- Electronics Engineers, Except Computer
- Marine Architects
- Video Game Designers
- Network and Computer Systems Administrators

Troubleshooting

- Signal and Track Switch Repairers
- Aircraft Mechanics and Service Technicians
- Medical Equipment Repairers   Bright Outlook
- Mobile Heavy Equipment Mechanics, Except Engines
- Heating and Air Conditioning Mechanics and Installers
- Refrigeration Mechanics and Installers
- Avionics Technicians
- Robotics Technicians
- Elevator Installers and Repairers
- Farm Equipment Mechanics and Service Technicians
- Industrial Machinery Mechanics
- Automotive Master Mechanics
- Electric Motor, Power Tool, and Related Repairers
- Camera and Photographic Equipment Repairers
- Wind Turbine Service Technicians

- Home Appliance Repairers
- Ship Engineers
- Musical Instrument Repairers and Tuners
- Robotics Engineers
- Electro-Mechanical Technicians
- Electricians
- Electrical and Electronics Repairers, Commercial and Industrial Equipment

Some of the occupations listed above are "short versions" of long lists of "specialty" areas listed in the O*NET site within these categories. Typically, physicians and teachers were shortened to avoid excessive repetition (even though there is still some across the various categories). You should spend time investigating any skill area that you feel you might possess or want to explore to locate that most rewarding job and career path unique to you.

We will talk more about what "rewarding" means in another chapter but for now, let's spend a little more time looking into O*NET. There is a section in the Workbook that accompanies this text, where you are asked to list your skills. Take a hard, careful look at the O*NET definitions of skills, there is more there than is included in this book. Write each and everyone of those skills down that you possess in some degree. Notice I said "in some degree." You did, didn't you?

Recall that there are levels, called job zones, ranging from entry level to highly advanced. If you possess skills, to any degree, you can use this information to look at jobs that your skills fit and find a level you can use to enter that occupation. In other words, combine your current level of skill, along with your knowledge, ability and education and training to find a career path. Start with what you can do, and work towards what you'd like to end up doing.

Not all jobs require extensive or advanced skill in an area, just some. Other jobs require a lot of the skill or considerable amounts of it. O*NET can help you sort out your level of the skill as that level relates to work, job and careers. Do not sell yourself short, if you have the skill, acknowledge it, write it down. If you didn't buy or receive the workbook along with this text, at least get out a blank sheet of paper, write "SKILLS" across the top and then write them down.

When you do have a fairly comprehensive or complete list of all the skills you possess (or if you want to use the workbook section named "Skills"), then you can summarize by your strongest skills or those you would most like to use or develop.

Your efforts in identifying your skills, along with your knowledge and abilities, will be useful not only in finding the right job or career but even in talking with others about yourself in the workplace and when interviewing for jobs.

Chapter 10: What Else Is There?

"Knowledge is of two kinds. We know a subject ourselves, or we know where we can find information on it." — Samuel Johnson (1709-1784), English writer, landmark work "A Dictionary of the English Language" (1755).

"Where is the wisdom we have lost in knowledge? Where is the knowledge we have lost in information?" — T.S. Eliot (1888-1965) American born, British playwright, poet, essayist, publisher, social critic.

"What we find changes who we become." — Peter Morville, (?-) American author of "Information Architecture for the World Wide Web", other books, lecturer, businessperson.

Background:

When looking at jobs and careers and using the Department of Labor's O*Net website, you will find a wealth of information and a well-integrated framework that can be very useful to you in your work project.

In 1939, the U.S. Department of Labor first published its landmark work, "The Dictionary of Occupational Titles" (DOT) as part of its effort to collect and disseminate comprehensive occupational data.

The goal of the DOT, was to make useful information available for "job placement, occupational research, career guidance, labor-market information, curriculum development, and long-range job planning"[9].

The last complete edition of the DOT was published in 1991 and contained over 12,000 job titles. During the 1990s, work was started to make the information it contained accessible through the means of an online database system. During this period, different approaches to making the information available were developed. One of these approaches converted the content of the DOT to webpages and the developers[10] of the website at www.occupationalinfo.org still provide that information.

The other major project was a re-thinking of the structure and accessibility of the content of the DOT. For more about the world of O*NET, visit the O*NET Resource Center at it's website: www.onetcenter.org. At that website you can learn about the resources of O*NET, its content, means of data collection, developer information, plans, products and more. There is information on career exploration tools, ways and means of accessing these tools (physical places you can go to be able to use them, and others are available on line). The new system now organizes jobs into 1,122 categories.

One more great resource is the Occupational Outlook Handbook, which is what it sounds like, the outlook for various occupation. You can find it at http://www.bls.gov/ooh. The homepage is shown below.

---

9 Robert A Schaerfl, Director, U.S. Employment Service, Dictionary Of Occupational Titles (4th Ed., Rev. 1991) — Foreword

10 1 Photius Coutsoukis and Information Technology Associates (1995-2011)

Figure 10 - 1: Department of Labor, Occupational Outlook Handbook.

Notice that you have a number of ways to look at occupations, such as by pay, education and growth rate. If you were to click on "select by 2012 Median Pay", you

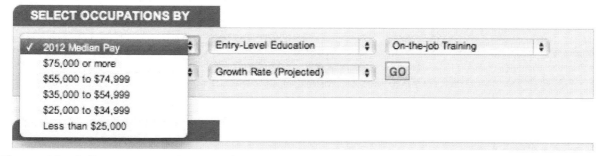

Figure 10 - 2: Department of Labor, Occupational Outlook Handbook, select occupations by wage.

would get a drop down list of pay ranges, as shown on the previous page, from under $25,000/year to over $75,000/year.

Click on one of those ranges, and then click on "go" and you'll get a listing of jobs that match that criteria, as shown on the following pages. You can even further refine your search by selecting additional criteria on this page.

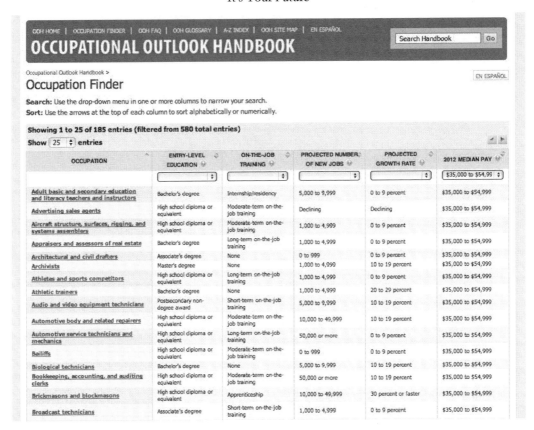

Figure 10 - 3, Department of Labor, Occupational Outlook Handbook, jobs by 2012 median pay. It might seem like there is too much information and it can be overwhelming but we have already covered some of the more important information in the preceding chapters. We will cover a little more in this and the next chapter.

When using O*NET, there are two general ways the material is arranged. One viewpoint is yours, as a worker (worker-oriented) and the other from the jobs' (job-oriented) point of view.

The worker-oriented material is broadly broken down into; Worker Characteristics, Worker Requirements and Experience Requirements.

Worker Characteristics are further refined into: Abilities, Occupational Interests, Work Values, Work Styles. Worker Requirements into: Skills, Knowledge and Education. Experience Requirements into: Experience and Training, Skills, Entry Requirement and Licensing. You may not have noticed but The three categories move broadly from being elements that go across occupations (Worker Characteristics) to occupation specific (Experience Requirements).

The general categories of job-oriented information also moves from cross occupational to specific occupations, which are: Occupational Requirements, Workforce Characteristics, and Occupation-Specific Information.

Occupation Requirements include: Generalized Work Activities, Detailed Work Activities, Organizational Context and Work Context. Workforce characteristics include: Labor Market Information and Occupational Outlook. Occupation-Specific Information includes; Tasks, Tools and Technology. For more detailed explanations on any of these, go to the O*NET website.

This is the basic types or categories of information *you* can access and use in *your* job and career planning.

In the next chapter, on we will talk more about your interests and they relate to jobs and job and career seeking, the O*NET tool, "My Next Move" but for now, let's take a look at the specific information that will show you how all that information is tied together in one job description.

When you go to the O*NET homepage, www.onetonline.org, you will see a box labeled "Find Occupations." It looks like this:

Figure 10 - 4: Department of Labor, O*NET, search for occupations with a "Bright Outlook."

The default is for occupations with a "Bright Outlook" defined as "occupations are expected to grow rapidly in the next several years, will have large numbers of job openings, or are new and emerging occupations ..." Clicking on the "go" button (a circle with an arrow in it, to the right of 'Bright Outlook') will lead you to another page and another box. The default setting for this box is "Rapid Growth" and it looks like this:

Figure 10 - 5: Dept. of Labor, O*NET, jobs with a Bright Outlook, Rapid Growth drop-down.

Before we go further, each of these boxes are called "drop down" boxes and contain multiple options from which you make a choice, kind of like mini-menus.

If you click on the "Go" button, and this time it really says go, you will see a list of jobs and occupations that are likely to see growth rates of more than 22% over the next decade. These certainly qualify as "Bright Outlook", "Rapid Growth" jobs. They are sorted alphabetically not by "fastest growing" as you might expect. You don't even get that option as a way to see the jobs listed. However, it is not a terribly long list and you can review it and pick those that seem interesting to you.

We'll pick just one, Bicycle Repairers, to learn more about the information O*NET can provide you with on any job, that's right any job.

In general, the Summary Report you get at this point contains the following information: Tasks, Knowledge, Skills, Abilities, Work Activities, Work Context, Job Zone, Education, Credentials, Interests, Work Styles, Work Values, Related Occupations, Wages & Employment, and Job Openings. That's fifteen categories of information, for those of you like to count things.

The information is presented in "Summary" form initially but you can obtain "Details" or create a "Custom" version that suits you. So that you can see what a typical report contains, the following is the Summary Report for Bicycle Repairers.

It's Your Future

Summary Report for:
49-3091.00 - Bicycle Repairers

Updated 2010
Bright Outlook

Repair and service bicycles.

Sample of reported job titles: Bicycle Mechanic, Bike Mechanic, Bicycle Service Technician, Bicycle Repairman

| View report: | Summary | Details | Custom |

Tasks | Knowledge | Skills | Abilities | Work Activities | Work Context | Job Zone | Education | Credentials | Interests | Work Styles | Work Values | Related Occupations | Wages & Employment | Job Openings

Figure 10 - 6: Dept. of Labor, O*NET, Summary Report for bicycle Repairers.

Tasks

Install and adjust speed and gear mechanisms.
Assemble new bicycles.
Install, repair, and replace equipment or accessories, such as handlebars, stands, lights, and seats.
Align wheels.
Disassemble axles to repair, adjust, and replace defective parts, using hand tools.
Shape replacement parts, using bench grinders.
Repair holes in tire tubes, using scrapers and patches.
Weld broken or cracked frames together, using oxyacetylene torches and welding rods.
Paint bicycle frames, using spray guns or brushes.

Knowledge

Customer and Personal Service — Knowledge of principles and processes for providing customer and personal services. This includes customer needs assessment, meeting quality standards for services, and evaluation of customer satisfaction.

Mechanical — Knowledge of machines and tools, including their designs, uses, repair, and maintenance.

English Language — Knowledge of the structure and content of the English language including the meaning and spelling of words, rules of composition, and grammar.

Engineering and Technology — Knowledge of the practical application of engineering science and technology. This includes applying principles, techniques, procedures, and equipment to the design and production of various goods and services.

Skills

Repairing — Repairing machines or systems using the needed tools.
Equipment Maintenance — Performing routine maintenance on equipment and determining when and what kind of maintenance is needed.
Troubleshooting — Determining causes of operating errors and deciding what to do about it.
Active Listening — Giving full attention to what other people are saying, taking time to understand the points being made, asking questions as appropriate, and not interrupting at inappropriate times.
Critical Thinking — Using logic and reasoning to identify the strengths and weaknesses of alternative solutions, conclusions or approaches to problems.
Equipment Selection — Determining the kind of tools and equipment needed to do a job.
Quality Control Analysis — Conducting tests and inspections of products, services, or processes to evaluate quality or performance.
Social Perceptiveness — Being aware of others' reactions and understanding why they react as they do.
Speaking — Talking to others to convey information effectively.
Service Orientation — Actively looking for ways to help people.

Abilities

- 68 -

Manual Dexterity — The ability to quickly move your hand, your hand together with your arm, or your two hands to grasp, manipulate, or assemble objects.

Finger Dexterity — The ability to make precisely coordinated movements of the fingers of one or both hands to grasp, manipulate, or assemble very small objects.

Problem Sensitivity — The ability to tell when something is wrong or is likely to go wrong. It does not involve solving the problem, only recognizing there is a problem.

Visualization — The ability to imagine how something will look after it is moved around or when its parts are moved or rearranged.

Near Vision — The ability to see details at close range (within a few feet of the observer).

Arm-Hand Steadiness — The ability to keep your hand and arm steady while moving your arm or while holding your arm and hand in one position.

Information Ordering — The ability to arrange things or actions in a certain order or pattern according to a specific rule or set of rules (e.g., patterns of numbers, letters, words, pictures, mathematical operations).

Deductive Reasoning — The ability to apply general rules to specific problems to produce answers that make sense.

Oral Comprehension — The ability to listen to and understand information and ideas presented through spoken words and sentences.

Speech Clarity — The ability to speak clearly so others can understand you.

Work Activities

Repairing and Maintaining Mechanical Equipment — Servicing, repairing, adjusting, and testing machines, devices, moving parts, and equipment that operate primarily on the basis of mechanical (not electronic) principles.

Making Decisions and Solving Problems — Analyzing information and evaluating results to choose the best solution and solve problems.

Selling or Influencing Others — Convincing others to buy merchandise/goods or to otherwise change their minds or actions.

Performing for or Working Directly with the Public — Performing for people or dealing directly with the public. This includes serving customers in restaurants and stores, and receiving clients or guests.

Communicating with Persons Outside Organization — Communicating with people outside the organization, representing the organization to customers, the public, government, and other external sources. This information can be exchanged in person, in writing, or by telephone or e-mail.

Documenting/Recording Information — Entering, transcribing, recording, storing, or maintaining information in written or electronic/magnetic form.

Inspecting Equipment, Structures, or Material — Inspecting equipment, structures, or materials to identify the cause of errors or other problems or defects.

Identifying Objects, Actions, and Events — Identifying information by categorizing, estimating, recognizing differences or similarities, and detecting changes in circumstances or events.

Communicating with Supervisors, Peers, or Subordinates — Providing information to supervisors, co-workers, and subordinates by telephone, in written form, e-mail, or in person.

Getting Information — Observing, receiving, and otherwise obtaining information from all relevant sources.

Work Context

Telephone — How often do you have telephone conversations in this job?

Indoors, Environmentally Controlled — How often does this job require working indoors in environmentally controlled conditions?

Deal With External Customers — How important is it to work with external customers or the public in this job?

Freedom to Make Decisions — How much decision making freedom, without supervision, does the job offer?

Spend Time Standing — How much does this job require standing?

Spend Time Using Your Hands to Handle, Control, or Feel Objects, Tools, or Controls — How much does this job require using your hands to handle, control, or feel objects, tools or controls?

Structured versus Unstructured Work — To what extent is this job structured for the worker, rather than allowing the worker to determine tasks, priorities, and goals?

Face-to-Face Discussions — How often do you have to have face-to-face discussions with individuals or teams in this job?

Frequency of Decision Making — How frequently is the worker required to make decisions that affect other people, the financial resources, and/or the image and reputation of the organization?

Impact of Decisions on Co-workers or Company Results — How do the decisions an employee makes impact the results of co-workers, clients or the company?

Job Zone

Title: Job Zone Two: Some Preparation Needed

Education: These occupations usually require a high school diploma.

Related Experience: Some previous work-related skill, knowledge, or experience is usually needed. For example, a teller would benefit from experience working directly with the public.

Job Training: Employees in these occupations need anywhere from a few months to one year of working with experienced employees. A recognized apprenticeship program may be associated with these occupations.

Job Zone Examples: These occupations often involve using your knowledge and skills to help others. Examples include sheet metal workers, forest fire fighters, customer service representatives, physical therapist aides, salespersons (retail), and tellers.

SVP Range: (4.0 to < 6.0)

Education

Percentage of Respondents - Education Level Required

74 - High school diploma or equivalent

25 - Less than high school diploma

1 - Post-secondary certificate

Credentials

There is a button to push "Find Certifications" to learn more about "Credentials" needed for the job.

Interests

Interest code: RCI (Realistic, Conventional, and Investigative)

Realistic — Realistic occupations frequently involve work activities that include practical, hands-on problems and solutions. They often deal with plants, animals, and real-world materials like wood, tools, and machinery. Many of the occupations require working outside, and do not involve a lot of paperwork or working closely with others.

Conventional — Conventional occupations frequently involve following set procedures and routines. These occupations can include working with data and details more than with ideas. Usually there is a clear line of authority to follow.

Investigative — Investigative occupations frequently involve working with ideas, and require an extensive amount of thinking. These occupations can involve searching for facts and figuring out problems mentally.

Just to see if you're paying attention and reading all of this, we will return to discuss the "Interests" and "Interest code's" in another chapter. These codes are called "Holland Codes" or "Holland Occupational Themes" and are named after psychologist John L. Holland, He theorized that certain jobs and occupations would hold more appeal than others for certain personality types. His work on theories of jobs and personality flourished and grew to create an entire system of occupational codes that relate to a combination of six vocational-personality categories.

Jobs and people are assigned three letters that "define" the job in terms of key personality factors. It is theorized that a person will be most satisfied in jobs where their codes and the job/occupations codes match.

Returning to the "Bicycle Repairer Summary Report" example:

Work Styles

Cooperation — Job requires being pleasant with others on the job and displaying a good-natured, cooperative attitude.

Attention to Detail — Job requires being careful about detail and thorough in completing work tasks.

Dependability — Job requires being reliable, responsible, and dependable, and fulfilling obligations.

Initiative — Job requires a willingness to take on responsibilities and challenges.

Achievement/Effort — Job requires establishing and maintaining personally challenging achievement goals and exerting effort toward mastering tasks.

Analytical Thinking — Job requires analyzing information and using logic to address work-related issues and problems.

Self Control — Job requires maintaining composure, keeping emotions in check, controlling anger, and avoiding aggressive behavior, even in very difficult situations.

Persistence — Job requires persistence in the face of obstacles.

Independence — Job requires developing one's own ways of doing things, guiding oneself with little or no supervision, and depending on oneself to get things done.

Adaptability/Flexibility — Job requires being open to change (positive or negative) and to considerable variety in the workplace.

Work Values

Independence — Occupations that satisfy this work value allow employees to work on their own and make decisions. Corresponding needs are Creativity, Responsibility and Autonomy.

Achievement — Occupations that satisfy this work value are results oriented and allow employees to use their strongest abilities, giving them a feeling of accomplishment. Corresponding needs are Ability Utilization and Achievement.

Support — Occupations that satisfy this work value offer supportive management that stands behind employees. Corresponding needs are Company Policies, Supervision: Human Relations and Supervision: Technical.

Related Occupations
47-2044.00 Tile and Marble Setters
49-3052.00 Motorcycle Mechanics
49-3053.00 Outdoor Power Equipment and Other Small Engine Mechanics
49-3092.00 Recreational Vehicle Service Technicians
49-9011.00 Mechanical Door Repairers (Tagged as Bright Outlook)
49-9031.00 Home Appliance Repairers
49-9063.00 Musical Instrument Repairers and Tuners

49-9094.00 Locksmiths and Safe Repairers
49-9098.00 Helpers--Installation, Maintenance, and Repair Workers (Tagged as Green)
51-2093.00 Timing Device Assemblers and Adjusters

We interrupt this report to point out that this section, "Related Occupations" may be one of the most valuable resources to you. Why? Because if you find a "job" that looks good to you, interesting, matches your skills, abilities and knowledge, and is something you want to look into, you now have additional potential jobs. There are 10 extra potential jobs for "Bicycle Repairers", all of them appear to be really good job and career alternatives.

Wages & Employment Trends
Median wages (2013) $12.22 hourly, $25,420 annual
State wages (has a button to click on for more state specific information)
Employment (2012) 11,000 employees
Projected growth (2012-2022) Much faster than average (22% or higher)
Projected job openings (2012-2022) 6,400
State trends (has a button to click on for more state specific information)
Top industries (2012) Retail Trade

Job Openings on the Web (has two buttons to click on for more information)

So, how's that for a getting your hands on job and career information? In the next chapter, we will show you one more way to get at jobs and careers using O*NET, but there are many ways and you should actively seek local centers that can help you access the information. The Department of Labor, through the Workforce Investment Act has set up many places, some near you, where you can get help with O*NET.

If you go to the homepage, and click on the first column, "Help", the drop down menu includes this option, "Job Seeker Help." Click on it and where you will find phone numbers to call for more help or you can enter a zip code or state in the box and be given detailed information about resources near you, such as the Michigan Works! Macomb Service Center, Southgate Service Center or the Wayne Service Center.

And oh yeah, these are _free_ resources, that's right, free. Their mission is to assist you in your job and career quest. They will not do your work for you but they will assist you.

Map of State American Job Center Web Sites

Instructions: Click here to find unemployment insurance filing information for your State. (you will be leaving the National one-stop website)

Click on a State on the map to move to a one-stop website.

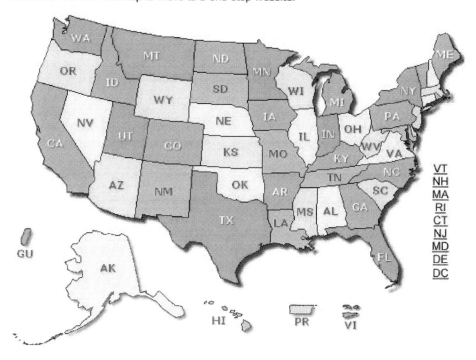

Figure 10 - 7: Department of Labor, Workforce Investment Act, interactive map to find Job Center sites.

Chapter 11: What's "My Next Move"?

"It is always your next move." — Napoleon Hill (1883-1970), American author of "Think and Grow Rich".

"I think there is something, more important than believing: Action! The world is full of dreamers, there aren't enough who will move ahead and begin to take concrete steps to actualize their vision."
— W. Clement Stone (1902-2002), American author, businessperson, philanthropist, co-author of "Success Through a Positive Mental Attitude" (with Napoleon Hill)

"Toto, I have a feeling we're not in Kansas anymore." — Dorothy, Wizard of Oz, L. Frank Baum (1856-1919) American author.

"Tell me what you pay attention to and I will tell you who you are." — José Ortega y Gasset (1883-1955) Spanish essayist, philosopher, professor.

Background:

It could be that you want to explore jobs and careers based on your interests. O*NET defines "interests are preferences for work environments and outcomes".

O*NET divides "interests," into six categories based on the work of the late psychologist, John L. Holland. He theorized that there are six categories of (work) personality type based on our interests and our approach to life situations.

The six are: Realistic (R), Investigative (I), Artistic (A), Social (S), Enterprising (E) and Conventional (C). Each person can be assigned a three letter code, a "Holland Code" or "Holland Occupational Theme" referring to those categories. This Holland Code signifies which of these six elements most clearly defines them in terms of their job interests (or the types of jobs whose content would most appeal to them).

Holland said that jobs and occupations can be analyzed for those same characteristics as well as individuals. Finding a satisfying job and career might then be as simple as matching an individuals codes to an occupations codes.

So what do these six primary themes look like? Here are the O*NET definitions of each[11]:

Realistic (R) — Realistic occupations frequently involve work activities that include practical, hands-on problems and solutions. They often deal with plants, animals, and real-world materials like wood, tools, and machinery. Many of the occupations require working outside, and do not involve a lot of paperwork or working closely with others.

Investigative (I) — Investigative occupations frequently involve working with ideas, and require an extensive amount of thinking. These occupations can involve searching for facts and figuring out problems mentally.

Artistic (A) — Artistic occupations frequently involve working with forms, designs and patterns. They often require self-expression and the work can be done without following a clear set of rules.

Social (S) — Social occupations frequently involve working with, communicating with, and teaching people. These occupations often involve helping or providing service to others.

Enterprising (E) — Enterprising occupations frequently involve starting up and carrying out projects. These occupations can involve leading people and making many decisions. Sometimes they require risk taking and often deal with business.

---

11 definitions are from O*NET Data Descriptors.

Conventional (C) — Conventional occupations frequently involve following set procedures and routines. These occupations can include working with data and details more than with ideas. Usually there is a clear line of authority to follow.

So a "Realistic" person might like jobs that are tangible, concrete as opposed to abstract and intangible. A Realistic person might prefer working alone or with other "Realistics." Some examples are: engineer, chemist, plumber, automotive technicians, electricians and other skilled tradespersons, and surgeons.

Investigative work involves using abstract or analytical skills to problem solve or work things out, as opposed to tangible, concrete problems and tasks. "Investigatives" like to work independently. They like to complete tasks. Examples are: political scientists, psychologists, bicycle repairers, business analysts, optometrists.

Artistic work is all about creating things, and requires imagination and the application of imagination. Examples are: writer, reporter, fashion designer, craft artists, hairdressers, nannies, and photographers.

Social work (not Social Work the field per se but it is included in it) involves interacting with people, and solving social problems and helping others. Examples are: hosts and hostesses, childcare workers, funeral attendants, nurses, community health workers, and teachers.

Enterprising work involves some form of leadership in the role. Their tasks involve challenges, and the people who perform in them are assertive, sometimes aggressive and outgoing. Examples are: chief executive officers, retail salespersons, attorney, wholesale or retail buyers, first line supervisors, telemarketers, and treasurers.

Conventional work encompasses structured tasks, paying attention to details, regularity in the work, and conservative people often are comfortable in these occupations. Examples are: accountant, bookkeeper, actuary, human resource assistant, loan officer, web administrators, library technicians, archivists, and pharmacists.

Keep in mind that few, if any, jobs are purely centered around one of these six factors nor are people who take interest surveys typically only assigned one of these codes. In general, people and occupations are assigned a Holland Code consisting of three of the letters. They are given in order of significance, so a code of RAE would mean that "realistic", "artistic" and "enterprising" are the prime descriptors for either the person or the occupation. In fact, if there is a good match on these three factors, the theory predicts a person would be successful in that occupation, at least they'd be a good theoretical match. That is a good place to start when you are looking for the right match between you and a job.

This is not say that a person may not score extremely high on one or two of the categories. They do but it would still be more likely that they would have a third code assigned. The balance between the three codes, in other words, "how much" of each code is present is meaningful. If you were "high" on "R", and low on "A" and "E" then a job or career that leaned heavily on "R" would be a better fit than a more evenly balanced "RAE" career.

Some examples, by the way, of an RAE job are: craft artist, jeweler, tailor/dressmaker, chef and graphic designer.

If you are using the advanced search option on O*NET, clicked on the "Interests" option, and then any of the categories, you would go to a page that would allow you to enter any of the 120 combinations of any three of those factors in the order you choose, whether it be RAE, CSI, or IAE or ERA. Figure 11-1: O*NET "Interests" three-letter interest code selection menu, as displayed on the following page, shows the entry screen for the codes.

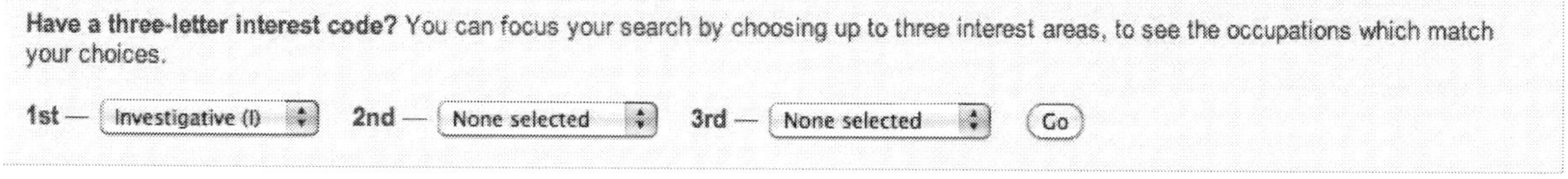

Have a three-letter interest code? You can focus your search by choosing up to three interest areas, to see the occupations which match your choices.

1st — [Investigative (I) ▼] 2nd — [None selected ▼] 3rd — [None selected ▼] (Go)

Figure 11 - 1: O*NET "Interests" three-letter interest code selection menu.

However, you don't have to go at it like this. There is a place where you can work through your interests as they relate to jobs. A place where there are no right or wrong answers. A place where you can "take the test" (it's actually a survey) and then go back and modify your answers and get new, modified results.

When you finish the survey, you obtain your personal RIASEC score on all six elements. You select the top three and put them in order of the value given and you have your Holland Code, like "CES"). Like the commercials say, "Wait, there's more."

This "Profiler" then offers you a way to look at occupations in terms of job zones, remember those, job zones? This will inform you of how much experience, education and/or training you might need for various jobs that match your personal Holland Code. Once you pick a job zone (either your current one or a projected one) you will be shown a list of jobs that match your RIASEC code. You can then click on one of the jobs listed and get a summary of information similar to but different from, the O*NET Job Summary Reports.

On the next page is a partial example of one of those reports, for a job as a Stock Clerk[12].

To access this superb tool, go to the webpage, www.mynextmove.org and click on the "tell us what you'd like to do" box, also shown on the next page.

Figure 11 2: My Next Move, sample report based on Holland Code, CRE.

---

12 excerpt from My Next Move, Sales Clerk, Sales Floor.

In the upper right corner is an icon for "Interests." Click on it and it will take you to the Interest Profiler, seen on the next page. There are a series of 60 questions that will help you see yourself in light of the Holland Scale and when you complete it, you will get your Holland Scale.

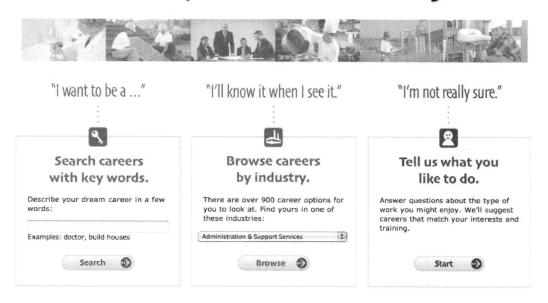

Figure 11 - 3: My Next Move "What do you want to do for a living?" screen.

Figure 11 - 4: My Next Move, "Tell us what you'd like to do" box. You can go to "www.mynextmove.org/explore/ip" directly and use the O*NET Interest Profiler as shown on the next page.

The answers you give are not "permanent." Suppose, for example, that you look at the first question "build kitchen cabinets" and select "unsure" as your answer to it. You can go back over the survey and modify your answers. When you finish it, you can save your profile and then revise it to see what impact different answers have on your Holland Code.

Why not plan to do it? You want to have as clear a picture of yourself as you can to get the best "fit" to occupations. Tinkering with your profile provides you the opportunity to get it right. So go back and modify some of your answers to see what impact that would have on your scale and more importantly your occupational matches. When you are comfortable with your Holland Code, print it out, or save it, or write it down (all six scores) because you can re-enter those scores on the first screen and jump over the "test" and use the rest of the information available to you.

The remaining information available to you is considerable, and in fact, is the point of using this "Profiler."

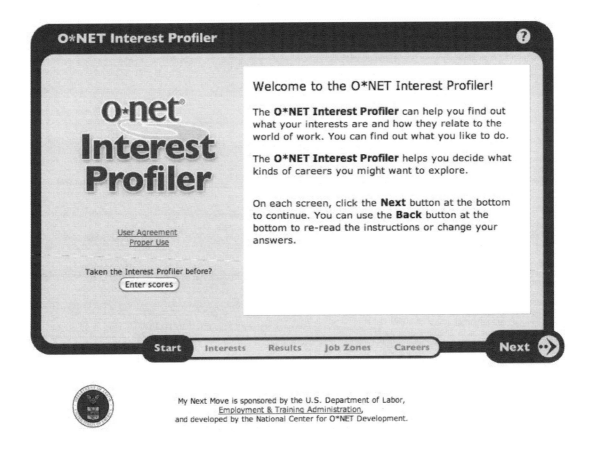

Figure 11 - 5: My Next Move Interest Profile screen.

You have the opportunity to look at "matching" occupations by job zone. In other words, you pick which job zone level you want to investigate and then move on to matching occupations.

For example, you could select, "Job Zone 1, little or no job preparation" for ideas on entry level occupations that matched your profile. You can then follow that to a page of potential jobs of interest to you, shown on the next page.

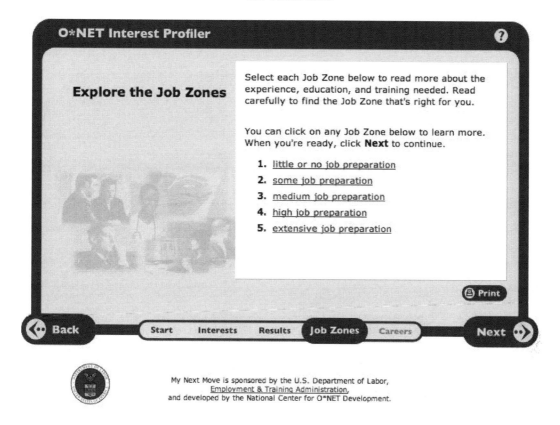

Figure 11 - 6: My Next Move, Explore the Job Zones related to your Holland Code. See
n on the following page is the report for "Hunters & Trappers".

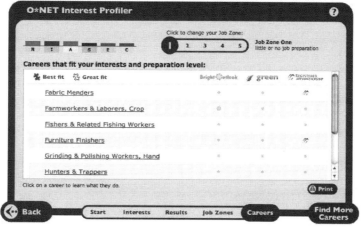

Figure 11 - 7: My Next Move, Careers for Job Zone for Holland Code "R."

Figure 11 - 8: My Next Move summary report for "Hunters & Trappers.

Notice that you can "See more details at O*NET OnLine" and that it is an active link so that you can easily obtain even more information!

Part 3: Tools

What are tools? Tools are things we use to help us do a better job or even make an impossible job possible. The next few chapters are tools for you to use to make your life better and make the impossible, possible.

Chapter 12: Problem Solving

"I suppose it is tempting, if the only tool you have is a hammer, to treat everything as if it were a nail." — Abraham Maslow (1908-1970) American psychologist, author "Toward a Psychology of Being."

"We always hope for the easy fix: the one simple change that will erase a problem in a stroke. But few things in life work this way. Instead, success requires making a hundred small steps go right - one after the other, no slip-ups, no goofs, everyone pitching in." — Atul Gawande, (1965 -), American surgeon, professor and author of "Better: A Surgeon's Notes on Performance."

"For every failure, there's an alternative course of action. You just have to find it. When you come to a roadblock, take a detour." — Mary Kay Ash (1918-2001) American businesswoman and founder of Mary Kay Cosmetics.

"Have you got a problem? Do what you can where you are with what you've got." — Theodore Roosevelt (1858-1920) American president.

Background:

Let's begin by defining "problem". According to Merriam-Webster, there are many definitions for "problem" among them are: "something that is difficult to deal with, something that is a source of trouble, worry, difficulty in understanding something, a feeling of not liking or wanting to do something, a question raised for inquiry, consideration, or solution, a proposition in mathematics or physics stating something to be done, an intricate unsettled question, and a source of perplexity, distress, or vexation".

Lots of things are problems, aren't there? You knew that though, didn't you? In this book we'll focus on the practical, career and life type of problems rather than textbook or real world problems involving math. This entire book is dedicated to helping you see solutions to solve the problem of finding your most rewarding job and career.

Everyone's got problems. Mostly we get experience solving them and then apply the knowledge we gained to help solve future problems.

Problems are everywhere, in abundance. Life is filled with problems. Plus, whether you're looking for them or not, they pop up all the time. A large part of our lives is spent dealing with our problems, finding solutions for them, devoting resources to them. Nobody is really looking for more problems, are they? Well, actually, yes, many people in business are looking *for* and *at* problems and *for* solutions everyday, that is how they make money. Problems are so much a part of life that it may be the most fundamental part of our lives.

Still, it is the solutions that are in short supply, isn't it? And if it isn't the solutions that are, it's the resources. In particular, since this is a book about your job and career future, we examine a problem solving model and then apply it to several job and career problems.

We'll also spend some time on your problems and how you deal with them (or don't). So, now let's take a look at your problems. Yeah you. You probably have a few, don't you? More problems than answers, solutions or resources. Some of them have answers but you can't implement them because of resources. Some have solutions, you just don't see the answer. What are you to do? Some of your problems are really big, some of them are small, but each and everyone of them is yours, in *your* life, affecting *your* life. It is *your* problem, until it is solved.

How do you approach your problems? Do you take them head on? Take them in order of appearance? In order of importance? Do you sort them out? Get help with them? Do you have a way to go about dealing with them? Do you avoid them? Do you have a problem (solving) plan?

Let's take a few minutes and talk about problem solving. It might surprise you to know that there have been a lot of people studying "problem-solving" in order to develop ways to make finding *solutions* easier. Or maybe you're not surprised at all.

We are going to assume that all problems have solutions. If it doesn't have a solution, how can you solve it? So no solution = no problem. It may be a situation but it's not a problem. It may be a problem even if you don't see a solution it just has to have one (or more).

In general, "problem-solving" involves applying patterns of general, or specific, methods, in an orderly manner, to find solutions to problems. We call these problem solving methods, "rules-of-thumb", algorithms or heuristics. Whatever we call them though, we want them to work, and to be able to refer to them whenever they are needed.

History

So, how do you go about solving problems? It depends on the problem, doesn't it? There are a lot of ways to solve problems, some are more efficient than others. People have thought about it quite a bit actually.

In1945, a mathematician, George Polya published a book called "How To Solve It", in which he discusses ways to approach and solve problems. Very simply he said it's a four-step process. Step One: understand the problem. Step Two: make a plan. Step Three: carry out your plan. Step Four: review your work and ask if there could be an easier or better solution. Polya said you don't even have to finish one of the steps, before you go on to the next one. He said you can even go back to an earlier one.

Okay, that sound easy enough, doesn't it? It is maybe not as easy as 1-2-3-four given that those four steps can represent a lot of work, lifetimes of it. Especially because that first step, "understand the problem" can be so difficult.

Problem Solving Model

Let's take a look at a another problem solving model built.

In this model we start with problem identification and then follow the flow around the diagram until we either solve the problem or identify new problems as a result. If that's the case, we start over again but this time with a clearer picture of the problem(s) we are trying to solve.

Let's look at each step of the diagram followed by questions you might ask yourself to help in the solution seeking process.

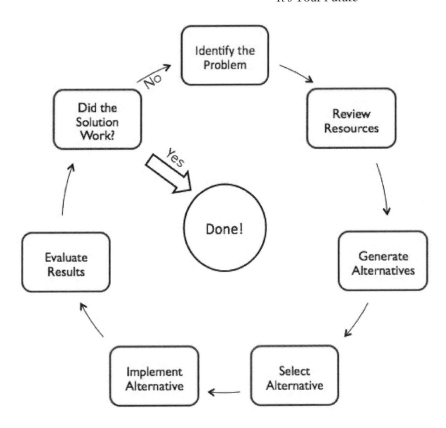

Figure 12 - 1: Problem Solving Cycle.

1. Identify the Problem
    1. Is it really just one big problem? If so, what is it?
    2. If it is a multi-part problem, what are they?
    3. If is a bunch of problems, what are they?
    4. How big a problem is it? Is it important to solve it right away or can it wait?

2. Review Resources
    1. Have you seen this problem before? How did you solve it then? Can you use the same solution?
    2. If it is a new problem, is it like any problem you've seen before? Would a similar solution work now?
    3. What might it take to solve this problem? Time, money, outside assistance?

3. Generate Alternatives
    1. What options do you have?

4. Select Alternative
    1. Pick one of the options, (usually the most efficient, economical, available, and likely to succeed, is a good starting point).

5. Implement Alternative
    1. Give it a try.

6. Evaluate Results
    1. See what happens.
    2. How did it work out for you?

3. Was the outcome satisfactory or could it have gone better? Was it good enough? Was it much better than you thought?

7. Did the Solution Work?
    1. Yes - you are done. Yay!
    2. No - start over again, this time with new information, new insights.

Referring back to George Polya's model, you can see this is an expansion on his theories. His second step or principle or phase is to devise a plan. Before we can devise a plan, we need to do a bit more work, like identify resources you have available to you and to generate alternatives and then weigh them.

Life, Job and Career Problems

To start, write down one or more of your problems. In fact, try writing them all down and numbering them in terms of importance to you. You can always look at the list and try to solve the easy ones while you work on the hard ones.

Try this technique. Just say it out loud. (You might want to do this when you are by yourself or alone). Say "My problem is (fill in the blank)."

Some possible examples are: My problem is I don't have enough money. My problem is I don't have a job. My problem is my car won't start. My problem is my kids won't behave. My problem is I'm _____ (too skinny, too fat, too old, too young, too stupid, too short, too tall, white, black, brown, Asian, East Indian, mean, ugly, uneducated, a felon, or whatever you think your problem is).

Some of those "problems" listed in the previous paragraph, aren't really problems at all. Some things are facts, facts of life. Your age for example, or your skin color, ethnicity, or that you committed a felony. Although your age does change, it only goes up. If you identified with those problems though, it does suggest you are having problems possibly related to that fact. What are those problems? Are they problems or aren't they? Yes and no. If they don't prevent others with them from finding a job or career, then they don't have to prevent you either, so in that sense, they are not problems.

They are also not problems in the sense that you cannot change them, and they do not have solutions. They may be problems though, in the job hunt depending on how you deal with or handle those facts. We do address some of these job-getting "problems" later in this book.

For now, let's start with the fallacy that your age, your race, your ethnicity, or a felony conviction mean you cannot or will not get a job or a career. Other people with your same "issue" or "concern" have. If they have, you can too! Unless.

Unless you want to use that as an excuse, the "reason why" you fail, fail to get the job or career you want. It is convenient after all, right? That fact may make it difficult for you but it is just an obstacle to overcome in the job hunt. First you must overcome it in your head, in your mind, and then in the mind of others. Get that? First you fix the problem in your mind. When you no longer see it as an obstacle, you are well on your way to removing it as an obstacle at all. You can then remove it as a barrier or obstacle to an employer. We will return to these types of job hunting barriers in subsequent chapters.

Did you follow that? Re-read those last two paragraphs again if you didn't. These problems are only problems because they are barriers in your own mind. They are not problems because, in and of themselves, you cannot change them, you cannot "solve" them. It is a perceptual issue in your mind. You can solve the real problem, your mental attitude about them.

So, what's a problem? If you said things like: "I don't have enough money," "I don't have job," "my kids won't behave," "my car won't start," then you've identified some problems. They have solutions, or do they?

A solution to "I don't have enough money" is get more money. No job? Get one. Got one but still don't have enough money, get a better paying one or a second job. Kids won't behave? Make them behave. Car won't start? Get if repaired and start it up. Do those answers sound kind of stupid? They are so simple and obvious that they aren't really solutions are they? They are goals. Goal attainment is a special kind of problem solving, and we talk about that in the next chapter.

Let's examine one of them, "no job," in light of the first phase or step in problem solving, "understand the problem." Is "no job" a problem. If you want or need one, it sure is but is it one problem? Assuming you want one, what seems to be the problem? Here are some possibilities:

- No job targets.
- No information about job requirements.
- No resume (one or two for each target)
- No knowledge of potential employers within a reasonable distance of home.
- No idea of what a "reasonable distance is.
- Haven't visit any employers to do an informational interview.
- No employer research.
- Haven't sent resumes with cover letters to a Potential Employment Target (PET).
- Haven't had any interviews.
- Haven't completed any applications?
- Unaware of how you look, your appearance, in an interview or of it's impact on your search.
- No transportation.
- Childcare issues or concerns that interfere with your job seeking.
- Other problems have cropped up.
- No job seeking plan.
- No job seeking experience.
- Poor interview skills.
- Clueless about how to go about finding a job or any job.
- Afraid to apply for one.

There are other significant things to do but for now, we are putting our focus on defining or understanding the problem. As you can see, there isn't one "no job" problem but rather a number of parts or pieces to the overall problem. Often in life, job and career seeking the problems are just too big to be solved in one simple step. They are actually composed of many smaller problems. That is a good thing and makes the job of solving "the problem" easier. Breaking the problem down gives you smaller problems to solve plus it offers you more solutions, more options, more alternatives, more resources.

Sometimes you need more information to solve a problem. Perhaps you noticed one or more phrases in the questions that you didn't understand. Phrases like "informational interviewing" and "Potential Employment Target (PET). Continue reading this book and you will get that information. If it is what you needed to solve the "no job" problem, then at least part of your problem, the need for more information, will be solved.

In another chapter, we discuss the concept of "Documentation" in more depth but for now, while you are problem solving, we suggest you write things down, also known as "documentation." The very simplest way to document things is simply write them down. When you, try this simple suggestion, "Put a date on it." Try it now, get out a sheet of paper, at the top (or the bottom, wherever you want, but try to always use the same place) write down today's date.

Then write down a problem you have. We're talking about "no job," so you could start with that. Then write down some problems that are part of the barrier or obstacles that get in the way of you getting one. Feel free to use some of those we already mentioned if they apply to you.

Problem Solving Examples

In the next few pages, we will use two examples. Problem No. 1 is about not finding a job. Problem No. 2 is the "need for clothes" for a new job. We follow both problems, step by step.

Problem 1:

Identify the Problem.

"I have been looking for a job for six months and haven't found one."

The simple answer to this is to find one. but that seems unlikely unless something changes but what? There are a lot of questions that can be asked about you and your job search at this point, like what kind of job have you looked for, why, and where have you "looked?" Your statement lacks clarity. It would be difficult for a professional employment adviser, or career development facilitator, to help you because they will have to start by asking you the same questions you should ask yourself. Are my job goals appropriate for my experience and skills? Do I have a (written) plan? Is my search organized or haphazard? What am I doing in my job search? Never forget to ask yourself, "How's my search working out?"

Review Your Resources.

I have a resume, a car, a cover letter. I am using my computer to apply for any job I think I am qualified for. I don't have a written plan but I spend a few minutes each day, using my computer to look for jobs. I got called to one interview.

As you begin to write out your resources, you might see that some of the resources you have, or do not have, may be part of the problem or part of the solution. In this example, the computer may be part of the problem or the solution. If you are only applying for jobs online, you have seriously limited yourself in your job hunt. Hopefully, you are beginning to see opportunities to improve the success of your problem solving.

What else haven't you done to solve the problem? What resources are available to you that you are not using, and maybe didn't think of? A plan? A written plan? An organized written plan? Looking in the paper for job leads? How about cold-calling? Using public and private job agencies? On-and-on, there are resources to be discovered that could be useful. There are available already, with a little work on your part.

Generate alternatives.

- Get professional assistance to improve job hunting skills, preparation, organization, etc.
- Go the library and study successful job hunting techniques.
- Use computer and get information about successful job hunting.
- Identify five potential employers (companies that employ people doing the job you are seeking) each week and then cold call four of them, one per day, each week. The fifth day, go to and do an informational interview. (We talk about information interviews later in the book).
- Develop an organized written plan. (You'll soon see why this is so important).

Make a Decision - pick an alternative.

Usually the most efficient, economical, available, and likely to succeed, alternative is a good starting point. How do you pick that right one? You could weigh your options. Sometimes you can't really narrow things down to just one "right" option. Doesn't really matter though, you are just looking for a starting point and if you pick the wrong one, you can always try another one, after you spend a few minutes thinking about why your first choice wasn't the right one.

You can even use a "magical" choice selection. What's a "magical" option? Relying on luck or some similar method. For example, suppose you identified six options. Write down the numbers 1 through 6 and next to each one write down the option. Get out one half of a pair of dice (a die), shake it in your hand and throw it down. The winning number is the option you go with. Or write your options down on separate slips of paper, put them in a bag, shake them up, reach in, pull the winning alternative. It's magic.

There are times when magic is as good a way to make a decision as any but, if and when we are talking about your future, your job, your career, it's not the best way to go. This is the time to focus and put good decision-making (still another chapter later in the book) to work for you.

You realize that out of all the options you've identified that it might be worth the time to go to a public employment adviser, sometimes called a Career Development Facilitator, and ask them for advice. You make a plan to visit them this week. You take a copy of your resume. You write down some of what you have done (as much as you can recall). Not satisfied with your plan or lack of an organized one, you put that into your "things to ask about" for the meeting. You also turn to the workbook and look at the "Organized Plan" section. There are examples of different plans and some blank plans for you to use. You also decide to visit the library and ask for books about job hunting. No one said you only had to choose only one alternative at a time. If you have more than one, why not choose more than one? In this case, you have chosen three things that are all likely to give you a good result or improve your chances for one.

Implement Alternative - Act.

Now it can't get easier than this. Do it.

So, you decide to go to the closest public Employment Center near you, in the morning, and to the library afterward. You open up the accompanying guidebook and read the "Organized Plan" sections in it. You want to think about which plan to use as your model before you start but you decide you will start when you return home tomorrow.

Evaluate results.

First, you did look at the guidebook and read over the Organized Plans. You plan to make a copy of whichever one you pick to use as a model.

Second, you went to the local public Employment Office and signed up to see a Career Development Facilitator and they will call you back for your first appointment. While you were there you took a look around and noticed a lot of things in the environment, books, computers, notices about workshops, and lots of people. "Hmmm," you thought to yourself, "wonder what all this stuff is?" So you asked and they told you that can come in for an orientation session tomorrow and learn about their resources. You signed up for that orientation.

Third you went to the library, and were shown five shelves of books about job hunting and career planning. The librarian also suggested some books on "selling" since they are related because she knew that job hunting is about selling. You chose several, including "Dress for Success." Plus, bonus, they also have DVDs and CDs about the topic so you can watch, listen and learn. You checked out one book, one DVD and one CD.

So you think back to what you did and how it worked out for you. You took action, a good thing. You made an appointment to meet with a Career Development Facilitator. You signed up for an orientation session at the center and even talked to a few people there, people using the services. You picked up some handouts too, and you saw a workshop on Resumes and signed up for that too. Your library visit opened you up to a number of books, CDs, and DVDs, on the subject of job hunting and career development. You also looked at Organized Plans.

Overall, you impressed yourself with all the things you did. It remains to be seen which of these things will make a difference but you are excited about your future because you are doing things, taking action to effect it. So far so good.

Satisfaction & Progress - satisfied with the solution, further action necessary?

By now you have realized your problem as stated, "I have been looking for a job for six months and haven't found one." is a statement of temporary failure, really a symptom of problems with your job search, not you, just the way you conduct your search. You are beginning to put your effort into uncovering a better way to go about your job search. Several of things you just did look promising, so although you didn't get a job, you are feeling success in learning new ways to go about the process. So, not done, keep going. Importantly, you feel a reduction in your stress levels, and by taking charge are feeling better about yourself. Results, good, but as said, not done.

Documentation & Problem Solving Example 2

Identify the Problem.

"I need new clothes for my new job."

Is that a problem? Maybe. If you got a job on a construction crew, you may need steel toed work boots. If you got a new job as a credit union teller, an office clerk, or a physical therapist, you may need clothes for those settings.

You need to analyze your problem. The first question is "Do you really need any new clothes?" Some jobs require, and supply uniforms. If that is the case, you may not need any new clothes except as directed by the employer (supplied by the employer or through an employer sponsored uniform company). You may or may not even need money for the uniform as they are often employer paid or deducted from your paycheck.

Some may require some special item, like steel toed boots, or special uniforms . Others may need nothing more than your current wardrobe because you will be supplied uniforms. You might just want new clothes, one of the reasons for wanting a job.

If you do find you need new clothes, you should sort out what you need to add to your wardrobe, like: 3 blouses, 1 skirt, 1 dress pants, 2 pairs of shoes, plus undergarments. Or maybe: one pair of steel toed work boots plus a hammer, steel rule, medium crescent wrench (tools needed for the new job).

Once you've challenged your assumption, "I need new clothes for my new job" and decided you do need something, you sorted out the problem into which things do I need. So you broke the problem down, sorted it out into smaller pieces, challenged the assumption and have small, solvable problems left.

Review Your Resources.

The resources available here are typically time, money, and transportation. Money is available in two forms, cash (or checks and debit cards) or credit (credit cards, owned or retailer accessible). Other types of resources might include, new clothing stores, clothing resale shops, online vendors, uniform suppliers. Another way to exercise your use of resources is to ask yourself if you can purchase items that can be mixed and matched, clothes that go together and will reduce what you have to spend now. Other options are to think in terms of a foundation wardrobe that you can add one or two items at a time to. For many men a few white dress shirts can be worn with many different ties to vary their work "uniform".

Generate alternatives.

You have two basic options if you don't necessarily need new clothes for the job. One, don't buy any now, wait until you're in the job and see what others are wearing and shop after you've received a paycheck. This is especially smart if you are considering using credit; after all you may not like the job and even stay. Option two is to go shopping. Pick your store based on your time, experience, and availability.

Make a Decision - pick an alternative.

Usually the most efficient, economical, available, and likely to succeed, alternative is a good starting point. So weigh your options. Or use one of the "magical choices" previously discussed. There are times when magic is as good a way to make a decision as any but, if and when we are talking about your future, your job, your career, it's not the best way to go. This is the time to focus and put good decision-making skills to work for you.

You decide to go to the local big box store and look for a (blouse, skirt, shirt, shoes, tie, whatever) but first look in the mark-down sections to see if you can save a dollar or two. Someone else might go to a resale shop and look for something really nice and save even more. Or you just go and buy those steel-toed work boots, they may not be pretty on your feet, like 3" heels but they will protect your toes (who said the construction worker was a man? Or that a man might not want to wear 3" heels, this is the 21st century, not the 20th).

Implement Alternative - Act.

Yay! You went out and bought three blouses, and two skirts, all that go together and cost way more than you should have. Or you bought your steel-toed work boots. Or you shopped and didn't find anything in your budget.

Evaluate results.

Person No. 1, the over-spender is feeling some remorse at doing that but at least she got some coordinated clothes that give her wardrobe flexibility. Call that mixed results and something to learn from, a little bit of concern over impulse control. Maybe she can work on it?

Person No. 2 got his or her work boots and can start work on Monday. Ta-da, perfect!

Person No. 3 still needs clothes but didn't buy anything she didn't need. Not a bad outcome just not successful. Perhaps a different store would work out? Maybe she doesn't need something new. Time to think about it.

Satisfaction & Progress - satisfied with the solution, further action necessary?

"I need new clothes for my new job." Depending on which person you were in this scenario, you are either done, or not. You may have surfaced a new problem to work on (over-spending), a new alternative to choose from (a different store), or realized you didn't need anything new just yet and can wait until you are on the job and have a chance to see what others in the environment are wearing. Other options depended on the circumstances (get required uniform) and you went with those. Overall, each of you has an answer, go on, or done. Yay for you!

In this chapter we looked at some ways people go about solving problems. It isn't some random, get lucky approach. It is the way you have gone about solving your problems, whether you knew it or not. One of the biggest problems for most of us in solving our problems is we don't have enough information, and getting the right information is priceless. One of those bits of information is having a problem solving framework to go, and you now have one. You can improve it (let me know if you do), or change it to suit yourself.

One last thing. You were asked to write things down, to document your process. If you did, you have a written record to look at that will help you see where you are stuck, what worked and what isn't working. It's much easier to see it when it is written down. Plus, you have the added benefit of being able to show your work to someone else who may be able to help you, like a friend, a relative, or a professional. When you show them what you've done, it is much easier for them to assist you. This is especially true with job-seeking professionals such as Career Development Facilitators at Workforce Investment Act facilities. Be sure to check in with them if you are having work-related, or job seeking related problems.

Chapter 13: Goal Attainment

"If you want to live a happy life, tie it to a goal, not to people or things." — Albert Einstein (1879-1955) mathematician, scientist, physicist.

"It's not hard to decide what you want your life to be about. What's hard, she said, is figuring out what you're willing to give up in order to do the things you really care about." — Shauna Niequist, (?) American author "Bittersweet: Thoughts on Change, Grace, and Learning the Hard Way"

"Shallow men believe in luck, strong men believe in cause and effect." — Ralph Waldo Emerson (1803-1882) American essayist, lecturer, poet.

"Goals are simply tools to focus your energy in positive directions, these can be changed as your priorities change, new ones added, others dropped." — O. Carl Simonton (1942-2009) oncologist, author.

"A goal without a plan is just a wish." — Antoine de Saint-Exupery (1900-1944) French author, "The Little Prince," aviator, aristocrat, poet.

"It's never too late. A determined mind and a positive attitude, will increase your ability to achieve and succeed any goal you want in life." — Ritu Ghatourey, female author in India.

Background:

What's a goal? What is goal attainment? What are objectives and milestones? How do they all fit together?

A goal is a desired result. It could be something you want, something you want to do, somewhere you want to go, something you'd like to achieve or accomplish or have, something you want to get done.

Some examples: I want a job. I want to see all 50 states. I want to build a house. I want to paint a picture. I want to write a book. I want to play a musical instrument. I want to be financially secure.

They don't have to be highly defined, but you do have to be able to know when the result was achieved. For example, you might want to play a musical instrument and will know you can when you can play one song that you recognize as the song you meant to play. For another person, "play a musical instrument" might mean playing a Bach fugue on a harpsichord in front of a sophisticated audience who would recognize it.

Objectives are goals and more often related to the implementation of a broader, more general long term strategy, plan or even mission.

Milestones are measurable achievements on the way to accomplishing a goal. Drive along a U.S. Interstate freeway and note the the mile markers along the roadside. Even the "Exit #" system, seen on the overhead signs, provide distance information and indicate how far from a border or starting/stopping point the exit is. These are milestones. They are a way of keeping track of how far you've come or how far you have to go. Their purpose is to provide you feedback and information to keep you on a predictable course.

Goal attainment is the process of getting the result(s) you desire. Goal attainment is one type of problem solving. The problem being, "how do I get whatever it is I say I want?"

For instance, you may have as a goal, getting into a satisfying career or buying a house or to become free of debt. In each case, you know what your desired result is; the problem is in how to attain or obtain that result.

One of the simplest techniques for goal attainment is to simply write down your goals. Get out a sheet of paper, at the top write today's date and "GOALS." Under that, write down "Things I want," "Things I'd like to do," "Places I'd like to go," "What I would like to be," "What I would like to change." Or you can turn to the section of the workbook called "Goals."

I recommend that you write these things down and then look at them every day for a month. Add to them. Think about them when you read your list. Picture them in your mind. Then put the list away. You don't have to keep looking at it, because your mind is an amazing thing. If you give it something to work on, it will guide you to it, if it is at all possible.

This worked for me. I wrote my own list in the mid-1980s. I put it away and found it after nearly twenty years. It was astonishing as to how many of those goals I realized. My top vacation goal and my automobile goal were obtained, along with many other things. It worked for me, it will work for you.

There are other Goal Attainment techniques. We mentioned applying problem solving to it as one. Another technique is called SMART. We'll discuss both. Let's take SMART first.

Before we proceed, you might ask "does the goal attainment process always have to be so formal?" The answer is "no." Life is filled with short term and long term goals. If you spent all your time writing formal goal attainment plans for everything would be exhausting and a waste of time.

It is helpful though to take time to make it more formal, for life's bigger goals. It helps to build a map of where we are and where we would like to be as clear as we can. You can refer back to your map to help you stay on track. One such formal plan is known as SMART.

SMART

SMART is an acronym for **S**pecific, **M**easurable, **A**ttainable, **R**ealistic, and **T**ime-bound and refers to objectives. Objectives are sometimes thought of as "little" goals, part of a general strategy, or as milestones (partial goals).

Here's an example of this model. You plan to spend at least one day in each of the fifty United States by age 50. The goal is to visit each state (Specifc). You can could get a US Map and put a checkmark on the map for each state visited or by creating a checklist of all 50 and checking them off after each trip (Measurable). It is Attainable goal, as well as Realistic (others have done it, why not you?). By putting a time constraint around it, "by age 50" you establish a deadline that you can look at later and determine if you've attained your goal. If you don't put a time constraint on it, even a wild guess, when will you decide if you've achieved your goals?

Of those elements of SMART (S), the "S" element is the most important. The more specific your goal or objective or milestone, the easier it becomes to focus your effort on its attainment. If you don't have a clear picture in your mind, how will you know if you attained it? The least important is typically T, Time-bound. It is nice to be able to achieve objectives within time limits, sometimes it is even necessary, but just as often it is not important. It also belies realities that interfere with your goal attainment.

It is best if you can Measure (M) your goal, such as lose 2 pounds per week for the next five weeks for a total weight loss of 10 pounds. Sometimes the attainment is more irregular, up and down. Lose 3 pounds this week, none the next, 2 the week after, then 3 again and finally 2 more. You hit your goal of a total weight loss of 10 pounds but blew your milestones of 2 pounds per week. That's okay though, isn't it. It helps to remember not to sweat the little stuff.

Why would you have an un(R)ealistic objective? Who decides if your objective is realistic or not? That's right it is you. No one else. Your life, your goals, your objectives. The human story is filled with stories of those who attained goals that no one thought possible. Thomas Edison failed to create an electric bulb 500 times before succeeding. Was "create an incandescent light" realistic? For some, maybe most people attempting it "no," but for him, "yes." Someone has to be the first, why not you?

This is not to say you should not be SMART in goal attainment, it is to say there is more.

One of the best ways to look at goal attainment, is to see it as a bridge. Build a bridge from where you are to where you want to be so that you can cross over it to get the results you want.

So, now let's return to goal attainment as a type of problem solving and apply it to finding a job and building a career.

The first step of problem solving is to define the problem. What is your job or career goal? Here are some examples:

"I want to be in the skilled trades as an electrician."

"I want to be a veterinarian."

"I want to sell medical equipment to hospitals."

"I want to be a realtor."

"I want to be a clerk in a government office."

"I want an entry level restaurant kitchen helper job."

Earlier in the book (and in the accompanying workbook) you performed some exercises that should help you state your goal in a few words or sentences. You could look to the work you did with O*NET and My Next Move as sources of job and career specific information. You could also incorporate the work you did looking at "Why People Work" and "Why People Volunteer." Those exercises can contribute to clarifying your values in the work place and your job objectives.

If you did select one or more potential job or career targets based on your research using O*NET, did you check to see if the values O*NET indicated for the occupation were similar to those you selected from "Why People Work" and "Why People Volunteer" as important to you? If so, those are things you should look for in the work place. If not, perhaps you should question why you want that job or career.

For example, if you selected "helping people" as important to you in those two exercises, does your job target or career target include that aspect?

If you still do not have a clear job or career goal that is your starting point, your problem is "I do not have a clear job or career goal." It might be a good idea to solve that one first.

Career Goal Attainment Problems

We're going to address too common Career Goal Problems and show you how to proceed if have these your problems. The first problem is "I do not a clear job or career goal." The second problem is "I have a clear job goal and now how do I get there?"

Problem 1: "I do not have a clear job goal or career path."

The goal is clear: Get one, develop one, make it a SMART one. A Smart one is specific, measurable, attainable, reasonable, and time-bound. It should also be a personally rewarding job for you.

Is this one big problem, a multi-part problem, a compound problem? It may feel like one problem, but it is a set of problems that can be solved. Actually, it is one problem with a number of things you can do to solve it. It is a big problem. Unless someone comes along and hands you a job, or you get "lucky" and find one that is available to you, you need to solve this problem.

So, how do you solve it? Helpful Hint: we pointed you at lots of great potential resources, so now let's apply more problem solving.

What are your resources?

O*net is one, the library another. How about going to a local public Employment Service Center, like those supported by the Workforce Investment Act? In Michigan, these are often connected to the MI Works! offices. There are similar offices throughout the country, to find one, go to this Department of Labor URL: http://www.doleta.gov/usworkforce/onestop/onestopmap.cfm and you will see an interactive map that will help you locate the center nearest you.

I mentioned where you are in life as an important factor for you. Your age, family situation, mobility, flexibility and health are some of those crucial factors. In your quest to develop a SMART rewarding job or career goal, you can use these factors to help guide you, too.

For example, if you are 18, just starting out after graduating from high school, or not, you have more time to develop a career that requires lots of time. You are most likely free to travel if you need to. You may be supported by your parents and are flexible as to work hours. You have the widest scope of opportunities. You have time to choose and pursue a goal. You may be able to develop more than one career over your work life. You have time to develop your career opportunities.

This is far different situation from that of a 45-year-old single mother of two. She has less time to prepare for a career that requires a long time to develop. She has less opportunity to re-locate, maybe even less flexibility in work hours. There is more pressure to develop and pursue one career goal, and less time to develop your skills to make a change later.

Still another situation is that of a 57-year-old worker who has been forced out of a long term job because of a plant closing. They may have narrow or broad skills, which are more or less generalizable to other situations. They may have savings to help tide them over, or they may not. They may or may not have immediate family depending on them for support, including aging parents. They need a job that requires little or no long term development, so they will need to focus on their current skills, abilities, knowledge, education and experience more. They will have more transferable skills and more experience to assist them.

As we continue looking at the problem, "I do not have a clear job goal or career path," we've identified a few resources to use. If you use the factors we just spoke about, or at least write them down as "influencing factors," you will be better able to proceed using those resources.

Practical Alternatives

Let's look at the development of some alternatives. Here are a few that might occur to you:

1) If you've had a job, look for another like it.

2) Use O*NET (www.onetonline.org), My Next Move (www.mynextmove.org), or the Occupational Outlook Handbook (http://www.bls.gov/ooh) and find jobs that match your background.

3) Go to a private employment agency.

4) Go to a public employment agency.

5) Read career and job development books at the library

6) Use the internet and Google "looking for a job". There are numerous websites that you could find useful. Nearly all, if not all, levels of government have websites and with some effort you can find their job application sections and apply for jobs for which you are qualified. There are employment websites where you can apply for jobs. There is America's Career Publisher, JIST, (http://jist.emcp.com/) where you can learn a lot about books about careers and jobs (some of which you can get at a Workforce Investment Act (WIA) site, or a library).

7) You can get newspapers and go to the "Help Wanted" section.

8) You can walk or drive around and look at businesses near you and go in and apply, if they have a "help wanted" sign up. You can try even if they don't.

9) Go to a military recruiter.

10) You could even take a wild guess?

This is not to suggest that any of these are specific recommendations for you to follow. Some are fairly weak, same-old-same-old solutions. There are better ways about finding your next most rewarding job, or the job that is your next career step. These are some of the potential things you could do to solve your problem, "I do not have a clear job goal or career path."

Pick An Alternative

So, let's pretend that those were your alternatives, though it wouldn't be difficult to come up with more. So, what is the next step? Pick one. You can choose more than one and probably should to increase your chance of finding alternative goals for yourself. Still, you need to pick one to meet the goal of your problem solving.

Try to pick one that is the most efficient, economical, available, and likely to succeed alternative you have. In many cases, this is going to be seeing a Career Development Facilitator (CDF) at a public Workforce Investment Act (WIA) site. They can introduce you to a wealth of materials, resources and aid you in developing a clear job or career goal. A good second choice is to use O*NET. Why not use them both? At WIA there are people who can help you with O*NET.

It's worth pointing out here that if you are like most people, you will have more than one career, and more than one job in a lifetime. If you pick a career path you later regret or no longer find rewarding, you can change it! You really can.

In either case, we once again urge you keep records of what you are doing. If you do, you can always show that information to a Career Development Facilitator (CDF), and help them understand you and where you are in the process, better, faster and easier.

Suppose you use the "My Next Move Interest Profiler" which reveals a few job clusters to which you seem well-matched. You add to these a few more from your own self-directed explorations using O*NET and found you have as many as 100-200 jobs you feel could be right for *you*.

Now, when you go to a Career Development Faciltator and show them what you have, they will readily see how they can help you focus on near term and long term opportunities. Even on your own, with that much information available to you, you should be able to narrow down your job and career options to a manageable few that are likely to be personally rewarding.

Okay, what are you waiting for? Do it. Go to the WIA site and sign up for a meeting with a CDF. Go online and take the "My Next Move Interest Profiler" (remember it's on the link in the upper right corner labeled "interests") and see what you learn about your possibilities. Better yet, do this and bring it to your meeting with the CDF.

Results

If you stopped here and then resumed after following through, how did it work out? Do you have one or more immediate job goals that match your background? Do one or more of these serve as a stepping stone or platform for a long term career? Did you develop an entry point for yourself? How satisfied with the results of your effort are you? If you are not satisfied, why not? Learn and grow.

Do you now have a job goal and career path? If the answer is yes, you are done and can move on to your next steps. If the answer is no, you need to continue to work on it.

What happened to prevent you from defining your job and career goal? Did the Interest Profiler fail to indicate any jobs or careers that interested you? Did you look into the Job Zones to find jobs that matched your skill levels. Were the jobs and careers "out of reach" given your age, social factors (like family needs), or need for training. Were the suggestions just not that interesting to you? Did you consider taking those results and then doing more research using O*NET? Or perhaps you "wrote yourself off" thinking you couldn't see yourself able to do one of the jobs suggested by the Profiler?

Maybe your initial session with the CDF requires further meetings and you've arranged the next one, along with some "assignments" to further develop your job goal or career plan.

It could be that your initial pass through both the Profiler and with a CDF will require more effort on your part to refine the information you've gathered into a solid job goal(s) and career plan. This is common.

There is so much information available to you using just these two approaches that you will usually need to put in more time with both of them. If you got a list of just 10 possible career options based on Job Zone 1, you could and should put in 5, 10 or more hours investigating these 10 options. On the first pass, you might print out the reports from the Profiler and read them and take them with you to the CDF.

You might even realize you could consider jobs and careers at Job Zone level 2 and print those out too.

Now go over those sheets and prioritize them from most interesting and best chance, or any other criteria you establish (your life, organize them the way you want, even alphabetical). Then go into O*NET and do more research. Type in the name of the job and get more information, including other similar jobs.

As you can see, even with just two initial steps how much effort you can put into developing the right choices for yourself. Your future is worth it. That is where you'll spend the rest of your life.

Problem #2: "I have a clear job goal, now how do I get there?"

What's the problem? You have a clear goal, which if it is SMART, means you are likely to be able to obtain it.

So, what's the problem? Let's analyze it, but to analyze it, we must state it.

Here are some potential places we might start (possible problem statements):
• I don't where to look for that job.
• I've applied but didn't get any calls.
• I've sent my resume with a cover letter but didn't get any calls.
• I've had interviews but no call backs.

There are three distinct phases of job hunting and career planning: 1) the Preparation Phase before the interview, 2) the Selling Phase or interview, and 3) the Closure Phase, at the end of the interview and afterward. Those three phases, again, are Prepare, Sell, Close (or Closure).

The first three of the previous statements ("I don't where to look for that job." "I've applied but didn't get any calls." "I've sent my resume with a cover letter but didn't get any calls.") were problems with the Preparation phase.

The fourth, "I've had interviews but no call backs", indicates problems with either the Selling Phase or the Closure Phase.

We will cover each of these phases or steps elsewhere in the book, but for now, to illustrate Goal Attainment as Problem Solving, we'll continue with one of them, "I've applied but didn't get any calls."

So, now let's examine that problem. Is it one problem? Seems like it and it is important too. Let's ask some questions though. Where did you apply? How did you apply?

If you said, "I applied online to 17 different job leads or openings in the past six weeks but that is all. I do look every single day for that particular job using the (fill in the blank) job website." That would be enough to continue the discussion.

You need more resources, so let's review some. On a sheet of paper, list the 17 companies to which you applied, if you can, some of them may have been "blind" ads (no employer named). Were they all in the same industry or different industries? Get out a phone book and see if they are all listed in it. Write down (or photocopy) the rest of the companies listed in the same category as the companies you've already listed. Or go to the library and ask for assistance identifying employers similar to the ones on your list with a 5-10-20-50 mile radius of your home (how far is up to you, though I'd suggest starting with 10 miles and only adding on if you have to). Now you have the makings of a "Potentials" list.

A "Potential" is any place of interest to you. It may not be a place you want to work though they often turn out to be. Don't start out viewing them as "job targets," start out thinking of them as places of interest to you. We'll talk more about them later.

Just because you have only used one or more online job banks or employment search websites, doesn't mean that is the only way to approach them. Doesn't even mean it is the best. Even if one of your POT's doesn't have an opening today, it doesn't mean you shouldn't plan on going there and applying anyway. New openings occur every day in companies for many reasons. People get promoted, or quit or get fired to name a few. Sometimes the company could use more help because it is expanding. If you are there at the right time, you may solve their problem on the spot. If you go there to do an Informational Interview (discussed elsewhere in the book), you might make a strong enough impression that they will create an opening for you.

There are more ways to create more Potential Organizational Targets (discussed elsewhere in the book) but for now we'll use the list you've developed, let's say you find one, named "MedRed." This is what you learn:

MedRed is a "cutting edge maker of medical equipment" whose corporate motto is "Tomorrow's Answers Today." It specializes in making diagnostic and treatment equipment that gives "the fastest, most accurate results possible." They have a manufacturing, warehousing and distribution center nearby and, in addition, a sales, parts and service department. The corporate home office is in another state.

You could be looking for a job in sales, warehousing, parts, service, or customer service. We're going to use "customer service" as we continue our discussion.

At this stage you have, at least initially resolved one of your contributing problems, "not having a target," by generating some alternative targets (employers intersecting with your job and career paths). You have another contributing problem to solve, which will require generating more alternatives, another problem identified. This time the problem is: "How do I approach them?" See other discussion topics, like resumes and applications, and researching a company for discussion elsewhere in the book.

What are your options, your alternatives? Here are some things you could do:
- Wait for them to post an opening online, at the website you use.
- Wait for them to post an opening in a newspaper.
- Wait until a public or private job developer discovers or uncovers an opening, returns to their office, and notifies you that there is an opening.
- You could call them tomorrow and ask if they have any openings.
- You could go to them tomorrow and ask if they are taking applications, and put one in if they are.
- You could go tomorrow and try to meet the supervisor of the customer service area.
- You could call them tomorrow and ask for the name of the Customer Service Supervisor (CSS) and ask to speak to them. You could ask the CSS if you could arrange to come out briefly to interview them.
- You could use your Network and see if you can develop a lead through it.

There are probably even more alternatives than this but we'll start with this list. Some of the options listed are fairly passive, the three that begin with the word "Wait ..." are. They don't require much effort but they also have a low probability, or chance, of landing you your next rewarding job.

The other options all have a better chance for success. They all call for you to take action. They do seem to differ a bit in terms of obtaining the outcome you want. Let's take a look at these more active approaches, one at a time.

You could call them tomorrow and ask if they have any openings. Assuming you actually speak to someone who can knowledgeably answer this question, you will get a "yes" or "no" answer which is true at that moment in time. If tomorrow is Tuesday, and you call at 10:00 am, that is when that answer is true.

Will it still be true on Wednesday at 3:00 p.m. or Friday at 4:00 p.m.? Or next week or next month? If you decide to call and ask, be aware that the answer is only true when you ask it. When you ask that question, why not follow it up with "Do you post openings on a particular day and time?" Some Human Resource Departments, and our fictional company MedRed is one of them, post all of their openings on Monday mornings. You could call every week on Monday morning and get that week's current openings. Or you could go there on Monday mornings, get to know the receptionist, or the HR clerk and ask to see the openings.

What if there was an opening at the time you called, but it got filled before you got there? Maybe you should have gone there directly.

What if you did. You got "interview ready" (discussed elsewhere in this book) and went to their offices. You asked the receptionist where Human Resources was and she directed you to them. You asked the clerk if there were any openings, learned there were not, but that they accepted applications any time. You took one, sat down and completed it. You gave it back to her (you did ask her name, didn't you?) and asked her when new job openings were posted. She told you that officially that was Monday at 9:00 am but they were already available the Friday before at 4:00 pm. You thanked her and left.

While you were there, you asked the receptionist who the Customer Service Supervisor was. She told you and you asked if you could meet with her or him for a moment. She called but was told they were busy. You thanked her and were on your way. You did realize that you covered two of your options with one visit, right?

You could call and get the name of the Customer Service Supervisor instead of asking while you were at the counter but either way, you can now call and ask to speak to them. If you are asked why, you could say it is personal. It is and that is true. Or you could say it is because you would like to conduct an informational interview with them, also true. Your purpose in meeting with them is not to apply for a job and you can stress that with them, you would just like up to a half-hour to talk to them and what day and time would be best for them. We discuss informational interviewing elsewhere in the book.

If you get the chance to speak to that supervisor, you have an opportunity to impress them with your interest in their department and company. You can learn what they consider entry criteria and on-the-job success. You can learn about their problems and opportunities and set about making them yours too. These meetings offer you clues for you in a future job interview. You can also ask questions about turnover in the department, how often they hire, is it a growing department and more. You have the opportunity to make a favorable impression with a hiring supervisor and develop a new contact for your network. Did you notice anything in their office or cubicle that suggests you have something in common with them? Pay attention.

You've just added this contact to your network but have you also used others in your network? When you researched MedRed, did you discover who their customers and their suppliers are? Their bankers? Did you ask your network if they knew anyone who worked for MedRed, their customers, suppliers or bankers? Depending on your own comfort level with approaching your network, you should know or be able to find someone who knows someone who works with MedRed, their customers, suppliers or bankers. Use those connections to try to make contact with a person in MedRed using your connections. Your goal is to speak to someone inside MedRed, or more than one. You want to use that contact to do things for you; learn of new openings before they occur, have someone on the inside who can vouch for you, someone to conduct informational interviews with or use to get introductions to others inside MedRed.

The more inside contacts you have, the better your opportunities become. There may be an opening in another department for which you are qualified, and once in, could transfer to Customer Service or stay in the position you obtain, as it may suit you even better. Sometimes jobs are created for people who make the right impression on the right person. Sometimes you might just need the right person to recommend you for the job. The more people you know inside MedRed, the more likely it is to happen.

One more thing about this is that these insiders often know of openings in other companies. They may know of one with one of their suppliers, customers, bankers or even competitors that they will pass on to you, since they have all become members of your network. These alternate potential targets should be explored by you as they may have the job you want!

Be courteous and always send everyone you meet or interview, a thank you note, preferably on paper but at least with an email. (You did get their cards, didn't you? Or at least follow-up contact information?) If you send a "hard copy" note or letter, always sign it, never, ever just print your name on the hard copy and send it.

So, now it is time to pick one of those alternatives. Since actually going there tomorrow has two or more possible benefits that seems like a good choice. (The "select alternative" problem solving approach to goal attainment).

So, you get up, get interview ready (dressed for the job you'd like to have, plus a few other things), and drive over to MedRed. (The "implement alternative" problem solving approach to goal attainment).

So, how did it go? Were you nervous? Maybe you should practice with employers you are less interested in working for?

Did they accept your application? How long will they keep it for? When do they post new openings? Who did you meet? Did you get the receptionist's name, the Human Resource Clerk's? Did you get to meet the Customer Service Supervisor (CSS) or get his or her name? Did you arrange to meet with her or him? Did you get called in for an interview on the spot (it happens and could happen to you, so be prepared)?

Were you satisfied with your results? Did you think you could have done better? What could you do better the next time?

The big question, did you get a job? Probably not, not that day. If there was an opening, you applied for it and may be included in the interview pool. If you got further than that and met the CSS, you improved your chances of being included if you made a favorable impression. If they did not have an opening, but you made an impression, you will be remembered when there is one and have improved your chances to be interviewed. If you also use your network, you may be able to improve your chances even more by having someone inside who will recommend you.

This is the "evaluate results" problems solving approach to goal attainment. You should feel positive about taking the initiative, taking action, going out and attempting to make things happen in you favor. You've taken big steps in taking control of your current and future job hunt and career development.

You could decide you're done and do nothing more but wait. That's probably not a terribly good idea. There are more potential targets to contact. There are more things in the process that you can work on. Keep working is a far better idea. Whatever isn't working for you can be worked on: your resume, your job application, your interview skills, job targets, and more. Whatever step isn't working as well as you'd like, you can work on until you get the rewarding job you want in your career development. This is the "Did it work?" phase of the problem solving approach to goal attainment.

Chapter 14: Documentation

"I'm a hoarder. For me, documentation has always been key, and I've kept everything from my past." — Diane Keaton (1946 -) American actress.

If you were part of Ms. Keaton's past, that might concern you, wouldn't it? She has a record of her past.

Background:

Documentation, what is it? Why should you do it? What if you don't like to write? What if you don't write well? Even if you don't like to write things down or are write well, you should consider making a habit of it in and for your job and career future.

It's easy! It could be as little as making a note on a daily calendar or keeping a journal. Many people use smartphones and synchronize it with their calendar. Expand your phone use a little and you should be capable of printing a compilation of your activities. Open that file and expand it by adding other information like what happened, what you did, any outcome or results to mention, follow-up action?

You could use a recording device, most cellphones have recording capability, many will take dictation and convert it to text messages and you can email and upload that on your computer. You could get a speech recognition program for your computer that can translate your speech into written text. You could also find someone to help you by writing things down for you. Even if you type slowly, you can document your activities in a word processing program.

Handwrite your notes on looseleaf paper if you have to, then put them in a loose-leaf binder.

There really isn't much reason for you to not document, now let's look at the other questions about what "documentation" is and why it's so valuable to you.

So what is documentation? How do we define it?

Documentation defined: keeping a record.

It answers the questions of who did what when. It is the process of recording information. It is information or evidence that serves as a record. It is sometimes referred to as "record-keeping". For our purposes, good documentation will be a record of what you did when. It will tell what happened, clearly enough that someone else could look at it and understand what you did, and with whom, if others were involved, but all that is required is for you to understand what you did. It is just a bit better if it is clear enough for someone else to follow along.

Job and Career Documentation:

The purpose of your job and career documentation is to help you identify and overcome problems. It will improve your understanding of your job hunt and career development process. It will help you make decisions about what to do next. It can help you perform your job hunt process more efficiently. The bonus is that it makes it much easier for others to assist you.

Documentation is a way of answering questions. It spells out the when, where, what, who, why, and how, of your process. It provides evidence that you use to improve your actions. It serves as a reminder to you of what you have done, empowering you, which can offset feelings of frustration that go with job hunting and career development. You will have evidence that *you* are taking action. Good documentation can reveal to you the need to modify your actions, or take other actions.

In short, keeping a record of what you've done, gives you guidance in what to do next.

Some documentation guidelines are:

- It should be timely.

- It should be done in whatever way works best for you and your needs.
- It should be easy for you access the information.
- It should be accurate.

A good minimum set of information to consider to include in your documentation is: 1) What did you do? 2) How long did it take? 3) When did you do it ? See, it's as easy as 1-2-3!

So how does it work, this documentation? Can you see how someone else might be able to *use it to help you?*

Before we go any further, it is not necessary for documentation to be "long." There are no rules for your personal documentation. Guidelines, yes, rules, no. It's *yours* after all. Keeping track of your actions can be covered in short, concise sentences or even with just a few words. Here are some examples of short, concise, not-even-a-sentence, but still good documentation statements:

- July 28, 20xx - called MedRed 8:15 am, 15 min.
- 7/28/xx - spoke to Jim L, at MedRed, 15 min.
- 7/15/xx - drove to and applied in person to MedRed for Customer Service Representative job, 2.5 hours (inc. travel time), was in the lobby at 8:00 am when it opened.

Note that in each example, we listed the date and then what happened. You could use a steno pad, a loose-leaf binder or any of a number of recording methods or devices but the key is to make a record that is clear enough to provide evidence of what you did.

As a way of asking yourself if this clear enough, try to think about telling it to a six-year old. They always have more questions. You don't have to answer them all, just try to be clear about what you did when.

Up to a point, the more you write the better your evidence becomes. Try to keep it <u>clear</u>, <u>concise</u> and <u>coherent</u>. In other words, don't spend too much time writing or trying to make it exactly right. Your documentation shouldn't take a lot of time, maybe one to five minutes to write. Keep it short, you do have plenty of other things to do.

It does take practice, so as you do some of the exercises in this book and the workbook, why not make entries in your documentation?

I do suggest you use a loose-leaf binder and that you keep your entries in chronological order. You can use one page for multiple entries. My reason for suggesting this approach is that you give yourself more options with this method than most. For example, you can take your loose-leaf binder with you to a Career Development Facilitator (CDF) and show them your actions. If they ask you a question about what you've been doing, you can show them.

With this flexible method, you can remove or re-arrange sheets into ways of organization that make sense to you, not me, your second grade teacher or your mom or dad or spouse. You can keep track of <u>calls</u> you make or receive (along with whom you spoke and about what) in one section. In another you could document people you've <u>visited</u>. In still another, other <u>actions</u> you've taken. You can keep copies of your resume in another section, and information from your research in still another. A loose-leaf offers this kind of flexibility. Your documentation provides tangible evidence and feedback that is qualitatively different form electronic forms.

Still, whatever works for you. The better you document, the more assistance you provide yourself. The evidence you gather about your activities helps you monitor what you've been doing. It can reveal to you things that you are doing too much or too little of. It may suggest to you what isn't working and prompt you to make changes in your program. It may reveal weaknesses in your approach which can be overcome.

Suppose over the past month you have been vigorously pursuing your job hunt and career development activities. If you did not document your activities, how many of those actions can you recall? If you did, you will likely be surprised at your work and your output. What does looking back tell you about you? Did you do a lot or a little?

Did you do much at all? Look at your documentation and note that:

- You applied to 12 jobs online,
- You applied for one job in person,
- You visited a Workforce Investment Act (WIA) site and met with a Career Development Facilitator (CDF) twice.
- You spent time nearly every day complaining about not having a job and trying to find one.

You add up the time it took you to do everything related to your job hunt, your career development project and program, and got a total of 15 hours in the month. That wouldn't be much would it? Unless you are already working and/or going to school and/or volunteering, dealing with life and family, friends and community, then it may be all the time you had.

Or maybe you did a lot. Look at your documentation and you note:
- You applied to 25 jobs online
- You went out and applied to 8 jobs in person
- You spent 6 hours each week using the resources of the WIA facility.
- You attended a workshop on resumes
- You re-wrote your resume in two different versions.
- You notice that you didn't send a thank you letter to each of the jobs you applied for in person, so you caught up on that correspondence, promptly.

Your research and work with WIA and a CDF helped you see that there are more jobs you can apply for, different job titles than the one you were looking for. You totaled up your time and you averaged 28 hours/week for the month, a good average for a job hunter and career seeker. Plus you found you have more options and that increases your opportunity for success.

Perhaps when you look at your documentation and you note:
- You applied for four jobs and got no calls for interviews but did follow-up and ask if the jobs were filled.
- You learned they were, so you asked why you weren't interviewed.
Suppose they said your resume didn't show you were qualified for the job, or that it contained errors or that your references did not support you. That is all important information for you, hard to take criticism maybe but still valuable.

Or you looked at your documentation and note:
- You applied for twelve jobs
- Got interviews for three based on the strength of your resume and your application.
- You had no job offers.
- You sent thank you letters to all twelve employers
- You did not follow up with a call to any of them.

(Helpful Hint: Here's something to mention to you now: You might want to make sure that your application and resume agree, most employers will compare what you say in a resume to the application and in an interview, so be consistent.)
You decide to follow up to see if you can find out why. Some employers may tell you, some may not; none will if you don't ask.
One employer tells you a more qualified candidate was hired. You alertly mention that you are still interested in working for them so that if another opening appears you'd like to be considered for it. You go on to say that if the other person doesn't work out, you are still available. Another employer you contact goes out on a limb and says it is your age, you're too old. Still another says you didn't seem interested in working for them. How would you fix any of those problems?

If you kept track of your actions, you documented what you did, you might want to check your resume in the first example. Consider having a Career Development Facilitator, or a friend or relative, or even ask one of the HR people you met with, if they would review it.

In the second case, you might want to question your interview skills. You were potentially right for the job but it appears you are not putting together a good in-person presentation.

It is difficult to always assess ourselves, ask anyone who has to proofread their own work and they'll tell you how very difficult it is. We see what we think we wrote, not what is actually there.

It is much the same with other things we do. We think we know what happened but it is good to get an outside opinion or point of view, what is sometimes called a reality check.

When it comes to employment and your career, it is critical for you to have a professional assist you. If you can get a CDF or other career advisor or counselor to look at your work and your "finding-work" effort they can be enormously beneficial to you. They are trained to see what you might overlook. They know what to look for and what a well-organized job seeking and career development program or project looks like. Taking a loose-leaf with your actions in it, along with a resume, can help them do a better job assisting you, faster.

When you consider how much is at stake, your potential lifetime earnings, your job satisfaction and happiness, and that of your spouse and children, it is well worth the extra effort.

Chapter 15: Tapping into your Motivation

"I've missed more than 9,000 shots in my career. I've lost almost 300 games. 26 times I've been trusted to take the game winning shot and missed. I've failed over and over and over again in my life. And that is why I succeed." — Michael Jordan (1963 -) American basketball player and businessman.

"The most difficult thing is the decision to act, the rest is merely tenacity." — Amelia Earhart (1897-1937) American aviator, author.

"The best time to plant a tree was 20 years ago. The second best time is now." — Chinese Proverb

"Whether you think you can or you think you can't, you're right." — Henry Ford (1863-1947) American entrepreneur.

"Ask and it will be given to you; search, and you will find; knock and the door will be opened for you." — Jesus, rabbi, teacher, prophet.

"You miss 100% of the shots you don't take." — Wayne Gretzky

"Do you want to know who you are? Don't ask. Act! Action will delineate and define you." — Thomas Jefferson (1743-1826) American president, diplomat, author, inventor, businessperson.

"The only thing standing between you and your goal is the bullshit story you keep telling yourself as to why you can't achieve it." — Jordan Belfort (1962-) American businessperson, author "Wolf of Wall Street," motivational speaker.

"Every strike brings me closer to the next home run." — Babe Ruth (1895-1948) American baseball player.

"All men want, not something to do with, but something to do, or rather something to be." — Henry David Thoreau (1817-1862) American philosopher, author "Walden", abolitionist.

"I said 'Somebody should do something about that.' Then I realized I am somebody." — Lily Tomlin (1939-), American actress, comedian, writer, producer.

"People who are unable to motivate themselves must be content with mediocrity, no matter how impressive their other talents." — Andrew Carnegie (1835-1919), American industrialist, philanthropist.

Background:

What is motivation? Is it constant or does it change or vary? Can you increase your motivation? If so, how? How is motivation related to needs and wants? What is ambition and how is it different than motivation?

Motivation is sometimes defined as the answer to "Why?" Motivation explains why we do things. It is the reason we give for acting, doing, or behaving, the way we did. It's the answer we give to "Why did you do that?" or "Why did I do that?" or "Why did he or she do that?" From this perspective it is an explanation of behavior.

Motivation is directed energy. It implies motion as its root is the word "motive," a <u>reason</u> for doing something. in particular Something happens, an event. Why it happened is explained in part by the motives of those involved. Motives may not be obvious or easily discerned.

Motivation is an explanation of an action or actions of a living creature. It is easier to see the motivations of animals than those of humans. Animal behavior is more straight forward and make it easier to illustrate some aspects of motivation that's why Aesop's fables have been popular for so long, they make motivation easier to understand.

If we think of motivation as "the why," we might want to look at "the why" in order to understand it.

Life and living requires a few basic things. Most life forms require food, water and air, a way to eliminate waste, a way to reproduce, and a host environment. Not all life forms require each of these (particularly air and water) but they seem to be special cases and nearly all of the rest of us sharing planet earth do.

These basic "needs" are sometimes called drives, or motives for doing things. If a dog, cat or any other animal is thirsty it will look for water until it quenches it's thirst thereby satisfying the need, also called "gratifying the need". The same holds true for food. When we, you and I, or a dog, cat and any other animals get hungry, we all do something about it (even if it is only to ask someone else to do what it takes to satisfy our hunger). Picture your dog or cat leading you to the cupboard and looking expectantly at it. Or you asking your wife, "When's dinner?" or asking your husband "to bring something home."

Thirst and hunger are words that describe two basic needs, the need for water and for food. Need to go to the bathroom? We have a few words for the need for elimination and when we have to go, we go, one way or another. Our pet dog usually lets us know when they need to "go outside." Our cat disappears to use their kitty litter or wants out.

The act of breathing is so basic, we take it for granted until it is obstructed. When we cannot breath, for any reason, we act quickly to resolve the problem, whether we are choking, drowning, having an anaphylactic reaction, or we will die fairly quickly. Our need to breath is so fundamental and can sustain so short a delay, that hospital emergency rooms give "not breathing" their highest priority.

These most basic of needs -- air, water, food and elimination -- are those without which we cannot live long; in other words, we are limited in how long we can delay their gratification (satisfaction). In normal, healthy individuals we are highly motivated to meet those basic needs, along with a few others like fuel, clothing and shelter.

With little effort, you can find lots of research into motivation, or motivational theory in psychology books. Many books are written solely on that subject, which is certainly fascinating but what does it have to do with jobs and careers? Well there is more to talk about on motivation be patient and we will get there.

Job and Career Motivation:

Earlier in this book, we introduced the work of Abraham Maslow and his "Hierarchy of Needs" and talked a bit about wants and needs.

We'll take a moment and talk about wants. Wants are expressions of needs. I need something to drink, I want water, milk, wine, tea, coffee, beer, etc. We may even have particular wants, like for a particular water such as Evian, Ice Mountain, or for a particular wine or variety, like or Chateau-Neuf du Pape or chardonnay. We've learned to want particular types of the things we need.

If we look at Maslow's pyramid, shown again here:

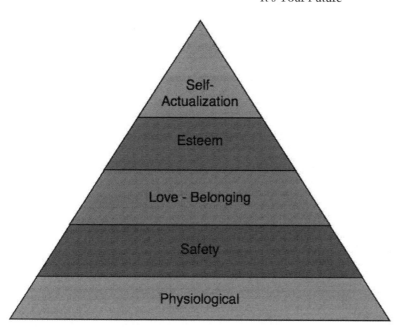

Figure 15 - 1: Maslow's Hierarchy of Needs

we can see that there are many other factors that we view as human needs. Safety, love, belonging and love, esteem, self-actualization are the major categories as Maslow defined them. He initially arranged these elements in a hierarchy and suggested that you had to meet lower level needs before you could move on to upper levels of needs. He later re-stated that you could work on many elements simultaneously and that your own growth as a human being (passive), and as a human doing (active) required you to.

There are other theorists and theories, many, many of them. If you are inclined to, look into theorists like Freud, B. F. Skinner, Hertzburg, Maslow, and even Masters and Johnson. They all contribute to understanding "the why" we do what we do. Schools of motivational theory, behaviorism, for example, and theorists abound. We're not going to spend more time with them, and instead spend our time looking at what motivates you.

So, what motivates you?

Earlier in this book we spent some time on O*NET and the "My Next Move" interest profiler. In part his was a practical exploration of what motivates you, your interests. The material contained in the "My Next Move" program is designed to look at you from the employment perspective and attempts to match your motivations, your interests, to workplace settings so that you can find a rewarding career.

How motivated were you? Did you explore O*NET and "My Next Move"? Did you? If you didn't, why not do it now? If you did, how far did you go? Did you complete the "My Next Move" interest profiler? Did you look at each job summary in each Job Zone that best fit you? Or did you look at "some" or a "few"? How much time did you spend with O*NET? Minutes, hours, days?

These are some measures of the strength of your motivation. Why you did what you did and how much you did is some indicator of your motivation toward developing your career plan and obtaining your next most rewarding job. You can measure your motivation by how much effort you put into what you do.

How motivated are you?

That's not all we've looked at though. How about the sections where we talked about defining your most rewarding job or why people work or why people volunteer. Did you do the workbook exercises? All of them? A few or one? Did you spend time thinking about that material? Or did you forget about it? If you didn't do any of them or only spent a little time on them, that implies low, little or even no motivation on your part. If you did them all, you are highly motivated to get your career life in order. If you did not, perhaps you need to get motivated. It doesn't take much effort, just start somewhere and do something because of what you want or need.

We've also spent a little time on problem solving and goal attainment. Did you do any of the exercises of just skim through them?

All of those things that you *could have* done, represent opportunities to work on your future. To the extent you have done some of the work, you have a measure of your motivation. The better the future you want, the more effort you need to put into it. The sources of your motivation are on your side for obtaining it. The obstacles, the barriers, the problems that get in your way, even your own inertia, pessimism, skepticism and disbelief work against you. So tap and use your motivation, change *could have* to *did*.

Ask yourself what you would do for a Klondike Bar? What would you do for a brand-new car, a secure future, a new house, a trip to Europe or Hawaii, or for a rewarding job? Did you complete the exercises asking you what you wanted, what you wanted to do, what you wanted to have or where you wanted to go? Did you put much effort into them? Again, these are indicators of the strength of your motivation. Maybe you should go back and complete them or at least work on them?

This is not to judge you at all, but rather to provide you with new perspectives and give you tools to have the kind of future you want and can have. So, if you haven't done the exercises or given thought to the material you've been presented with, perhaps you need to ask yourself, why not? Are you going to be content and satisfied with the least favorable life you can have? Will you take whatever job comes along or falls in your lap? Will you live life "small" and on other people's terms or will you live "Large" and on your terms? Will you spend you days wishing and wanting, or will you emerge a champion?

You can change. You can change yourself, your life and your future. Will you? Are you motivated?

As humans it is one of the things that separates us from other life forms. A tree is a tree, never a blade of grass nor a bird on the wing. A dog is a dog, a tiger a tiger. They are what they are. But we, we human beings, we have potential. We can change. We can leave our past and change direction completely, entirely. We can build our lives up, constantly improving and adding to what we already do and know how to do.

Delayed Gratification & Motivation

Let's talk a little about delayed gratification as it relates to motivation, wants, needs and desires.

As we said earlier, there are some basic, biological survival needs and their gratification needs to be "immediate." The need for air is one of the most immediate needs. Try holding your breath. Right now, go ahead and do it. How long can you do it? Thirty seconds, a minute, not many of us can go much further than a minute and a half or two minutes. There are a few, though, who can but even they can't go hours without it. That's a very immediate need. It is a need because we die without it, and we cannot go very long without it.

We can go days without water, though not many, and weeks without food but not too many. How long can we go without relieving ourselves? For most of us, that is a daily activity, several times a day for many of us.

All of these are examples of immediate biological survival needs. So "immediate" implies "fairly soon". Waiting, on the other hand, is what delayed gratification is all about.

How long can you wait to satisfy a need or a want? Often in our quest for a job or developing a career we find ourselves dealing with long term goals. How long we can delay gratification is another measure of the strength of our motivation. The reward of attaining our goal or fulfilling our goal attainment plan is offset by how long it takes to reach the goal and be gratified.

What is a long term goal? Goals that take more than one year to obtain are long term goals. That is at the shorter end of the continuum though. Many people serve two or three years in the military in order to obtain benefits along with doing their duty. Many people spend 2-4 years going to college to get undergraduate degrees. Advanced degrees and law and medical school educations take even longer. Apprenticeships can take many years to complete.

Striving to obtain long term goals are examples of delayed gratification. You don't get to expend your time and energy doing what others may be doing, instead you make the sacrifice necessary to meet your long term goals and obtaining the reward(s) that go with it. What you sacrifice, what you give up in order to realize your goal is yet another measure of your motivation.

Motivation & Rewards:

No discussion of motivation is complete without taking a look at the "rewards" side of things too. Earlier we said we work because it is rewarding. We said that we are motivated by our needs and wants. In short, we do things for the rewards, the satisfaction of our wants and needs.

Various theories about motivation always include a discussion about the "rewards" side, in order to explain the relationship between motivation and behavior. In fact, one cannot be discussed without the other. The various schools of thought attempt to explain the relationship between motivation and reward. Some of them would even disagree with the use of the word "reward," preferring to speak of "drives", "drive reduction" or "dissonance reduction" (dissonance being the difference between our feelings and actions and our views of the world around us, or a difference between what we think and what we feel).

Without elaborating on the various theories and philosophies any more than this, we need only to recognize and accept that we simply do things for our own reasons, our own motivations, some of them we aren't even aware of. We are complex beings. We have our own tastes, preferences, wants, desires, etc. Why we have them isn't important to our discussion. We just need to recognize that we do and the apply that information to help get us on track and stay there.

If you want a fur coat, a new car, a boat, to get out of debt, take a trip to France, and know how to get one or more of them you might do so. Then again, you may not. Certainly the economics of your life will have an influence on whether you get one or more of those things. There may be more important things for you to spend your money on.

There is competition between all the things you want, all the rewards you are interested in having. You may work to satisfy more than one of them simultaneously. You, to the extent you possibly can, get to select which rewards you want and are motivated to satisfy.

Let's look at putting our knowledge of motivation, rewards and the workplace and combine it with our self-awareness, or knowledge of ourselves.

There are a set of dynamics at work in attempting to find our next rewarding job and building our career.

Time. How long do we have or can we wait? Job zones are a reflection of how long it will take to acquire the knowledge and skills necessary to perform a job. These might range from little or no time, as in becoming a stock clerk, or extensive training and experience as in becoming an ophthalmologist. Where are you in life? Do you have the time to invest in building a career that takes months or years? The more immediate our needs are, the less time we have to invest in and wait for long term rewards.

Desirability. What to do you want? What are the economics of what is important to you? It is possible to have a highly paid job and be very satisfied in it and all it affords you. However, high pay doesn't equate to happiness. As we've looked at the reasons people work or volunteer, other things emerge as important. Using the "My Next Move" Interest Profiler relates our interests to occupations that satisfies or matches those interests.

Motivation. What do you want and what will you do to get it? What actions will you take to get the things, the rewards you want? If you have a burning passion to do something, you are more likely to go after it then if you merely feel it a little.

Along with these factors are the skills, abilities, values, knowledge, education, experience and training you currently have.

We suggest that you examine yourself to determine who you are and what you want. Do you need to increase the strength of your motivation to obtain the next most rewarding job? Why?

Chapter 16: Decision-making and weighing alternatives

"Good decisions come from experience, and experience comes from bad decisions." — Mark Twain (1835-1910) American novelist, journalist.

"When you have to make a choice and don't make it, that is in itself a choice." — William James (1842-1910) American philosopher, psychologist, and physician.

"The hardest thing to learn in life is which bridge to cross and which to burn." — David Russell (1953-) Scottish musician.

"I must have a prodigious amount of mind; it takes me as much as a week, sometimes, to make it up!" — Mark Twain (1835-1910) American novelist, journalist.

"The most difficult thing is the decision to act, the rest is merely tenacity. The fears are paper tigers. You can do anything you decide to do. You can act to change and control your life; and the procedure, the process is its own reward." — Amelia Earhart (1897-1937) American aviator, author.

Background:

What is a decision? What is a good one? Are there "decision skills," "decision tools," "decision techniques or methods"?

A decision is a choice between options or alternatives. Go to the show, go bowling, stay home? Buy a black car or a white one? Get a dog or a cat? Where to eat and what? Those are kind of easy.

Get out a phone book and pick a new doctor or dentist. Not as easy. Do we pick one based on how close they are or their specialty? Maybe, but then again, maybe not. Doctors and dentists aren't found in Aisle 6 of our local grocery store, so it is much harder to shop for one. You need more information.

Where should you take that next vacation? You have a budget, but a world of possibilities. Get a cabin near a lake or fly to Las Vegas? Different prices to be near rent a cabin or go to Vegas. Is it off-season or in-season? Expect to pay more for the same thing in-season than off-season, even though the experience may be nearly the same or even better depending on what you like. Again, you need more information.

Should you take a job that pays better but is farther away than one nearby, everything else being equal? How much farther? How much time will it take, round trip for either job. How much will that trip cost in wear and tear and usage of your vehicle or on you? More information is needed and some of it isn't even clear, like what is the wear and tear on you to commute one hour instead of twenty minutes?

Should you take a high-paying job, doing work you don't like, or a lower paying one that you do? Should you take a job that you are qualified for now or go to school for 2-4 years and get a better one but sacrifice some lost opportunities?

As you may suspect, a lot of times there isn't a "right" answer to our decision-making. There is a "best" answer based on the information we have at the time. Sometimes we need more information but can't always wait for it or get it. Sometimes it is fairly trivial choice, like "go bowling, to the show or stay home." Sometimes though, the decision is hugely important.

Either way, typically, we only find out if a decision is a good one or a bad one, after we've made it and the results are in. Was it a good one or was it as Mark Twain put it, more "experience".

We all make bad decisions at times, some of us seem to make more than others. Usually we don't know this or realize this until after we've committed ourselves, made the decision, and are now "stuck" with it.

There are some tools, techniques and methods that can help us improve our decision making. It is also helpful to understand a little about our styles of making decisions so that we change, or adapt a new style if it might better serve our needs. Just like your wardrobe, where you can mix and match styles, there are tools, techniques and methods to different decision making scenarios.

Decisions and Personality:

So, what kind of decision maker are you? In general terms, there are four major ways people make decisions; Intuition (we'll call intuitive), Thinking (thinker), Feeling (feeler) and the Feeling-Thinker (Emo-Thinker).

The Intuitive style trusts their instinct and their gut-level feelings about the decision they are about to make. They do not rely on details, facts or information. They play their hunches.

The Thinker style is detail-oriented; they trust in facts, information and details -- not feelings -- to make their decisions. They analyze the information available to them and make the best possible decision with the greatest or best pay-off.

The Feeler style is not inclined to analyze information choosing instead to focus on everyone's feelings about an impending decision. Their decision is often a choice of what they like, or don't like. They aren't playing hunches or using their intuition, which seems like using "feelings", these folks are using their emotions, and others to find a solution that everyone will feel comfortable with.

The Emo-Thinker style is detail- and fact-oriented but goes by their perception (their **emo**tional feeling) of the information rather than analysis to arrive at their conclusion or decision.

Decision Making Context:

There are also a few types of decision situations that we are confronted with. These situations or "decision considerations" are: 1) Is the situation irreversible or reversible? 2) Does the decision have to be made (required) or can it be postponed or delayed (does delaying a decision, in effect become a decision, as opposed to a need to make a decision quickly or soon) 3) Can the decision be tested or pre-tested, or done in steps, or "bite-sized" pieces?

Can all outcomes be determined, predicted beforehand with some reasonable degree of accuracy based on the information at hand? If you think of "decision making" as simply one more type of problem to solve, you can to some extent. You can apply the same steps to making a decision as you do to any other problem that must be solved.

So let's review those steps one more time.
- Identify and define the problem or opportunity.
- Gather information and review your resources.
- Identify and analyze your alternatives.
  - Estimate or "guestimate" the probability (chance) of their outcomes.
  - Estimate or "guestimate" how desirable the value of those outcomes are.
- Select an alternative or preferred course of action.
- Implement the alternative or preferred course of action.
- Evaluate the results and follow up and adjust as necessary.

Remember too, that you may have options such as "do nothing", or "delay making a decision" that are choices but they are choices that can buy you time that you can use to get more or better information.

There are aspects that make "decision making" a slightly different type of problem. One thing that is different is that you usually know what your options are and are trying to pick or choose from them. You do not always know the choices you have. You may lack the information that would reveal more choices to you. However, you often do have a set of choices to pick from and you have to decide which one.

The second aspect is that there may or not be a "right answer." After you've made your decision, you will find out how good you choice was but it is not as clear cut as in other types of problems you solve.

A third difference is there is a continuum of possibilities in your option environment. Your range of choice or options environments are: 1) Certainty -- you can clearly determine the result of your choice *before* you have to make it. 2) Risk -- you can estimate the chance that the choice will lead to a certain result or how close to that result you will be. 3) Uncertainty -- you have no foreknowledge of what the outcome will be.

Suppose you are hungry and decide to go to a particular restaurant. You can go either this way or that. Your experience and knowledge tells you that either way is about the same. You will get there in about the same amount of time, everything else being equal. You decide to go "that way" and get there. That was a fairly certain decision-making environment. Inside you review a menu and decide to choose between two dishes. You've had them both before and like them. You make a decision and enjoy the meal. Another fairly certain decision environment.

Now suppose you are going to go out to eat and have no particular restaurant in mind. Which way should you go? You may choose based on the number of different restaurants along your optional paths. Road A has 5 restaurants, road B has 2. You've eaten at them all and think they are about the same. You choose Road A because it has a better chance of having a restaurant you want to eat at. You pick the third restaurant you approach and sit down and look at the menu. You decide to pick a beef dish because your experience suggests you like restaurant beef more than chicken dishes.

These decisions were "riskier" than in the first case, but you had some idea of what the chance the outcomes would be favorable to you.

Finally, you are in a hotel room in a city you've never been to before. You are in an unfamiliar downtown area. You know there are a variety of restaurants in the area within walking distance. What do you do?

This example is that of an uncertain environment. You literally have no idea which way to go or what restaurant will have food you like. You might just walk out and take your chances. You might stop at the front desk and try to get some information to help you improve your chances, which is still risky. What if you tell the concierge you like seafood and they send you to a place that turns out not to be good by your standards? Or it's out of your price range?

Major Decisions:

Depending on what kind of a decision-maker you are, different decision environments are more or less comfortable for you to operate in. This is why businesses often use teams to make "big" decisions, realizing that different types of people can all contribute to different types of decision making.

You probably do something similar with your family and friends when it comes to decision-making, using their skills, abilities, knowledge and styles to help make decisions.

One more important aspect of decision-making is that making the decision has some value and significance to the decision-maker.

Little things like which dinner choice to make to big things like whether to go to college or join the military, and which college or branch of the military to join, are *big* life decisions. It's easy to see more "big" decisions; get married or don't, buy this car or that, this house or that one.

We often see people agonize over small, seemingly insignificant decisions, while others just make them and move on. No matter who you are or what your approach is, it is inevitable that you will have to make decisions, really big and important ones all the way down to small and insignificant. Try using a problem solving approach to make your decisions. It is at least one systematic way to go about it.

Successful Decision Making:

When in doubt, here is a something you may find helpful:

I was once asked how I could tell if a person might be a successful writer. I said I cannot predict their success but I know this about a writer, a writer writes and they must write before they can be "successful".

So, when in doubt about making a decision, if it won't cost you to put it off, put if off, but when the time comes to make the decision, make it.

Don't be someone who is so afraid of making a decision they are paralyzed by the fear. Make one. No matter what the importance or magnitude of the decision, you taking charge of the process gives you control over the outcomes.

Part 4: Finding the Most Rewarding Job

"I am a humanist, which means, in part, that I have tried to behave decently without expectations of rewards or punishments after I am dead." — Kurt Vonnegut (1922-2007) American writer.

"The reward of a work is to have produced it; the reward of effort is to have grown by it." — Antonin Sertillanges (1863-1948) French Catholic philosopher and writer, "The Intellectual Life: Its Spirit, Conditions, Methods."

"Being in control of your life and having realistic expectations about your day-to-day challenges are the keys to stress management, which is perhaps the most important ingredient to living a happy, healthy and rewarding life." — Marilu Henner (1952-), American actress, producer, writer.

"If you want to be an entrepreneur, it's not a job, it's a lifestyle. It defines you. Forget about vacations, about going home at 6 pm -- last thing at night you'll send emails, first thing in the morning you'll read emails, and you'll wake up in the middle of the night. But it's hugely rewarding as you're fulfilling something for yourself." — Niklas Zennstrom (1966-) Swedish entrepreneur.

"Start with good people, lay out the rules, communicate with your employees, motivate them and reward them. If you do all those things effectively, you can't miss." — Lee Iacocca (1924-) American businessperson, author.

"The reward for work well done is the opportunity to do more." — Jonas Salk (1914-1995), American medical researcher, virologist

Another Direction

If you've spent time doing the various exercises designed to help you discover or uncover those things that are rewarding to you, you are on your way to finding your Most Rewarding Job.

That is only part of the picture. You need clear job and career goal, that align your abilities, interests, values, skills, knowledge, education, experience and training with occupational requirements. You need occupational understanding. that you can gain from self and occupational exploration. This work will provide you with potential targets that you can set your sights.

If you already know jobs and careers that will be most rewarding for you, then you are in a great position to pursue your goal of getting your most rewarding job. You should still consider working through self and career exploration because it provides you with alternatives for now and *in the future*.

Make a distinction between your most rewarding career options, and potential employers. The employers have the jobs. Which employers have the right jobs for you can best be discovered by understanding what jobs you want. Linking the two is one of your jobs. You can think of self-employment or entrepreneurship in this context as well, will it be a rewarding career option for you?

In the broadest context you will have many potential employers in thats jobs exist all over the world and there are millions of employers. Locally though, you will have a smaller pool of potential employers. If you have one, or more, job targets, each target can be found in more than one employer. You control how many potential employers you have based on where you are, or plan to be geographically, and how many potential job targets you have

As an example, you, as a salesperson have decided that you like to sell equipment but not be in retail sales. Your background suggests you could sell material handling equipment or with a little orientation, medical equipment or major construction equipment. Those job targets can be sought out at many different employers.

Continuing you decide you want to stay within 20 miles of home, but are re-locate for the right job. A starting point, for you, could be to investigate makers of material handling equipment, construction equipment or medical equipment. (As a reader, try using a search engine to identify all the makers of any of those kinds of equipment.) There are literally hundreds of makers of one or more of those types of equipment and even more distributors.

Your task, in this example, is straightforward: Get one of them to hire you. Should you wait until they advertise for a salesperson, apply and get the job? Well, you could do that. It is an option. Not a very good one, but still, it is an option.

This is where you need to stop and make a plan. Apply your problem solving skills to the task. The task is this: How do I market myself so that I find "the right buyer me" so that I get my most rewarding job? What is my Personal Marketing Plan. The next chapters will take you through the process.

Chapter 17: Targeting Targets & Target Practice

"To be sure of hitting the target, shoot first, and call whatever you hit the target" — Ashleigh Brilliant (1933-) English author and cartoonist.

"Men nearly always follow the tracks made by others and proceed in their affairs by imitation, even though they cannot entirely keep to the tracks of others or emulate the prowess of their models. So a prudent man should always follow in the footsteps of great men and imitate those who have been outstanding. If his own prowess fails to compare with theirs, at least it has an air of greatness about it. He should behave like those archers who, if they are skillful, when the target seems too distant, know the capabilities of their bow and aim a good deal higher than their objective, not in order to shoot so high but so that by aiming high they can reach the target." — Niccolo Machiavelli (1469-1527) Italian writer and statesman, Florentine patriot, author of 'The Prince'.

Targeting Targets:

What is a target? It is something to take aim at and hit. In the job and career marketplace though, it is a person, place or thing that has caught your interest.

Why are job and career targets important? How can they be targets if they aren't all places you might get a job?

Let's start with how they can be career targets even if they aren't all organizations or businesses.

Suppose you happened to read an article about monkeys, or St. Croix, or Save the Whales, or Dow Chemical, or National Geographic, or Jeff Bezos (CEO Amazon) or Bill Gates and it caught your eye. You were interested in something the article had to say. Perhaps you were driving down a road and saw a brewpub or some other building that looked interesting. Maybe you heard about a new business. What might you do?

You could copy the article, clip it out, or write a note about it, with enough information to get back to it or follow-up on it. If you did, you could put it in a file, an "Interests" file or a "Targets" file. A file of "Things of Interest" to you, because that's what they are.

What kind of file should you use? It could be as simple as a large brown paper bag, a brown accordion folder, but something with some room is best. You could make hard copy print outs of online items to put into it too. So, why not just keep everything on a computer? For one, it is hard to store some of the material you'll be gathering. For another, when you want to spread it all out in front of you, it's easier when you can put it all on the floor in front of you. Granted you can tab through lots of files on a computer but sometimes it is just easier to work with tangible things in front of you.

So, how can those notes, clippings and articles be job and career targets? Easily. Nearly everything we come across in our lives is in some way, shape or form is connected to a business or many businesses.

As an example, take "monkeys" in the article you might have read, maybe in National Geographic or on National Geographic, the Travel Channel, or some other cable or broadcast channel. The article you may have seen was about a new exhibit at your local zoo, or maybe it was one further away. How many businesses did you just cross paths with? The zoo for one, the tv channel for another. How about the supplier who obtained the monkey and brought it to the zoo? What about the monkey food producer? Could you contact any one of them and ask for more information? Sure you could. Could you go to them and see what kind of work the people do in those places? Sure you could.

Or maybe it was an article in a travel magazine about St Croix that caught your eye. How did it catch your eye? Was it a commercial for tourism in St Croix? What was the article about? Was it about people visiting there, working there, having fun there? Maybe it was about the weather in the West Indies (and where are those West Indies at exactly) Could you locate any or even all the businesses that are listed in St

Croix? Sure you could. Could you contact any of them that seemed to have work you might like? Could you visit someone or someplace local and find out more about the work with that business and then find out if that work was available in St Croix? Yes, you can!

How about Bill Gates? Did you read an article about his charitable foundation? What does his foundation support? Does that interest you? Could you look for employment at his foundation, or one of those it supports or maybe just get involved in the cause?

Could you contact someone in any of those or any other organizations that catch your eye? Of course you can, why not? All you need to do is write a letter and ask if you can talk to someone. You can do that can't you? If you can't write a letter, can someone else write one for you?

What we have been talking about is identifying things, people, places, activities that draw your interest. They are potential clues for you to use in looking for work, jobs, and careers, clues that you might find rewarding. It is a custom-made interest survey for you, designed by you! Don't eliminate anything because "you couldn't get a job" associated with it, instead just freely toss it in your file.

So, start today. Write down, cut out, tear out, or copy things that catch *your* eye, *your* interest.

Target Practice:

If you do decide to start and keep a target file, open it up and look at it from time to time. Do there seem to be things that pop up more frequently, maybe clusters of similar things? Look for these kinds of clusters because they are stronger interests and potential targets for you, than items for which you have few or one article. When you look at what you put into the folder, are there themes, trends, or patterns that stick out to you?

For example, did you find that you had 7 or 8 articles and notes about charitable foundations or a particular kind of charity? Maybe you found 5 or 6 articles and notes about sports and the minor leagues of baseball or greens-keeping in baseball and in golf.

If you did see the TV program about monkeys and you noted it in your target file, ask yourself, "What interested me about this program?" What kind of program was it? Were the monkeys in a zoo? Were they in the wild? Where were they? Did the program study the behavior of the troop? Did it show threats to the troop from man or a changing environment? Did it show what man is doing to help them survive? Was it about people helping the monkeys? Where was it set, in some exotic location or nearby? Did that interest you? Was there a moment in the special where you said to yourself, "I could do that" or "I'd like to help" or even "I'd like to do that"? Maybe it was just the travel that was interesting, seeing new places for example.

Suppose you noticed that you have put a number of articles about "beer" in your file. You put a booklet about craft beers made locally in your file. In fact you clipped and put in 22 ads for craft beer festivals within 100 miles of your home. You've seen two documentaries about it. You have articles on growing "hops" locally. Plus you have articles about wine-making and alcohol distilleries. You even noted that you have been to several craft beer festivals, and visited one brewery. This industry could be a strong Target Industry for you. Why not look further into it? Why not try to find your Most Rewarding Career in that industry? Why not? And look at all the beer you'll get to try!

To be sure, some of your notes and clips will be "dead-end" stuff. Interesting articles, or notes, that aren't that interesting on second thought. Some may become places you decide to visit. Some may be local, like a new building or business you saw. Why not go investigate and learn more? Don't be too timid or shy, these are your interests after all. Pursue them. Ask a few questions like: What do you do here? Or when do you open? Or what kinds of jobs do the people who work here do? Use your eyes, what do the people seem to be doing? How are they dressed? Would you be happy doing what they are doing?

Most typically, businesses employ more than one kind of worker. A scientific lab may have researchers, guards, secretaries, accountants, bookkeepers, at least one boss, and cleaning people. A zoo has staff who handle the administration of the zoo, zookeepers to care for the animals, clerks to sell food and souvenirs, greeters, guards, drivers, and cleaning people, not to mention someone who works in personnel. A new dealership, of any sort, may have sales people, service technicians, service writers, parts department people, administrative people like accountants, secretaries, and a cleaning crew.

Not only can you look at one potential target that has caught your interest but you might consider other companies or businesses or organizations that are related to this company or business. As you look into this particular company, or industry, you might want to identify their competitors. They can easily be identified by finding the company in a business directory. Their competitors will be right there too!

Ask yourself what is it about this business, company or industry that interested you. Then look for companies and businesses that share that aspect. You might not like this or that company as a potential employer but you might like one of their suppliers or a competitor! (Always worth remembering if you have a job: your employer's competitors all hire someone to do what you do. All of them.)

Learn from your interests, they are trying to tell you something. Are you listening?

Fund Sources To Create a Career

Some charitable foundations offer grants to people to do things others to organizations. Some of these are things you could do if you were given the opportunity. Perhaps you can give yourself that opportunity. If you did a bit of research, you might find a perfect grant to apply for but then say to yourself "I don't know how to apply for a grant." Do a little more research and you will find that there are professional grant writers, and you can hire them to write one for you. A CPA can set up a company for you to own or operate that can apply for grants as an organization (they can also help guide you to a loan to afford a grant writer). Using your interests and a little motivation you can create a job for yourself!

There is no end to the things people are interested in, and no real limits on what you can pursue. You can find and develop dream jobs or careers with some effort. Your personal target file can be a great, free, resource for you to mine to find your next most rewarding career. Why not start it now?

One more thing, if you are really troubled by the notion that people, places, things cannot all be Potential Targets because they are not all "organizations," that's just a word ("organizations"). Loosen up a little. Create the file and name it whatever _you_ want to name it but do it, you will be glad you did!

Chapter 18: Researching A Company and what's a SWOT?

"Research is creating new knowledge." — Neil Armstrong (1930-2012) American astronaut, first man to walk on the moon.

"Research is the process of going up alleys to see if they are blind." — Marston Bates,(1906-1974), American Zoologist, epidemiologist, professor, author "The Nature Of Natural History"

Background:

Do you <u>have</u> to research a company? No, you don't <u>have</u> to research a company and you don't have to make your bed in the morning either. Should you research a company? Yes! We'll show you how in this chapter.

You never have to research a company. It is not necessary. Your life will go on if you never do any research on any company. You can spend your life "looking for a job" and if you try hard, you will find one. You might get very lucky and get a great lifetime job. It happens, even without research. Then again, you might find one, and then another and another because, well, they just didn't fit *you*. Job hunting without doing research is like trying on different size shoes trying to find a pair that fit. If you took a few moments to research your size, it would make finding a good fit easier.

You put yourself at a huge disadvantage if you don't learn to do a little research on a company.

Research gives you new knowledge about a company. That new information and knowledge is there for you to use to your advantage.

Here are two job hunting, or career building situations where you may want to research a company. One situation is after you have applied for a job and now you are waiting for them to call you for an interview. Another situation is when you have identified a company or business as a Target and want to get "inside" information. In either case, you want to be prepared to answer the question "what do you know about that company?" If you can answer that question, you can interact with anyone within the company.

You should consider doing research for even more reasons. You may actually find a job just by doing research. Doing research will put you in contact with a company and that act alone is one way to uncover a job waiting for you.

What do you want and need to know? You will want to gather general information and specific information. Like a football coach or a battlefield commander, you want "Intel". "Intelligence" in this case is information about the "other side". The more you know, the easier your task becomes. Think about this a bit before you start. Wouldn't you want to know about the company's future prospects and your own before you attempt to go to work there?

Why do you want to research a company and gather information? It is vital that you do your research, in order to obtain *your* next most rewarding job and to build *your* career.

There is no almost no limit to the kinds of information you could collect, but you should look for information that is important and useful to you. What is important and useful information? It is important if it helps you understand the employer better. It is useful if it helps you get a job, or decline the wrong one.

There are several types of information that you will be seeking, as you'll see next.

Target Research:

The first type of information will be useful for you to see and understand the company in light of your goals. Is this a place you belong? A place you want to be, now and in the future? Is it the right place to find that rewarding job and to build your career? Is it right for you? Are they a suitable place for you to spend your work life?

The second type of information that will be useful for you, is the kind that will help you to infiltrate the company. We don't usually call this infiltration, we call it marketing yourself to the employer. Either way it is "getting inside". When you do, you want to be able to show them that you belong there, that you fit. (We talk about Your Marketing Plan in another chapter.)

So now let's look at the first type of information, information that helps you screen the company to decide if you want to work there.

Some things you might like to know are what the company prospects are for long term stability. Is it a growing company or stable and unlikely to grow? What products or services does it sell or offer? How many people work there? Is it in one location or several or many? Is it a local business or a local outlet of a chain? Is the chain regional or national or international? Is the company in an industry that seems likely to last. Is the company in an industry where change occurs frequently? Is it in a disappearing industry?

Elsewhere we spent a great deal of time developing an image of you in the workplace, your interests, your skills, etc., as they related to occupations. It is assumed that the places you are now investigating qualify as potential work sites for you, that they are on your "might fit" list and you are just weeding out the potential targets.

For example, if you like or have a strong interest in working outdoors, then at least some of your Target employers on your "might fit" list should offer some kind of outdoor work. If you like and want to do "lab" work, then these Targets, or employers, must have labs to work in. If you like helping or serving "people," then those Target employers must need people-oriented staff.

What we're talking about here is that you learn details of a particular company so that you can screen them in or out as an employer. They do this for potential employees and you can for potential employers! When you make contact with them, seeking information, you send two messages. "I'm interested in you" is the first message. "I take initiative" is the second. Doesn't this approach seem to empower you? It gives you control over where you will work, or won't, plus it gives an employer a favorable impression of you, makes you desirable in their eyes.

People are people and fitting in with them is likely to be about the same wherever you go unless you've gone to a radically different culture. The people at the places you may work will also be part of a corporate culture that you can investigate. The better your values and those of the company align, the better it is for you and the better the fit between you and the employer will be.

What is in your job and career plan? Are you looking for a fast-paced, rapidly evolving technology company, like a Microsoft, Apple, Amazon or Google. Maybe you want someplace youth oriented, with opportunity for long term growth and abundant promotional opportunity? Maybe you are looking for a more stable, mature company with fewer opportunities for promotion but a more predictable long term job, like a management role in a beverage company?

Regardless of your job goals, your job seeking and career development research goals in researching a potential employer are identifying potential and compatibility. The more you know about yourself and about potential employers, the better positioned you are to find the right one(s). As you do your research, you should be thinking in terms of this employer as compared to others like it.

There are many beverage companies, realtors, insurance companies, banks and credit unions, manufacturers, retailers, branches of government, non-profit agencies out there. No two are alike. If you are researching a company and find that you like a lot about it but not some aspects, you might look to see if one of their competitors, large or small, might be a better fit for you.

Another answer to "why do research?", is to assist you in marketing yourself. We talk more about this in the chapters on Interviewing and Marketing. For now, though put yourself in their place, the potential employer.

Market Research:

Read the next two examples and then decide who you would hire Jaye or Kaye?

Jaye walked in with a referral from a manager in the company and says that they are there to put in an application for the job. Jaye tweaked their resume and it exactly matches the job opening that's just opened up. The HR Department was alerted to them coming in by the manager, and "brings Jaye back" for a preliminary interview. After a few questions by the HR person, Jaye clearly has shown an interest in the company, its mission, what they do at this location, the important values the company seeks in an employee, and its strategic plan. They ask questions that reveal they know about the company and its competitors.

Kaye showed up unannounced but with a resume and asked to complete an application. There is an opening but their resume and application don't quite match the opening. Nevertheless Kaye seems qualified and so HR does a preliminary interview. Kaye doesn't seem to know much about the company, or what it does at that location. Kaye's only questions were about the wages and benefits.

Who would you hire, Jaye or Kaye?

If you answered Jaye, you're right! Jaye went to the trouble of being prepared. They were prepared for the interview because they used tools at their disposal, just like you can. They researched the company, its industry, its competitors, its current and future potential. They developed an inside contact through their personal network. When they met with the contact, they were able to impress them with their knowledge of the company and the work done in their department as well as at the general location. They shared values that displayed their capacity to fit in. They were given a "heads up" on the opening because it was created by their contact person who was so impressed they wanted them in their department. All they needed to do was follow-through. Being better prepared meant they were able to focus on what was important.

Interestingly, Kaye was in many ways a better candidate. Kaye had a little more experience, had slightly better education and training. Their resume -- one of two versions they had (a functional resume and a chronological resume) -- actually showed Kaye to be the better candidate. Either of them would have been an excellent fit for the company. Unfortunately, Kaye's lack of preparation showed and put them at a decided disadvantage for the job competition even though Kaye knew there was going to be an opening because they had regularly contacted HR in this company.

Research Questions:

So, with that said, let's list a few questions that you might want to answer before you meet anyone in the company, either for an Informational Interview, or as part of the hiring process, as in the job interview. You don't have to get answers to them all but you should aim for most of them to be thorough.

Questions to get answers to (in no particular order):
- How old is the company?
- How large is the company?
- What are its products or services?
- Who are its customers?
- Who are its major competitors?
- Who are its up and coming competitors?
- Do the Consumers demand changes, improvements in products or services?
- Do the Consumers resist changes to products or services?
- Are there environmental changes that may affect company?
- What is its reputation or industry standing?
- Where is the company's headquarters?
- What are the company's short- and long-term goals?
- What problems is the company dealing with related to:
    - Competitors or competition
    - Products
    - Location

- Labor, fuel, other supply issues
- Legal issues
- Management issues
- What are the company's strengths?
- What are the company's weaknesses?
- Have there been recent employee layoffs?
- Are they family friendly?
- Do they have part-time jobs?
- Where do you see the company in the next few years?
- What are the current products or services?
- What plans do they have for new products or services?
- What are the company's plans for growth?
- What are the current goals the company is working on?
- How large a department is the one you would be working in?
- To whom would you report (supervisor and title) (or find out the chain-of-command)?
- What are the company's plans for hiring in the next six months?
- Are they technologically current?
- What is the condition of the building?
- What are the working conditions?
- Do they invest in their appearance?
- How modern is their information system?
- What kind of a company is it to work for?
- How would you describe the work environment?
- What do they seem to value most in employees?
- What makes working here unique or different?
- What are the opportunities for training, development and growth?
- What are the top priorities?
- What's the best thing about working there?
- What's the company history?
    - Innovations
    - Milestones, in growth or achievements
    - Milestones, acquisitions and mergers, spin-offs
- Mission or Vision Statement
- How do they describe themselves?
- Recent awards?
- Grants?
- Can you determine "dress for success" patterns for the company, the employee look and style?
- What are your own connections to organization:
    - Alma Mater, fraternal/sorority ties
    - Personal Network
    - Social Network - LinkedIn
- Who owns the company?

Those are some ideas of what you could and should be looking for but why stop there? Take this list and add to it. Cross out any questions you don't like. Add questions you want answers to. It's about *you* after all.

Research Resources:

Today, using computers and the internet, makes research much easier than it once was. However, you can still go to a local library and ask for assistance. This is especially true if your computer skills are not strong or if you are not good at sorting out the enormous amount of information you can be overwhelmed with when you do computer assisted online searches.

So, go to your local library and ask a librarian for assistance. Tell them you are looking for general information about businesses.

Books on "private for profit" businesses:

The Yellow Pages; Headquarters USA (by year, 2012 for example); Directory of American Firms operating in foreign countries; The Directory of Business Information Resources; Companies and their Brands; Walker's Corporate Directory of US Public Companies; Thomas Register of American Manufacturers; RL Polk Marine Directory, Beesons Marine Directory (no longer published); Dun & Bradstreet; Dun & Bradstreet: Business Ranking 2010; Dun & Bradstreet: The Career Guide 2010 (look what you could have stumbled upon just by going to the library for information about businesses), Community Profile Analysis.

Books on Charitable Organizations:

Guidestar; The Foundation Directory (by year, 2012 for example); Annual Register of Grant Support (by year).

When you choose to use the internet, two searches you may want to use are to:

- Search for the company by name with the word website added for example enter "GM Company Website", "Ford Motor Website" or "Toyota Website". Then go to their website and read everything. Somewhere on it you will almost always find not only a link to employment but lots of information about the company products, product lines, and a sense of the image the company wants to portray. Take your time and try to understand the company.

- Search for the industry and add the word "news," for example "beverage industry news," and you get a list of news sources for the industry, like "bevindustry.com." This information is vital as it gives you a wide "insiders" overview of potential employers and news and information to those who work in the industry. If the news and information you see on the website interests you, the industry may be a good match for you. Plus you have access to all that "insider" information.

Other online resources you may want to use include:

• Jobhuntersbible.com (a superior resource hosted by Dick Boles, author of What Color Is Your Parachute) filled with useful information of value to you.
  • Websites with information on general for-profit companies:
    • LinkedIn.com
    • Hoovers.com
    • ThomasNet.com
    • dnb.com (Dun & Bradstreet)
    • Glassdoor.com
  • Websites with information on general not-for-profit companies:
    • http://www.guidestar.org/NonprofitDirectory.aspx/

You could and probably should (Google/Bing or your preferred search engine) type in "company research job hunters" and follow up on all those leads too.

Still more resources for local information:

Your local Chamber of Commerce: "2001-2002 business community referral & community directory" by Central Macomb County Chamber of Commerce (Mt. Clemens, Mich.) is an example of a Chamber of Commerce directory.

Better Business Bureaus, where you live and work or may want to live and work are valuable resources for you to use.

Your local government, county, city, township and village office will have information about business in their (your) community.

We're not done yet, here's more:

Direct contact:

You can and should consider writing to, or calling, a company's headquarters and requesting any and all kinds of literature that they might have. Some companies will not have much, maybe a sales brochure, others will have booklets. All of it, and any of it, will give you valuable information and insights into the company. Ask for the Public Relations Department in larger companies or the Sales Department in smaller ones. Ask for, or seek out, company newsletters.

Have you considered asking a company if they have a tour of their facilities? Depending on what company you are researching, they may offer group tour. Some companies will do individual tours if they are large enough for a marketing department. Try contacting them. Some companies host open houses on a regular or irregular basis, you should try to find out if they do and go to one. A good way to find out if they have open houses is to go to their website or call and ask.

Still one more way to get a tour is by contacting the company and arranging an informational interview. This is covered in another chapter but it is a great way to see the inner workings of a company. There is almost always someone with the time, expertise and interest in showing people around within a company. Your mission is to find that person.

Government Jobs

You need to approach government jobs and research for them differently. They almost all post their jobs online, on their own websites now. It is still important to learn what you can about them. Realize that "government" jobs are of three types: elected, administrative/bureaucratic and civil service. There is also a fourth type; quasi-governmental, jobs that sound like or seem like they are government jobs but the work is delivered through an outside contractor. You can identify each of these types of jobs and increase your opportunities to getting one.

If you want an elected position, you need to identify which one, and then affiliate or not with an organization such as the Democratic Party, Republican Party, Tea Party, Libertarian Party, others, or run as an independent. Depending on what level of elected position you are targeting, you can prepare and win the position. You can go to your local elections office and obtain the necessary forms. You can try to get a "job description" for the official position but they typically don't exist. We won't talk further about this but it is a job and career option for every citizen. If the position is state or national in scope, it is probably advisable to consider affiliating with the party of your choice which gains you access to funders and funds.

If you want an administrative/bureaucratic job, you can sometimes be appointed to the positions by politicians, those who were elected. That might be an incentive for you to get involved and work on a campaign. You can be involved in projects that form a basis for your selection. Think of the top advisers to almost any governor, or all of the jobs considered to be "political appointees."

A starting point for your research is to contact your local representative to whichever level of government you are interested in. It will help you if you develop a contact network of people who are in party politics and use their assistance to access your representative, although technically they should all be willing to assist you. Ask them how you can learn about political appointment.

For civil service jobs, you have to apply for the positions when they are posted but that does not prevent you from making contact with the department you would like to work in. It is usually more difficult to even "get in" and visit because there is a tendency for bureaucracies to be more closed to the outside world than private sector businesses.

Often, there are "open house" days that can give you that access. Call the governmental office you are interested in and ask about this. My local county government offers a two-day open house program that permits you, the citizen, access to most of the government offices to see what they do. You can usually find a department responsible for stimulating business interest in the geographic area they serve and they may be able to provide more information for you. One thing they can provide you with is a list of private contractors that they do business with, which you can then use to attempt to obtain a quasi-government job.

When it comes to government there is an old adage that they are largely employers of "friends and family." It's true, so if you have a relative or a friend, they can often help you to get a job. Use your network. If governmental agencies cannot fill their employment needs with people with inside connections, they do hire "outsiders." Do not give up.

One more aspect to getting a government job is to be aware that they give preference to internal employees for whom a job represents a promotional opportunity. You should aim for whatever job level is appropriate to you. If you do not get that one because someone gets it through promotion, that means there is an opening one level down. Consider trying for that one.

"The better prepared you are … the luckier you get."

Chapter 19: Informational Interviewing

"There's only one interview technique that matters ... Do your homework so you can listen to the answers and react to them and ask follow-ups. Do your homework, prepare." — Jim Lehrer (1934-), American journalist, newsman

"When I interview someone, I know in the first two minutes if I like them or not. I find that if it's easy to talk to someone and I see an openness and honesty and integrity, then I usually hire them." — Bobbi Brown (1957-) Professional Make Up Artist, founder Bobbi Brown Cosmetics,

"I think an interview, properly considered, should be an investigation. You shouldn't know what the interview will yield. Otherwise, why do it at all?" — Errol Morris (1948-), American film director.

Background:

So, what is Informational Interviewing?

Definition: Informational Interviewing is a semi-structured interview that *you* conduct with people who have information *you* want.

Let's break that down and look at those three parts. An Informational Interview is; 1) a semi-structured interview, 2) *you* conduct with people who have, 3) information *you* want. The people you interview are those whose careers or occupations interest *you*. It really is all about *you*.

The first part of the definition is that it is a "semi-structured interview". What does "semi-structured interview" mean? It means that you have a reason for using your time and the time of the person you are interviewing. Since you are investing your time and asking the other person to donate or volunteer theirs, you will want to have a clear idea of the questions you would like to discuss. At the same time, since you are fact-finding, exploring, and learning during this interview, you will want to be alert to comments made by the other person that might lead you to ask questions you had not anticipated. Therefore you come to the meeting with a set of questions you would like to ask but are prepared to be flexible based on the person with whom you are talking.

You should plan on asking for one-half to one full hour of the other person's time. Fifteen minutes is too short a time to conduct a meaningful interview, a half hour can be sufficient, but probably will not be. However, if the other person has time and is willing to continue, be prepared for one hour. You should be prepared for a one hour interview but only plan and ask for a half hour to an hour. Once the interview begins, if they do not have time to continue, ask if you can follow up with email, phone calls or evan a follow-up interview.

If you do get a full hour or more, you will get a lot of information. Informational interviews often go longer, much longer than this. You are exploring information with someone who "lives" your topic and they often find more time for you. You should be prepared for an entire morning or afternoon to conduct one informational interview. It is recommended though, that you ask for one-half to one hour and be aware of when that time is nearly up. Be courteous to your host and let them know when you are nearing the time limit established beforehand, but if you have more time, let them know that you are free to continue as long as they are.

Later we discuss questions that you might ask in a semi-structured interview. The workbook contains more material on the topic for you to use a start or place to work from.

The second part of the definition, "you conduct with people who have," means that you are going to lead the interview with another person. That does not mean that you should plan on doing all the talking; quite the opposite. The other person has the information you are seeking. You will want to let them do most of the talking but you want to prompt or direct them when needed to get the information you want.

You will have your list of the top 5-10 questions you want answers to but prepare yourself to say, "Could you tell me more about that?". It is your task to use your listening skills. After listening carefully to what the other person says, you may want more information. Ask for it. If something is unclear to you, ask for clarification. If they say something that is new, unfamiliar or interesting to you tell them you want to know more. It is flattering to someone for you to ask questions about the topic they are discussing, it shows you are listening and interested.

Easy Ways to Acquire Information Interview Skills:

It is difficult for most people to keep from speaking during a lull in a conversation. One thing taught to people who "listen for a living" (like psychologists, and reporters for example) is the trick of how to say nothing during conversational lulls. Before you do an information interview, you may want to practice with someone. Get a friend or relative to carry on a conversation with you and see how long you can go without opening your mouth. Learn to keep your ears open and your mouth shut for 30 seconds. Learn how long 30 seconds feels like. Resist the urge to comment or say something. It's harder than you think at first. It gets easier with practice. You should practice it though even simply sitting and timing how long 30 seconds is. Look at a watch or clock and then look away, and look again when you think 30 seconds have passed.

Once you've read through this chapter, you may want to practice or rehearse an informational interview with someone you know. Take the starter questions, and then practice asking them and waiting for a response. This will make it easier for you to not only conduct a "live" or real Informational Interview but will aid you later when you are in a job interview. You will be more accustomed to the interview situation which will make you more comfortable and a better interviewee.

One barrier to Informational Interviewing for many people, is being shy or hesitant because you think no one would want to talk with you. Why wouldn't they? Get over it. Really. People love to talk about themselves. They love to talk about the things that interest them. Sometimes they are dying to talk about it but the people in their world are tired of asking or hearing about it. You represent a new ear, a new opportunity for them. Some people love the subject of their work or workplace, and are glad to talk about it because it gives them an opportunity to inspire, or at least inform someone about their life's work.

There are people who won't want to talk. That says more about them and not you. They may not like talking to others. They may have very little spare time. They may be uncomfortable talking with others because that's just how they are. There may be rules that prevent them talking about their work. Maybe, maybe, maybe. It doesn't matter, if you can't speak with them, move on and find another person to interview.

The same logic holds for doing Informational Interviews as rehearsing them with friends or family. If you get comfortable meeting with strangers in an interview situation, you will conduct yourself better in a job interview.

Finding Interviewees:

The third and final part of the definition was "information you want." That will help you determine what questions to ask. What do *you* want to know? That is up to you but take a moment now and think about a few things. You, and the other person, do not have lots of time. Time is precious so do not waste it. By the time you are considering doing an Informational Interview, you should have a fairly clear purpose for targeting a particular person in a particular company or industry.

Suppose you wanted to work as an independent producer of documentaries, who would you think you might want to talk to? Independent producers of documentaries, of course. Where might you find one? At a film festival or by searching online for independent documentary film makers in your area. You might look to Youtube and look at the general subject of documentaries and work your way to one in your area based on a subject or two of interest to you.

Perhaps you would like to work as a lab technician. Who do you think you might like to talk to? Lab technicians and supervisors. Where do you find them? Working in labs. How do go about meeting them? One way would be to look into associations and other organization that they belong to. You could go to schools that train people for that career. By the way, that is a very broad description, lab technician, as they are found in numerous industries and settings, hospitals, independent medical laboratories, agricultural labs, crime labs, and more. You might want to narrow your search and research down to a particular category, like nuclear medical lab technician.

Once you have located a potential person to contact, you now have to work through making that contact and getting that interview.

How to make contact:

So, how do you go about it? Thanks to your research, you know who you want to talk to and you have their street address, right? Or an email or phone number? You do have their name, right?

Okay, let's start with you have their name and an email address. So, fire off an email. What should you say?

For a subject line, something along the lines of a reference to something specific about them or their work is good, like the following:

Subject: "Your work on robotics" or Subject: "Your recent documentary entitled "XY and Z." or Subject: "Your lab work at MedRed medical device makers". And If you happen to be fortunate enough to have a referral through your Network, try this: Subject: "My friend Johnny J. Johnston suggested I contact you".

For the body of the text, you objective is to get a phone number or street address so that you can call, send a letter or make an appointment to conduct your interview. To meet your objective, you will need to provide them with a reason for giving you that information. They need to trust you enough to share information.

Your sincere honesty and clear, coherent purpose in making contact will do it. You may not "get it right" on the first, second or even fifth try but practice, make the attempt and see what happens. It is typical that you will be able to get through to that person. On the next page are some examples that you can use as models.

Mr. Tobor;

I am writing to you because I read about your works on Robotics in an article in last months Robotics Monthly. I am a beginning robotics engineer and share your interest. Would you be willing to talk to me about your article and your work? May I have a phone number I can reach you at to talk with you?

My name is Joe E. Jones and

Thank you.

Joe E. Jones
555-678-4321

Example 1:

Mr. Hudson;

I recently attended a screening of your documentary, "X, Y and Z" at the Sunset Film Festival in Sunup Michigan. It was a thought provoking work that held my interest throughout the four hours it ran.

I am a budding documentary film maker and I would be so grateful for a few minutes to speak with you about your work. Here is my phone number, 555- 333-2424, so that you can call me when you have a few minutes to talk. Or, if you would like I can call you. At what number may I reach you and when is a convenient time to call? Thank you very much.

Bob Babinsky

Example 2:

Ms. Smith;

I was researching leading medical device research and design facilities and your name came up as the lead R & D Lab Manager at MedRed. I am contacting you because I would like to speak to you about your work there. Would that be possible? My number is 555-333-2424. Please feel free to contact me at a time of your convenience.

Sincerely
Melanie T. Johnson

Example 3:

   Alternatively, since you do have a location for Ms. Smith, you could call her directly and ask to speak with her. You should consider sending a letter to any contact that you plan to interview before you make that call.

You want to "set the stage" before you make that call asking for an appointment for an Informational Interview. Your "set the stage" letter prepares the recipient for a call they will receive and fills them in on the purpose of your call. That way, you don't put them on the spot, which oftentimes will raise barriers and prevent you from getting your meeting.

There are examples of these "set the stage" letters, and of phone scripts, in Appendix B, "Informational Interviews - Sample "Set the Stage Letters" and Phone Scripts."

Take a look at the example of a "set the stage" letter below.

Do you see what this letter accomplishes in six sentences and only four short paragraphs?

Sandra Smith, Director
Research & Development Laboratories
MedRed Inc
1234 Fifth Street
Fiction City, MI 48999

Dear Ms. Smith;

I am writing to you because of my interest in the development of new medical devices. My research revealed that MedRed is an international leader in Research & Development of medical devices and that you are a key individual in their success.

I am sure you have a very busy schedule but I would like to arrange a brief meeting with you to discuss your own growth and development to become the leader you are. We could even meet during a lunch period if that would be convenient for you.

I plan to call you on Monday, between 3:00 pm and 4:00 pm to make arrangements with you or you may feel free to call me at 555-333-2424 anytime.

Thank you so very much and I look forward to meeting you.

Sincerely

M.l. i T I l

First, you've identified why, your purpose, for making contact with this specific person. No one else can speak for her, can they? It must be her. Then you acknowledge that she must be a busy person but that you can be flexible as to the time of a brief meeting. Again, this recognizes her value. You then forewarn her and alert her to when you plan to call, so that she is prepared to speak with you. You convey a business sense of fitting things into schedules. It is vital that you call at that time. If you do, you have shown that you are someone who follows through on commitments and can be trusted to do so again. Fail to make that call on time and you are seen as someone whose word cannot be taken seriously. Finally, you conclude your letter.

You have not wasted Ms. Smith's time. You've given her a clear, concise letter to read which business people and busy people respect. You've shown good business judgment. Just be sure to mail that letter out a week before you plan to make the call. That will give your letter time to reach her or her secretary and be read.

On Monday, you make the call. The only two possibilities are: You speak to her or you do not speak to her.

If you speak to her, all you need to do is find out when it will be convenient to meet with her and set up the appointment. It is likely that she will want to discuss your reason for needing to meet with her and/or trying to cover the meeting over the phone. Stress that it would be better to meet in person as you have a few questions and that you would really like the opportunity to meet with her and see the facility at the same time, if that is possible. You should also ask if she received your letter. You can refer to it during your conversation to help refresh her as to your purpose.

Be sure that you stress you are not looking for a job and that this is an Informational Interview. (Be sure you know it, believe it and act like it.)

If you call and she does not take your call, you need to find out why she did not if you can. If she has a secretary, perhaps she can tell you that she is in a meeting or out of town or on vacation or in the middle of a project. Whatever answer you're given is fine, just use that opportunity to find out a better time to call back.

If you get her voicemail, listen to the message. Sometimes people will leave a message as to why they are unavailable which will suggest to you an alternative time to call back. Sometimes they don't. If all you can do is leave a message, you should state your name, your phone number and that you are calling in reference to a letter you sent to her last week and that you will call again tomorrow at 9:00 am or suggest that she can call you back when it is convenient.

Anytime you leave a voice mail, speak slowly and clearly. All too often people speak too quickly to be heard clearly. Don't do that. If the recipient can't make out what you said, you will be dismissed and not responded to, which is not your desired outcome. It is common for people to speak too rapidly when leaving a voice mail and often their words and numbers slur together, leaving an annoying and useless message.

In your voicemail message, by indicating when you will call back, you are showing that you will be persistent and mean business. This will let the person know that it might be best to just call you when it is convenient. You have reminded them of your purpose and purposefulness in calling. They will look for the letter if they set it aside, and will read it.

After the interview, be sure to send a thank you letter. In the letter express your gratitude for their time and some key element that was of special value or import to you, which will show you were actually listening and learning. These elements give them feedback as to their value to you and your overall recognition of their value.

Example of a thank you letter:

Dear Ms. Smith;

I want to thank your so very much for meeting with me last Wednesday and fitting me in your busy schedule.

Your discussion of your career path based on achievement, accomplishment, preparation and opportunity was very helpful. I will use your insights to help me in achieving my own career goals.

I appreciated your enthusiasm about the new project you are designing. It sounds very exciting to me.

Again, thank you for your time and patience with me.

Sincerely
Melanie T. Johnson, BA
(address & telephone)

So, you've made contact and have an appointment for the meeting. You plan to send a thank you letter. What about those 5-10 interview questions you need?

Your Informational Interview Questions

The questions you ask should be designed to get the other person talking and sharing useful information with you. *You* should think about what you want to know. Here are some possible questions you could ask. Notice they are like some of those pesky questions you are asked in job interviews. They ask them for the same reason, to get information by getting you talking and then listening to what you have to say. We will explore those job interview questions in Chapter 23: Interview Ready.

Here are some questions you could ask (though there are many others throughout the book that you could ask too):

- How did you get started (in robotics, or making documentaries or doing research and development, whatever)?
 - When did you first get interested in _____?
 - How long have you been doing this _____?
 - What do you like most about your work?
 - What do you like least about your work?
 - What advice would you give someone who is interested in _____?
 - What is the work like?
 - What are the prospects for someone entering the field today?
 - What kind of training was required?
 - What do employers look for in someone in this field?
 - How much freedom do employees have to set their own work schedule?
 - Does the company support further education and training opportunities?
 - What are the company's core values?
 - What determines success in this company?
 - What determines success in this field?

After the interview, think about what you've learned. Do you now have a better understanding of the work? Does this work or company still interest you? Would you like this work? Who should you contact next if you want to pursue this employer or work? If this isn't the field or employer, ask yourself "what should I look into next? Should I try another employer in the field?"

Keep in mind that you've already benefited in *many* ways by doing one or more Informational Interviews. You've gained valuable insights into an employer or work in a field of interest. This information is useful to you in your job and career decision making process.

You have made contacts, hopefully with interesting people and added them to Your Personal Network. You've learned some of the jargon in the field and learned of important issues in the field. You've practiced interviewing skills and become more relaxed in interview situations. Yay you!

It is a low pressure way for people to become aware of you, which is one of the techniques in self-marketing, making potential consumers, employers, aware of your product, you.

You may have eliminated employers or fields from your search, saving you time and who knows what else if you got a job with the wrong company.

Part 5: Your Marketing Plan

"To establish oneself in the world, one does all one can to seem established there already." — François Duc De La Rochefoucauld (1613-1680), French author of maxims and memoirs.

Background:

When you are ready to engage in the job hunt process, three elements become immediate needs to prepare for. These are; Resumes, Applications and Interviews. They represent an inter-locking cluster of tasks that your mastery will enable you to find and get your most rewarding job and career. These three components form a package that will represent you to a potential employer.

They are not you. They are a representation of you. You are not a few words on a sheet of paper. You are not the person who gets interviewed. Rather these form a set of pictures in the mind of your potential employer that permit them to decide if you are the employee for them. That is who they want, the employee
.

You are so much more than your resume, your application and interview, right? Honestly, most of us dislike the whole resume-application-interview thing because we are good at what we do, not because we are good at resumes, applications and interviews.

If there were a good alternative process to offer you, the offer would be made. There just isn't.

Even if you get a job offer from one of the techniques described in this book, you still need a resume. You will still need to complete an application (for the records), You will still have some kind of interview.

As a group, the resume, the application and the interview, represent you. They form an image of you to those who read them and who meet with you. You should want that image to be as positive and attractive to those people as you can.

It is not only important that your image be appealing but that the message be consistent across all three elements. Dissonance and discord should be avoided. You don't want a reader or an interviewer to find that your application and your resume don't agree. You don't want the interviewer to find that you don't know what you've said in your resume or that what you say doesn't match what you've written.

When that happens, it is like hitting a jarring bump in the road or the warning strips alongside a freeway. Interviewers respond negatively and that can cost you a potential job.

In the next few chapter we address each of these elements individually and spend time on your image and marketing plan. Your goal is to put them to work for you rather than looking at them as "something you have to put up with." Unless you've found a way to skip them, you need to work on them and put them to work for *you*!

Chapter 20: Your Marketing Plan

"There are those of us who are always about to live. We are waiting until things change, until there is more time, until we are less tired, until we get a promotion, until we settle down - until, until, until. It always seems as if there is some major event that must occur in our lives before we begin living." — George Sheehan (1918-1993) American physician, author and running enthusiast.

"Two-thirds of promotion is motion" — (Unknown).

"Networking is marketing. Marketing yourself, marketing your uniqueness, marketing what you stand for." — Christine Comaford-Lynch (?), leadership and culture coach.

The Market Plan

Suppose you were an Employment Coach and your next client came in and said:

"My name is Joseph K. and I'm looking for a job as a Chief Financial Officer in a conservative manufacturing company, or warehouse and distributing company. My 25 years of successful growth and experience in accounting and finance, in banking and in manufacturing, positions me for this next career step. My familiarity with the needs of manufacturers and the resources available to them assures my capacity to enable their business plan. My leadership skills and vision can help any manufacturer take the next step in their success.

My marketing plan is simple, straightforward. I know who I am and I know what food manufacturers need in a Chief Financial Officer. I am currently the Vice President of Finance at FarmFresh Foods.

I know where I want to live and where I am in my career. I have identified all the types of manufacturing companies within 25 miles of my location, in order of industry preference, food manufacturing, beverage manufacturing, then aero and auto supplier manufacturing. Within each industry, I have arranged the companies in order of my preference as places I want to work. I have written out what I am looking for in terms of the type of company I will enjoy working in, which are closest to me in style. culture and values. I have a list of contacts into more than half of my targets. I've done my research and I'm prepared to activate my plan.

I plan to call a contact in each of the food manufacturing companies, starting with my first choice. My network was developed through the contacts I've made over the years in banking and manufacturing, at trade shows and in trade associations, and through my volunteer work with and for my employers. Added to that are my personal friends.

When I call on my contacts, I have a prepared "informal" script to follow that includes a plan to not only get a copy of my resume in their hands but to their Board of Directors, Chief Executive Officer and the current Chief Financial Officer.

Since I am re-locating from the southwest back to my home state, I don't know as many of the people personally as I would around here, I do not know the current scuttlebutt as to who's growing and who's stable, who has an aging or unsuccessful CFO, but I plan to try to find that out, during my contacts with my network."

What would you think? How would you see this person, Joe K? Are they prepared? Likely to get the job they want? Wish you were Joe? Who is he? Joe is a man with a plan, a marketing plan.

Marketing Plan:

What is a Marketing Plan? What you just read was an example of one. Not yours, just an example of one. So, what was in that Marketing Plan and what should be in yours? What are the key elements and how can you use them for your most rewarding job hunt and career development plan? Why should you have one?

Let's answer that last question first, "Why have one?." A good marketing plan will aid and assist you in optimizing your next most rewarding job search opportunities. Optimizing means to make the best possible use of your resources to get the most benefit, in this case to get *your* most rewarding job and career. It save time, money and offers you the best results for your effort.

A "marketing plan" is a business term that applies to finding the best way to reach your customers and motivating them to buy from you. It is a program or plan to find the most rewarding way to offer your product(s) or service(s) to a marketplace, i.e. to buyers. Ideally, as a business, you want to sell 100 percent of the product(s) or service(s) that you produce or offer, at the most economic production point and thereby maximize your profit. That may sound like gobbledygook but it boils down to a few key things: 1) make the most profit you can by 2) selling all you can at 3) your lowest cost. We could, but mercifully won't go into this any further than that. What we will do, instead, is apply that business thinking to your job search and career development plan.

Definition: a Marketing Plan is the best way to reach you potential customers and motivating them to be your customer.

Background:

Not surprisingly, businesses spend a lot of money on this concept "marketing plan" and universities and colleges worldwide expend a lot of research and money on the subject. It is a key component to "making money." It is not the only component but it is so fundamental that there are many business schools courses and many more books about "Marketing." Successful marketing equates to business success. Poor, bad, or non-existent marketing and market planning lead to failure. Let's use some of that research and thinking to develop Your Market Plan.

So, what does "marketing" do? It examines the features and benefits of a product or a service. It designs a strategy to communicate them to the right market or audience. It then delivers the "goods" to the consumer.

If you had the world's greatest product or world's best service and no one knew about it, your business would fail because no one would buy it or use it. Some fairly bad products and weak services have succeeded because of good marketing campaigns. I won't name names here, but have you ever bought something on the strength of a really good commercial that made you want it, and then were seriously disappointed when you did? Thank a good marketing manager for getting you to try it and buy it. Your purchase is the ultimate fulfillment of the marketing plan. There is a summary of this in Appendix C and a plan of your own to complete in the workbook.

Marketing You!

Along the way in this book we have looked at you and where you have been. We've looked at where you are now and where might you go.

We could also look at you from the standpoint of "what if you do nothing" and we will. What if you do none of the exercises in this book and the workbook? What if you do nothing to find your next most rewarding job? What if you do nothing to develop your career?

Most assuredly time will go by. Weeks will become months and months, years. Years will pass. During all this time, your remaining time, you will work. You will find jobs. And at some point in time you will look back over your life and see what you did. You may even reflect on what you *could* have done with that lifetime of work. You will probably not see all that you *could* have achieved, and accomplished. You will not see how much more *money* you could have made. You will know how much you made, thanks to the Social Security Administration but you will not know how much you *could* have made. Another $50,000, $100,000, $250,000? You will not see what else you could have accomplished. You will not know what other rewards could have been yours, in the workplace and out. You will just never know. That is sad, and a terrible waste of your life. These lost and unknown opportunities, are called opportunity costs.

Yes even doing nothing comes at a cost. Whatever you choose to do, is at the cost of not doing what you *could* have done, the *opportunity* cost.

That's why it is so worth the time for you to explore yourself, your potential and then to develop a Personal Marketing Plan to realize your potential. This is why we asked you to examine and determine where you want to go with your career.

Once you have a plan, you can define the action steps you can take to make it happen. The problem solving and goal attainment material can assist you with this. Those tools can help you overcome obstacles, break through barriers, and give you the ways and means to adjust and change your plan when it needs to be done.

Personal Marketing Plan

What might a Personal Marketing Plan look like from a business perspective? We'll start by examining something called the "4P's" of the marketing mix. These are the four most basic building blocks of a business marketing plan: 1) **P**roduct 2) **P**romotion 3) **P**lace and 4) **P**rice. These elements are all under a businesses' control and are the fundamental factors of how a business plans to bring it's product or services to market. They are the factors that you control in the job search process.

Product:

What is your product? Well, in a word, _you_, but not just you, _you_ in the context of being a successful employee. In the chapters on the Department of Labor O*NET material, and in the workbook, we spent considerable time looking at you. We examined your abilities, interests, values, work styles, skills, knowledge, education, experience and training and relate that information to occupations and jobs. Now that you have identified them and even selected those that are strongest or most important to you in each category, you have also identified them as key elements to help you stand out in the eyes of an employer as compared to your competition.

Unique Selling Proposition

For the purpose of creating Your Marketing Plan, you may want to think about developing something called a Unique Selling Proposition (USP). What makes you unique and attractive to an employer? What makes you a better employee to an employer than the next person. Try to describe yourself in 15 words or less using this USP concept.

Start by looking at your potential employer and job targets are. What do these employers need a potential employee to be or to do? What problems, barriers and obstacles do they have in getting the right employee for this job?

Now, how do you solve that problem or eliminate that barrier or overcome those obstacles? How are you the solution?

Write down 3 - 5 of your features as an employee that apply to the problems, barriers and obstacles of the employer. Your unique combination of those features, or benefits, forms the basis of your Unique Selling Proposition.

When you present your qualities that solve their problems, it eliminate barriers and overcomes obstacles. You imply a "guarantee" a promise or pledge that says "if you hire me, your problems are solved." Try to expand this and state which problems are solved if you are hired.

Take everything you've been jotting out, brain-storming, and taking stabs at and try to write it all up in one paragraph. Don't worry about how long it is or how many sentences you've got. Just write it out. Set it aside for one or two days. Then get it out and start to polish it. Combine some things. Eliminate some. Move the most important stuff to the top, the least to the bottom. Try to get it to flow.

The big challenge, can you write one sentence that sums up your Unique Selling Proposition best. Or two or three sentences? Try to sum it up in one sentence though if you can.

Example:

You want a job as a Computer Numerically Controlled (CNC) Machine Tool Programmer in an established, stable machine shop. You've done some research and learned that they place a premium on experienced and trained new hires willing to work overtime or on second shift. They often have applicants who say they can do the job but haven't worked out, so that there is some steady turnover because of that. They have several competitors and it is always a constant concern for all of them that they turn out high quality product, in small batches, rapidly and consistently.

You have ten years experience producing high quality, small batch production runs. You are especially adept at rapid re-tooling and programming and minimize down time due to changeover. You were trained at one of the leading technical schools in your area, before you entered the industry but you also routinely take refresher courses, and read-up on advances in your industry.

You also worked for one employer for your entire work career.

You can promise an employer, "a loyal, stable, committed, trained, experienced CNC operator programmer who will make it right the first time, quickly and with minimal downtime".

Your USP boils down to: I am an experienced, high caliber CNC Programmer committed to rapidly producing high quality product with the flexibility and knowledge to rapidly be a successful contributing team member for you.

Nice, huh?

Positioning

You will also want to think in terms of positioning yourself in your marketplace. Imagine this to be a series of comparisons of you to others. Who are you relative to other potential employees. Are you young and they are old(er)? How are you positioned to compete? What are your competitive advantages to an employer? Are you a seasoned worker, or an eager new, recently trained, entrant? Are you familiar with modern computerized accounting systems or adept at using a wide range of bookkeeping methods? What advantages do you possess, what qualities or qualifications make you a better choice then someone else?

Keep in mind that different employers look for different qualities, different strengths and skills. That is one of the reasons we spent time on Researching a Company and on Informational Interviewing. Some of that effort was to help you identify what those things are that an industry and an employer would find important so that you can use this knowledge when you target that employer.

Finally, you need to be able to communicate all of this information, your message, to the marketplace. Once you've spent time with this, you will see how it helps you tie together your resume, cover letter, job application, informational interviews and job interviews. Your package of you as "product" will stand out as different from everyone else.

Now that you have looked at your Product, what you are in terms of features and benefits to an employer(s), you can work on the second "P", Promotion.

Promotion:

Suppose you had a great product and no one knew it existed, what would you do? You'd promote it. How? How would you promote it?

You might try different types of advertising to reach your potential customers. You would probably try to figure out who your potential customers were and then what the most cost-effective way of reaching them would be. TV, Radio, Magazines, Direct Mail. Which TV shows, which radio programs and where? Which magazines and why? What literature would you mail and to whom?

Fortunately as the person marketing you, your promotional efforts are easier in many ways.

Think of it this way, if you could identify the one person who is in a position to hire you for your most rewarding job, how would you reach them with your message? Your message that says "when you need somebody and not just anybody will do, you need me" or more simply "you need me." Better still they do need you, want you and would hire you on the spot.

That's the work you do in promoting you. Get "you" in front of "them" and get them "ready to buy." You want them aware of you and motivated to hire you. You've already spent time on finding the "who." How are you going to reach them? Have you created a consistent message for them to receive? You do this through a combination of actions on your part. Your cover letters, resumes, job application, phone calls, informational interviews and job interviews are all part of a bundle of tools for you to pick from. You want to work on these tools and get them as sharp as possible.

Now that Product, you, and Promotions have been covered, we now look at Place.

Place

In business marketing place refers to the how to get your product or service into the hands of the consumers. Where can they encounter you? Where can they get you? How will they find you, in what locations?

How are you going to get you into the hands of your consumers, your potential employer?

Some resources to consider are using:
- Job Postings/Recruitment Advertising
- Job Fairs
- Cold Calls
- Using Your Network
- Job-hunting on the Web
- University Career Centers Job Postings(they aren't limited to students as a rule)
- Alumni Offices of schools if you went there
- Headhunters & Recruiters at Executive Search Firms
- Public & Private /Employment Agencies
- Informational Interviews

Most career experts suggest that networking is crucial to a successful job search. It is not for all of us but if you are good at using yours, it can turn about that job offer that you are looking for.

Price

The fourth "P" in Marketing is Price. What's yours?

You may have noticed that much of what you buy is sold at a fixed price, you don't get to set it. Somebody else does. When you buy a gallon of gas or of milk, that vendor delivers it a price they set. It may change, up or down. It may change because of changes in supply or to try to lure you in to make other purchases or to make a sale to you that their competitor won't make.

Price for some things, though, is negotiable. If you are buying a new car, you can typically find a variation in the price depending on the dealers you shop. Furniture and appliances at the same store, can often be sold at differing prices depending on the skill of the buyer.

Whatever the situation though, you are paying a "price" for a product or service that contains a bundle of benefits. The benefits vary if you are willing to pay more or want to pay less.

When it comes to your "price" in the employment market, you should keep in mind that there will be some range in what an employer could pay you. Your task is to get as much as possible while theirs is to pay a sufficient amount (not necessarily the least they can get away with). In theory, you should only accept less pay, and benefits, for a job that requires less. Looking at it the other way around, the more benefits you bring to an employer, the more you should receive. Some of what you earn will be "market related". The "market" in this case is all of those who could do the job, the "labor market" that you are in. The "real labor market" you are in is you plus your direct competitors. More competitors lowers wages, fewer raises them. If you are good at marketing yourself, you should still find that you will get more than your competitors, all other things being equal.

It is easy to see this in sports, where agents negotiate "pay" for athletes. In theory, the better the athlete, the more they will make (assuming their agents are equally talented, and everything else being equal, which it never is).

So, what is your "price"? It is not only your wage or salary but should also the following:
- Insurance
  - Medical
  - Dental
  - Optical
  - Life
  - Accidental Death
  - Disability
- Extra Pay
  - Raises
  - Bonuses
  - Overtime
- Leave
  - Vacation
  - Paid and Unpaid Holidays
  - Sick/personal
- Retirement
  - Pension Plans
  - 401(k) Plans
  - Profit sharing
  - Stock options/ESOPs
- Other benefits
  - Tuition Reimbursement

- Dependent Care
- Employee Assistance Programs
- Parking
- Expense Reimbursements
- Travel Expenses
- Expense Accounts

One indirect benefit to consider is how much time and money it will cost you to travel to and from an employer. It is a cost to you. Another is, clothing costs. You may want to consider what clothing you can wear on the job, as it may increase or decrease you costs as well.

When you consider a "job" you should take into account your costs, plus the bundle of benefits you receive, your wage plus the other benefits, as a total package price. This total package price can then be compared to what other employers will give for the job they have. You should then compare what you have to offer and will be expected, willing and eager to do, in light of what is offered to you.

It is not widely known but there is a range of pay (including benefits) that most employers can and will pay their employees. They will pay more if they have to, or want to for someone they really want or need. They will often pay less if they can. Shouldn't you position yourself at the high end of their scale as someone they see as highly desirable?

So, now let's go back and tie together some of the work you've done elsewhere in the book and design Your Marketing Plan. The next section is laid out in "outline" format, and you can easily use the headings in either a word processing program or even on paper, to create your own marketing plan.

Your Marketing Plan:

We purposely designed this section to be in outline style, as you will find the outline in the Appendices. We added discussion to the outline here.

Phase 1: Preparation

1. Goals: What are your goals for finding your most rewarding job? You can use the material you developed in the sections on Why People Work, Why People Volunteer, why you work and volunteer. Use the knowledge you gained in the Dept of Labor O*NET work you did. What elements of "your most rewarding" job are most important to you? Are your goals SMART (Specific, Measurable, Attainable, Realistic, Time-Based)?
   a. What are your personally rewarding factors? Here are four examples:
      i. love working with people and being of service to them
      ii. like moving around, not stuck at a desk
      iii. like promotional opportunity
      iv. would like to work within 5 miles of home
   b. Job Targets - what are they, in order of highest to lowest?
      i. Target 1 - State it. Some possibilities are CEO, CFO, CNC Programmer, Lab Technician, Territory Sales Representative, Head Chef, landscape laborer.
         1. What are the requirements for each job you listed, at your current Job Zone Level? (list the requirements and how you meet them). (This list is based on "My Next Move" but you could use the O*NET model, or create one of your own for that matter). As you work on this section, you should be thinking about how you can demonstrate you have that particular factor.
            a. Knowledge

       i. what knowledge is <u>required</u> (this could be 1 or more elements, more likely to be more than on element, more like 4-5 or more. Example: customer service, management, math, good use of English).

      ii. what knowledge <u>do you have</u> and where did you acquire it? (Example: Customer service work at Piedmont Stores return desk, Assistant Manager at Piedmont Stores, excellent math skills and took and passed courses in Public Speaking at Pine Valley Community College).

  b. Skills

       i. what skills are required

      ii. what do you have

  c. Abilities

       i. what abilities are required

      ii. what abilities do you have

  d. Personality

       i. what personality factors are involved

      ii. what are yours

  e. Technology

       i. what technology is involved

      ii. what do you possess

  f. Education

       i. what education is required

      ii. what do you have

  ii. Target 2 - (Examples: CFO, Vice-President of Finance, or if not Head Chef, Pastry Chef, doorman)

  iii. Target 3 - (Examples: CFO or VP of Finance, Corporate Controller, Parts Deliverer)

  iv. Target 4 - You can of course have as many as you would like but it is more manageable to stick with your top three. You can always drop one and add another as circumstances dictate.

2. Where do you want to live?

  a. Are you willing to re-locate?

  b. How far from home are you willing to travel?

  c. How much are you willing to travel away from home for the job?

3. What kind of company do you want to work for?

  a. Do you have preferences? Preferences like a new, flexible versus old, established, or perhaps small, one owner - family owned versus large, or enormous worldwide or local government or national, private-for-profit, private-non-profit, public, whatever they are, write them down. You might have, and probably do have, several potential employers "types" that you might like. Try to look at each of your target jobs in light of what kind of employers employ them. Example: If your target is a biological lab assistant, you might think of employer types that would hire you to be: 1) university research centers, 2) private research centers, 3) hospitals, 4) local lab's, 5) pharmaceutical companies. Four of these are likely to be facilities but with smaller labs within them. The "local lab's" are likely to be smaller. When you write out this section, ask yourself why you like or prefer these business type environments.

  b. Prioritize your preferences. If you really like the notion of working in a university research center, and hospitals, make those your number one and two choices. (You might even think of combining them, why not a university hospital lab?) You should include what about it appeals to you. Is it the chance to contribute to science, be of help to mankind, the opportunity to be around bright, educated people, possibly get further educational cost underwritten. It's okay, you are working on becoming as self-aware as possible in relationship to work settings.

4. Establish decision-making criteria. How will you evaluate the job offer made to you? List the factors important to you. You can obtain some of this information during your research phases if you do Informational Interviews, and through other business research. You may have to wait until you have a job offer and can then ask about them but you can list what you would like now and then evaluate an offer against that criteria. Government jobs, and public employment jobs, like at universities and hospitals, are usually very open about the benefits that go with the job. If you are applying for a particular job posting, it will often expressly state the benefits included. Even though you may not be applying for a particular job at a particular employer, you can still obtain much useful information beforehand for jobs you subsequently apply for. You can also tap into your network, and you may learn all you need to know before you have an interview!

   a. Does it pay enough to meet my budget needs? What are my needs?
   b. Will it pay enough to meet my financial growth plans?
   c. What specific benefits are included?
      i. Insurance
         1. Medical
         2. Dental
         3. Optical
         4. Life
         5. Accidental Death
         6. Disability
      ii. Extra Pay
         1. Raises
         2. Bonuses
         3. Overtime
      iii. Leave
         1. Vacation
         2. Paid and unpaid holidays
         3. Sick/personal
      iv. Retirement
         1. Pension plans
         2. 401(k) plans
         3. Profit sharing
         4. Stock options/ESOPs
      v. Other
         1. Tuition reimbursement
         2. Dependent care
         3. Employee assistance programs
         4. Parking
         5. Expense reimbursements
         6. Travel expenses
         7. Expense accounts

5. Pre-search Preparation (Resumes and cover letters are covered in more depth in the chapter on resumes):
   a. Resume. You should have three prepared. The first is a "most generic" type that you use to accompany online applications. The second is a "chronological" resume, your experience in

"time order." The third is a "functional" resume, which list what you've done and can do with less detail about where and when you did these things. See the chapter on resumes for more information and insight. As you have done all your personal "homework" you can see what information you want to appear in whatever type of resume you create based on employer needs and your fulfillment of those needs. If they need a person with retail management experience, and you have that as a chain-restaurant assistant manager, make sure that is something you clearly state: "retail management experience as an assistant manager in a fast paced environment" for example.

  i. References. Line up 4-6 references, be sure to have addresses and phone numbers for them and that they are all working. Check to be sure you know what they'll say about you.

b. Cover letter. Create a generic cover letter that you can readily modify or customize for each employer to whom you will send it.

c. Your commercial where you pitch your Unique Selling Proposition. Suppose you had a ton of money and could create a TV ad about you. You would want the world to know about you and where you can be found, that's the first thing. The second thing is to motivate the world to buy you. Think something like this example: "Hi, I'm Tim Bucktoo here to tell you about leading lab technician Tim Bucktoo. Tim has worked for years at Foremost Laboratories, with over 5,000 perfectly performed, and on-time, blood analyses delivered to more than 250 medical doctors and clinics in and around Waterborn, MI. You can count on Tim to deliver timely, accurate lab results, with little or no supervision, for you! Tim is leaving Foremost Laboratories to find a position in or near the State University Hospital System as a laboratory supervisor. So, when you need it fast and accurate, Tim Bucktoo delivers. Let Tim take charge for you." Okay, it's a bit hokey but realize that it does hit the key elements of timely, accurate work without a lot of supervision. If that is what your lab wants and needs, that commercial would position you well.

d. Phone preparation. Be sure you have your phone response record pad near your phone and a copy with you. Avoid noisy, casual settings to take calls from employers. Be sure you capture all necessary information.

e. Online preparation
  i. Depending on what kind of job you seek, you may want to go over your social media presence (Facebook, LinkedIn, others) to be sure that any potential employer sees only what you would like them to see. A "hard partyin'" image is fine in some youth oriented positions, such as an entertainment director at a Las Vegas Hotel and Casino, not so much for a job as an accountant at a conservative CPA firm (unless their clientele include entertainment, showbiz and sports figures).
  ii. Email. Be sure you spell out your email address on your correspondence and that you check it frequently (check your "spam" folder frequently too, because you'd hate to have a job inquiry go there and then lost forever).

6. Tracking System. Remember how we've repeated throughout the book, document everything. You have been doing that, right? Who did you talk to last April 12th, at MedRed? Who called you in March about an upcoming hiring program for a planned expansion when? Can you tell from your documentation? You do use some sort of calendar system, too, right? Use it not only for upcoming events (interviews, job fairs, etc) but to record what happened and when.

7. Documentation. Letters of reference. Training certificates. Diplomas. Driver's License. Proof of insurance. Trade certification. If you are going to be asked to "prove it," do you have physical, tangible, proof? Some applications will require you to arrange to have it sent directly, like college diplomas. Do you have the address to contact to make those arrangements? If not, get it. Prepare, remember?

8. Interviews. Practice interviewing with family, friends, professionals and get feedback on how you do and what you could do to perform better. Practice will make perfect so be sure you find out what you can correct and improve upon. Give them questions you are fairly sure to be asked, as well as problem questions, at least problem questions for you, such as long periods of unemployment, felony convictions, career changes. Practice having good, comfortable answers to them. If you can get someone to record your interview, view or listen to it. Learn from yourself in a safe situation.

9. Develop job leads and contacts. You haven't waited until now to have a list of potential employers. Get that list of people and places you've targeted and get ready to go after them and others like them. Some of the others you can use are:

   a. Job postings/recruitment advertising
   b. Job fairs
   c. Cold calls
   d. Using your network
   e. Job-hunting on the Web
   f. University Career Centers job postings(they aren't limited to students as a rule)
   g. Alumni offices of schools if you went there
   h. Headhunters and recruiters at executive search firms
   i. Public and private employment agencies

Phase 2: Action (Implementation)

Nothing is accomplished without action being taken. Nothing. You must <u>activate</u> your plan. Use it to guide your actions. Take action!

Apply for Jobs:

1. You should consider varying your approach. Apply for one job that is near the outskirts of your geographical limits. Apply for one job at your third or fourth choice of employers. Why? If you are going to make mistakes, it is better to make them with a company that you can say to yourself, "Well, I messed that up but I can learn from the mistake." You might get a job offer from one of them and wouldn't it feel good to say, "Thank you but no thank you?" because you don't want to travel that far or work there. If you do get an offer, you can always accept it and look for a better one, right? This is not to suggest you spend a great deal of your precious time and effort trying to get a job where you don't want to work. You did do a lot of research and development on jobs, employers and yourself to put this company on your list, so it isn't like you don't have good reason to apply for a job with them.

2. You have a list of potential employers. You have a list of ways to add to your list of potential employers. You should consider the economics of your effort. How much time will each of the major activities you do take? If you have been keeping records, documenting your actions, you should also be noting how long each activity took. Go back through the actions. How long did it take you to write a resume? How long to modify one for a particular employer? How long to tweak a cover letter? How long to conduct informational interviews? How long to get from home to the library or to the closest Workforce Investment Act site? How long to get downtown in rush hour? How long to get uptown in rush hour? Or crosstown? It isn't just about your time either. Being economical with your postage, your travel expenses permits you to accomplish the most with the least.

3. *Do it!*

4. Do you have a calendar? A paper one? One that has one month or one week on a page? Is there enough room for you to write down appointments on it? The details aren't necessary here, you'll have them in your records. You just really need to keep track of what you are doing. Not only is this useful looking ahead, but also for going back over your activities to evaluate your performance.

5. Be sure you follow an employer's instructions completely when you complete their application. If they want proof of graduation, get it to them if you didn't happen to being it for an in-person application.

6. Look at a one week schedule and look at all the things there are for you to do. Which things should you do first? "First things first" is one of the ways to attain goals. Should you go online and complete as many local applications as you can? When should you do it? You could do those at night, when it is unlikely that you could meet with a private or public employment service center, or someone for an Informational Interview, or apply for a job or go through and interview. If you are dressed for an interview and on your way to one, could you stop and fill out an application at another employer on the way home? Could you put in 2-3 applications within a geographical area, all in a morning or afternoon? There isn't a lot of spare time if you are seriously working on your most rewarding job or building you career plan. Do what you have to do when you have to do it, do everything else around those events. Need to do online research, whether into employers or using O*NET? Weekends and nights are perfect. Need to read and write and work on your plan? Again, weekends and nights. Need to visit someplace in person? Weekdays, normal business hours should be reserved for those actions and activities.

7. You already know this: Try to engage the "hiring manager" or person before you apply at a place of business. It's why you have worked on your network, why you did so much employer research, why you arranged and performed an Informational Interview. If none of these approaches surfaced the "hiring manager," two things: First, why not try to figure out why you didn't turn this person up with all those efforts. Second, what could you do turn up the next one who is in a similar position in a similar company? Learn from your work and experience. This isn't even a mistake but you can learn from it just the same.

8. Did you get this interview or apply for this job as a result of your cover letter? What did you commit yourself to doing in the cover letter? Did you say you would call on a particular day and time? Did you follow through? Did you put that "follow through" on your calendar to-do list?

9. Remember from the discussion elsewhere in the book that you could get a telephone interview almost anytime out of the blue. Usually they seem to come in at the worst possible time. If you get "that" call at a really bad moment, it might be better to let voicemail handle it than to attempt to catch it. If you're in the middle of one life's daily crises, like your washing machine just decided to stop and flood, or a toilet overflowed, or your kids are in the middle of a fight over anything, maybe you should let voice mail handle it. Handle the crisis and then call back when all is calm. If it is a good time to take the call, be sure you have both your resume, and your "call sheet" available. Always. You may find you have to answer questions about your resume, or your cover letter. You should record the information on your call sheet, whether the caller sets up an interview or not. You should plan to follow up with them if they did not schedule the interview at that time, unless it is clear you are not being considered for a job. Sometimes, they are trying to

narrow down their applicant pool. Your job is to be included and you should plan to be in that pool or to find out why you are not being included. Sometimes, they are pre-screening for subsequent callbacks for interviews. Find out when they plan to make those callbacks and assure them you not only want that opportunity, but will call back to follow-up.

10. You should plan to answer the phone in as professional a manner as you can. Ask a friend or relative to role play it with you until you are comfortable not only taking the call, not only answering questions just as though you were in an interview, but also completing a "call sheet." Yes, you need to be as ready to answer questions just as though you were in an interview in person. Why? Because it is an interview. Try not to have your mouth full, or be chewing gum, when you get that call. Spit it out or swallow it quickly. No one likes to hear the person on the other end of the phone chewing food or gum. Don't be having an afternoon treat that might keep you from being at your best.

11. You did take our advice to bring a "cheat sheet" with you when you apply for jobs, right? Having that information at your fingertips not only makes it easier for you to fill out an application, it will be accurate and match the resume you remembered to bring, too.

Interviews:

1. Even if you are "just" going in to complete an application, you should dress as though you were going to be interviewed. It sometimes happens and even if it doesn't, you will make a better impression on the people you encounter if you are dressed appropriately.

2. Be sure you have all your supporting material with you: resumes, references, copies of transcripts, certifications, etc.

3. Use the Interview Checklist and review it before you leave home, and before you walk into the interview.

4. You're prepared, you've practiced, have answers to typical and tough questions, have a "pitch" or Unique Selling Proposition (USP) or a "commercial" you can deliver on the spot, any time. Got a good closing statement? Just like professional salespersons are trained to surface and overcome objections, they are not afraid to "close the deal," you shouldn't be either. Ask what the next steps in the hiring process will be and when they will be completed. Be sure you ask questions to show you really are interested in the job and the company. Use a call back closing.

5. Relax yourself on the way into the interview. Be alert, focused, attentive, calm in the the interview. Smile.

Post Interview:

1. Within 24 hours send a hand-signed thank you letter or note. It is alway good to put it in writing. Make a specific reference(s) that show you are interested, and were listening. Make an extra pitch. Typed or printed is fine but not a generic letter of "thanks." Put some effort into it. It could be the final deciding factor. Hand sign it, don't print or type your name at the bottom. Don't be overly friendly either. They are Mr., Ms., Mrs. Whomever, not Tom, Bob, Betty, Nancy or June. You aren't Nick, Bill, or Lisa, sign your first and last name.

2. Follow up when you said you were going to, if you said you were going to. Follow up near the time they said they were going to make a decision. Be sure to make it known that you are interested in working with and for them.

3. If you don't get the job, and no matter how they let you know, call them and thank them for the opportunity to interview. Assure them you are interested in that job with them or *any similar opening* they might develop. Also, they should keep you in mind if they must resume their search for the right person, for whatever reason. Sometimes the first person hired doesn't work out. Sometimes the new hire is actually someone promoted from within and now their job is open. Find this out if you can when you call back.

4. If you were offered the job you should be prepared to negotiate. They may say we can start you at "some amount" and if you know there was a range and this was low or middle and your skills, experience and knowledge suggest more is appropriate, indicate that it is a tempting offer but you think you might be worth "that amount plus" or indicate that you would like to know what benefits that would include before you accept the offer. It is up to you to try to negotiate for as much as you can get before you accept the job. At that point, it is what it is. If you want or need more, then do not be shy and say so. You should have already determined your value and potential value to this employer so it really shouldn't be much of an issue. If their offer is inadequate, and they will not negotiate upward to meet your needs, wants or desires, you can say, "No thank you but that is just not enough for me to accept that position." It does sometimes happen that they make a better offer, especially depending on how much they want you, how much competition there is, how great their need is, and so on. Sometimes the person who calls cannot negotiate but has to speak to someone else before they can increase the offer, or go above a certain range. Businesses prefer to pay the least they can for "talent," i.e. you. They do not hire people unless they need them, no matter what any politician tells you when they want to give employers tax breaks. Got that? They only hire people when they need them. They typically pay no more than they have to. Even "super" employers who get raves about how they treat people do it. They offer more and do more because it is good business and this is how they get and keep their employees but it is still the least they have to pay! If they paid less, in whatever fashion, they wouldn't get and retain the people they want. And they only hire people they need when they need them. Here's a suggestion, ask for 5-10% more than they initially offer. If they offer $10/hr ask for $11 or $10.50. The worst they will say is "no" but they might have the lassitude to say, "We can go to $11," and you just got a 10 percent raise before you started.

5. You were offered the job, accepted and you're done, right? Nope. You need to contact in writing, by phone, by email or in-person everyone who helped you get there. You should let employers with whom you recently interviewed but haven't heard back from (maybe their decision isn't even due yet) that you are "off the market" but thank them for considering you now, and possibly in the future. Turn off any online "job searcher" postings you've "put out there." Thank your references, your network, the professionals who've worked with you whether their efforts got you this job or not. Be grateful and express it.

Evaluate Routinely:

What needs to be changed? When and how to determine success with each step of your plan. How will you evaluate *your* performance?

Daily: Take a few minutes each day and write down the 2 or 3 most important things you can do tomorrow. Start with anything scheduled. See what time is left over and add a few items to do with the leftover time. Cross off what you got done each day and set that aside. If you have time, write down what happened, good and bad, with your job and career efforts. Note things you could use help with and find a resource to help you work it through.

Weekly: review your work activity and look ahead to the coming week. What is scheduled and what do you need to do to prepare for it? What time is leftover and what "best" things can you do with that time? Are you putting things on your schedule that are "personal renewal" items? Things that help you rest, relax, recuperate, fun? It isn't all about getting the next job. How about distractions, have you identified what time you spend doing counter-productive things? How much time watching TV, playing video games, hanging out with friends? Some is okay but too much is just not putting your effort into your present and future job hunt and career development. Look for things you committed to doing (thank you notes, callbacks etc.) and didn't, then do them.

Monthly: look back at what you've done. Impress yourself with the effort you put out, the new things you've tried, new places you've been, new people you've met. Think about what you've done that has gone well. Think about the things you can cross off your list as done, freeing you up to spend more time on the other things you can, could and should do. Got three top job targets that are SMART? Got 5 employers for each of them? Got resumes for each job and target? Don't keep doing things that are done. Work on something else that can be improved or expands your opportunities.

Are you keeping track of which resume(s) seem to work best for you? Are you getting interviews? Suppose you have three resumes, one of which got you 4 interviews, the other two got one and none. Keep using the "hot" one, drop the cold ones. Can you improve the hot one? How'd the interviews go? Stymied by any of the questions? Stumbled and stammered out an answer to a tough new question? Did you follow up to see how you did even if you weren't selected? Sometimes an interviewer can tell you what they saw and give you insight into how you appeared to them. Maybe you were distracted by something that day and you came across as neutral about the job, not enthusiastic enough. Especially when you go on an interview, let the interviewer know that you would appreciate any feedback they can provide you after the selection process is over. Let them know you are always seeking ways to improve, it is your personal quality improvement plan, and you are open to feedback. How else will you do better without feedback? It applies in business and can in our personal lives. It also doesn't hurt to tell an interviewer that you always work on quality and self-improvement. Most businesses do.

What you need to ask yourself is what changes or adaptations do you need to make to your plan as the days, weeks and months go by. As you fill in the blanks, get things done, find out what is and isn't working, modify your approach. If something isn't working, ask why. Get outside help when you need to, especially with a Workforce Investment Act Career Development Facilitator. That is their expertise and their calling.

Remember it will take time to find the most rewarding job, or any job for that matter. The DoL Bureau of Labor Statistics indicated a search time of about 33 weeks for the average person, that is almost seven months. You can find "just any job" or "your Most Rewarding Job" in that same time period.

Other ideas, concepts and approaches:

How are you going about your search? Are you using a shotgun, spray and pray, or a rifle, highly targeted and focused? Are you a good-old solid go-to product or the latest and greatest coming down the pipeline? Who are you and how have you presented yourself to the world of employment?

Segmentation -- There are many different kinds of companies and many different kinds of jobs that you could apply for. That means many different career options for most of us. Segmentation is finding which of the markets best fits our product, us. What do these places look like, what are their characteristics? We spent time on this in the O*NET section and you may want to go back and work on that material.

Competitive Alternatives -- This is a list of alternatives your potential employers have to hiring you. The aim is to help you see and understand what the others all have and what makes you really different from them and therefore more appealing as a job candidate. Do you have such a list? No? Well, that's not so bad, there is only one you which makes you unique and means in a way that you have no competition, who could be better than you at being you. On the other hand, a potential employer has options like: hire no one, hire the first person to walk in, hire someone with more, more what, skill, ability, need?

Differentiated Points of Value -- For each segment, what are the top 3 or 4 most important factors that drive decision making for the job you want? Identify these differentiators to help know what features to bring up and bring out to potential employers. Is it success, stability, know-how, sociability, adaptability, eagerness to take on workloads and long hours, flexibility and willingness to do alternative jobs, opportunity for upward mobility, being a family-person, being a church member and attendee, being in social clubs or organizations, being a volunteer in certain settings. On and on, the possibilities may seem endless but they are not, just try to identify what employers look for and want (in your research and in Informational Interviews). Be sure to include or mention these in your pitch.

Message --When you are creating your "pitch," "personal commercial," or "Unique Selling Propositions (USP)," try this technique: Think about someone you've run across or are aware of. Write down what you know about them. Since we're talking about people as employees or workers, do this when you think of that person, ask yourself how you see them as a worker or an employee. Especially pick a successful person in the field(s), or occupations or industries you're interested in working in. Then try to describe that person and what makes them so valuable in their job. It is easier to practice writing a pitch about someone else than ourselves. We might be shy or hesitant when talking about ourselves but that wouldn't be a barrier about that other person. Next, re-state the pitch but make it about you, as the person being described.

In your Informational Interviewing, did you interview someone who is a success in their field? What made them so. Not just in terms of the achievements and accomplishments that are the outward manifestations but in terms of who they are. Is he or she a self-starter? Tenacious? Curious? Hard-working and industrious? Maybe they are good at getting others to talk? Perhaps they have a gift for making speeches. They are good with complex problems. They are a real people-person. Pick 3 people and write out a paragraph on each that describes who they are and why they are successful in their occupation. Do a few more. Read about someone, and try to identify what makes them tick.

Then, try looking at yourself in light of those same kinds of qualities. Which ones do you share? You might find you share one quality with one person, none with another, and 2-3 with still another. As you write them out, you are building that "Personal Pitch" or USP.

SWOT:

Strengths, **W**eaknesses, **O**pportunities, **T**hreats (**SWOT**) are a business concept used to identify and analyze a business' situation. You can apply these concepts to your life and your most rewarding job hunt, long term career development and career building plan.

Suppose you identified a particular job and job zone that fit you well. Suppose you would like to advance your career in that job. What steps would you take?

Take a few minutes, more than a few actually, and describe your strengths. Look at all the areas covered by the Department of Labor's worker and occupation characteristics and requirements. Look at yourself, which ones describe you?

Look at every one of the skills listed by the Department of Labor, all 53 of them. Which do you possess and at what level? What could you do to improve on those you care about or fit you?

Look at the 35 skill sets they list. Which do you possess and want to work with? What is your skill level and what can you do to improve it?

How about your personality? Look up "personality" online and then look at "personality types." If a trait seems "to be you" then jot it down. Honest, forthright, guarded, warm, cold, friendly, aloof. Find yourself with words that describe personality. Everyone and every type of person isn't right for every job but there are jobs that fit types of personalities. Are you "guarded," a "loner," "aloof," and have technical and analytical skills, maybe you should be in investigative or laboratory work.

Once you have looked at yourself from the standpoint of strengths, do it again in terms of your weaknesses. Maybe you don't have much education (so what) and would need more training for a particular job path. Can you get it on the job, or through the job, before the job, or alongside the job. You aren't going to try to sell yourself based on your weakness but rather you need to be aware of them and know what you *could* do to correct or improve them. If they keep you from success in obtaining the rewarding job you want or career you want to build, then doing something about it should be on your long term personal plan.

Opportunities are all those possible jobs and careers you can step into now, almost immediately. You can narrow them down to those you can and want to step into. Your opportunities are even greater when you can see and identify those choices, "if." "If" you had more experience, more training, more experience, were in another area where the demand is greater, all the job and career choices that would be yours "if".

Threats on the job and in the employment marketplace are much tougher to see and deal with. Were horse breeders prepared for the impact on their business of "horseless carriages" back in 1905 and neither did buggy makers and buggy whip makers. Unskilled auto factory factory workers probably didn't see the impact of robotics in their workplace. Key punch operators probably didn't see the need for them disappearing. Downtown retailers with limited parking didn't foresee shopping malls as business killers. Computerization has changed the face of the workplace and many jobs have been lost or reduced to far fewer people doing them. Globalization has made its impact felt in lost jobs that have been off-shored and out-sourced. Still, you need to look at the work you are doing and planning to do and try to determine what the threats are to you. It is certain that times change and businesses come and go along with their philosophy toward employees. Therefore, the threat of losing your job is always imminent.

Have you found yourself unemployed more than once? Maybe the type of work you have been doing is the problem, not you. But you can look at making a change. The days and times when we could find lifetime employment at one company are fading. The new normal is to have two or more careers, not jobs, careers in a lifetime. So, prepare for change and you improve your lifetime opportunities.

Chapter 21: Resume? Cover Letter?

"When you first start working, you take whatever job is offered, because you have to build your resume. But you don't think about what you're building." — Chris Hardwick (1971-), American stand-up comedian, actor, screenwriter, musician.

"I asked all of our recruiters to give me all resumes of prospective employees with their name, gender, place of origin, and age blacked out. This simple change shocked me, because I found myself interviewing different-looking candidates -- even though I was 100% convinced that I was not being biased in my resume selection process." — Eric Ries (1979-) American entrepreneur.

"One day, I looked up and saw I had an extensive resume and saw how I did that and did not realize it because you are constantly working and trying to build a body of work." Ruben Santiago-Hudson (1956-) American actor and playwright.

"No one has a resume that they are 100% comfortable with, nor does anyone have a life that they are 100% comfortable with." — Jay Baruchel (1982-) Canadian actor and comedian.

Background:

What's a resume? What's a "cover letter"? Do you need one or both of them? The answer to the last question is, yes, you need them both.

If you answered "what's a resume?" something like "a written summary of my qualifications, work history and education that I can use to find a job", you're not wrong but you're missing what it really is. It is a selling tool, and advertisement. It is one of several in your arsenal.

Think of your resume as an ad about you. Imagine it as if it were an advertising "slick." A "slick" is a colorful, attractive, informative piece of sales literature on glossy paper (hence "slick") designed to sell. You most likely imagine one that is colorful, with pictures, and on glossy paper. If you are looking for an advertising job, why not create one like that?

The point is that a resume is advertising. The purpose of advertising is to inform and motivate customers to buy! The purpose of your resume is to inform and motivate employers to hire *you*! You want them to buy what you're advertising from you! "Buy it from you." They not only want the product, they want yours. They want yours so badly that they will drive past the other guys just to get yours. Your resume, your ad, needs to differentiate (make clearly different) you from your competitors and motivate an employer to want you.

Whose french fries or hamburgers do you buy? Whose telephone? Whose car?

Companies and advertisers spend a great deal of time and effort on creating an "image" and cultivating it to become the one you want.

Shhh, don't tell anyone but very often there is really no big difference between the products. Minor ones, sometimes yeah but nothing really big, something worth basing a decision on.

I was once took part in a group that wanted to know if we could tell the difference between various products. Our group tried different brands of cigarettes, beer and soda pop, to name three things we "consumer tested." Turned out, those who were most certain they could pick out their favorites, couldn't any more often than they could by chance. It wasn't scientific but still a learning moment for us.

Try it yourself. Get a group of your friends together and pick a couple of products and do the "taste test". Think one brand of milk is better? Try the taste test. It's not just taste either, try a "smell test", Think one brand of air freshener is better? Do a "smell test".

Even better, try to rate how much of a difference you perceive betweens brands. Try to include a cheaper alternative, and a pricier one, certainly try two head-to-head competitors. Try it on paper towels, cars, canned goods.

What you will likely find is that there may or may not be a difference that you can reliably detect. Yet, we still find we "think" there is a difference.

So why do we get so focused and determined about the "one we want"? The answer is image and advertising. Companies spend considerable money "branding" their products, creating an image in your mind, that sets their product apart. Their reason is simple, money. They advertise to increase sales and create customer loyalty, which equates to long term sales, or "buy and buy again" consumer behavior.

The job of advertising is to create a perceived difference between products and desire for their product. They do this by creating an "image" for the product. The features could be status based, age based, LAGs (Latest And Greatest) based, or countless other differentiators. These differentiators are sought out by marketing people to determine what factors you, as a consumer, will respond to when considering making a purchase.

Surprisingly, the attributes that surface in their research may have little or nothing to do with the true values, functions and features of the product. If they can associate these features with their product, you are buying those perceived values and not just the product when you make a purchase.

Is there something wrong with your phone? What, it doesn't have the latest "talking to you" feature? Better get a new one.

That thing you use to go from point A to point B and back again, a car or truck. Reliable, dependable, reasonable gas mileage. You gotta get a new one? Something more upscale? Something that makes you think of "getting out there" or a rugged mountain truck and you live in a flat city? You're sure you need a new one though.

What perfume would you buy? What store do you shop at? What brands do you buy?

Stop and think about these things for a few minutes. It is important to understand what the value of advertising is, which is it directs consumers attention to purchase (rent, lease, buy, however they obtain it) certain specific products.

Your Personal Advertising Campaign and Marketing Plan

Your personal Advertising Campaign and Marketing Plan involves many of the same concepts. In particular you want to differentiate yourself from everyone else. So much so that there really isn't any competition because there is no one else like you. That is true, right, you are unique? Of course it is. There is only one you. You have your own gifts, talents, experience, education, training, interests, skills, knowledge, ability and your own relationship to the world, your community, society.

During your exploration phase, the research efforts you undertake, are designed to find out what "they are buying." When you do research on a company, you are looking for what they say about themselves because their self-image, the one they promote, tells you if they are the kind of company you might want to work for. It also tells you what features about yourself might be decision-making features for them.

Are they a "safe, reliable product"? Then you might mention safety and reliability in your advertising campaign. Are they "new and exciting"? You should be too.

Your advertising campaign consists of "cover letters, resumes, follow-up and thank you letters, telephone contacts, applications, and interviews." It is anything and everything that your potential customer sees of you. Your campaign should consistently sell the same features and bundle of benefits.

This is much easier for you than it is for the maker of a toilet bowl cleaner. Look at what they sell, the image, as opposed to what it does (think about it).

Picture yourself walking into an interview. You have a smile on your face. You're dressed appropriately for the position. You are confident. You have answers prepared and rehearsed for most questions you anticipate being asked.

Now what happens? Do they ask you questions about what your wrote in your application or resume? About details that don't quite line up? Do they ask questions that imply your verbal answers don't match what you put in writing? Did you create doubt in your consumer's mind when this happens.

So one of the first rules is consistency.

Once you've created your image, in a resume, in applications and in interviews, you will find it easier to convey that image, each time you need to repeat it. The practice effect will work for you.

If you are interviewing with a new, expanding, exciting company and your cover letter letter and resume show you to be an innovator, adaptive and on the cutting edge, how should you approach the interview?

Here's a suggestion: a few days before you go into an interview, you "stake out" the place. Who is going to work and what do they look like? Don't make assumptions. Check it out. If they are all young moderns, dress to fit in and look like one of them, unless it would be too jarring and in conflict with your image. In other words if they are young moderns and you are too, go in like that. If you are older by a wide gap, but are someone who is an innovator, a cutting edge person, what can you do to display that without looking out-of-character? Maybe jeans and a sport coat, and the smartest smartphone?

If it is a conservative, traditional place of business with conservative values, maybe you should put on that three-piece business suit, or other conservative apparel. That is, unless they are hiring someone to handle the new "youth" account.

It is important that your resume, and impersonal elements like cover and "thank you" letter should look and feel like they match you and your image.

Image

That's right, your image. How do people see you? How you see yourself? How you present yourself? What personal message do people perceive when they see you? What message do they get when they look at you? Is it the one you want them to perceive? You've heard the phrase, "image is everything" before right? It may not be but it is very important.

Get dressed as if you are going to an interview and go stand in front of a mirror. Look yourself over. Slowly.

Are your shoes shined, or not? Does your belt match your shoes? Are your clothes cleaned and pressed? Stains or spots on your clothes? How about your hair, clean, combed/brushed and in place?

Does it matter if all of these things are "just right"? Maybe, that will depend on the type of job, where it is, and at what level it is, for starters.

If you are going to work in a "head shop" or a motorcycle dealership the image you present, or may want to present, will be different than the one you would present in a an old, well-established CPA firm. You can be that same tattooed, pierced, "just-out-of-bed-haired" person in either setting but you will want to show that your are aware of which one you are in when you make your pitch, your presentation. You should be able to explain how and why you fill their need for an accountant who can handle the certain accounts in particular like the motorcycle, craft brewery and nouveau dining accounts. You may want to show this using Your Personal Network (covered later).

If you are the razor sharp banker-looking guy, you might want to leave the three-piece suit to apply for the job as a motorcycle salesperson, then again maybe not. Go look at what motorcycle salespersons are wearing, and match it. The best advice is to be yourself but respect where you are applying.

For a chapter on "resumes and cover letters" we've not talked about either of them much so far, but by now you have a different concept of what they are than simply "a written summary of your qualifications, work history and education used to find a job", right?

So, let's talk about them as advertising "pieces" starting with the resume.

The Resume

There are two basic types of resumes: chronological and functional. What's the difference? Which one should you use? How long should it be? And what the heck is a CV?

A <u>chronological</u> resume arranges your work history, also called work experience, your education and a few other elements, in order of when they occurred. A <u>functional</u> resume puts the focus on achievements, accomplishments, skills, abilities, and experience.

A "CV" or Curriculum Vitae, is a type of resume that reviews your "professional life" and is typically used for advanced academic, research and scientific positions.

How long should your resume be? Long enough. One or two pages is the standard length. Readers of resumes do not have a lot of time to devote to reading resumes. They have many to read and are looking for certain specific "qualifying" bits of information that demonstrate you have the qualifications of the person they seek to hire. They may have dozens or hundreds to read, so each gets little time beyond the "basics". Long resumes suggest you cannot condense your information into the acceptable 1-2 page length.

Look at it when it is in finished, typed form. Did you get one and half pages? Try to either expand it to make two nice-looking, balanced pages, or cut it down to one. Don't waste space. Don't leave a big chunk of space left over. It doesn't feel right. A CV is an exception to the 1-2 page rule, it should be as long as it takes to tell the story.

Oh, and don't get tricky with tiny-sized or over-large letters (font size) or play with line spacing to try to make things work out. It looks and feels weird. Typically, as you build your resume, you put one line of space between things. One space line between education and work history, one between employers. Visualize each section as a paragraph and put a space line between the "paragraphs."

Which one should you use, chronological or functional? You should prepare one of each, and then decide when to use them. Some employers are not prepared to cope with the newer functional type of resume and that could disqualify you from a job. It is not so different that it should be that way, but it might. If you have more than three pages of material for your resume, you should consider the functional type as it is easier to squeeze a functional resume down to two pages than a chronological. If you are an older worker, or one with a long gap in your work history, the functional resume lends itself to your needs as well since it focuses on the what not the when.

There are examples of chronological and functional resumes in Appendix D. You should look at them now.

Resume Construction - Chronological:

Now that you've looked at both types of resumes, how do you go about constructing either one?

Let's start with and breakdown the traditional, chronological resume down into it's components. What common features did you see? In a traditional, chronological resume these are:

- Personal Identification
- Goal or Summary statement
- Work history
- Education & training
- Other items
  - Skills summary
  - Awards
  - Achievements
  - Accomplishments, etc.
- References

These elements are usually presented in that order.

Personal Identification: Who you are and your contact points. Name, address, phone number and email address. Usually centered at the top of page 1, on 5-6 lines (depends on your address). Your name should be in **bold** letters, and be your legal name, not your nickname. You might want to use a font size, one or two points (sizes) larger than the rest of the resume for extra emphasis.

Your goal statement (Job Objective, Objective, Position Desired) should be a brief statement of the type of position you want and may include skills, knowledge, and experience that support your claim on the position.

So, now how about the rest? By now you probably have a work history outlined, and a list of your key educational experiences. It is easier to start with the Education section. Where you went, when you graduated and your degree, like this: Top Notch University, Somewhere, State, 19xx BA - Psychology and then, Some State University, Someplace, State, 20xx - MBA. If you earned additional awards, or earned citations, like a Certificate of Special Distinction, a Dean's Listing, Phi Beta Kappa award, etc., be sure to include that information here. This is also a place you can include membership in a fraternity or sorority.

Note: as a working approach to constructing your resume, you may want to drop in placeholders for some of the other elements, like Summary Statement, References and the "Extra" statements. You can put the details in later. This way you allow for them and you can use them to "fill a page" or shorten the resume to one page by trimming them out.

The most important thing to work on is what you want to say, or highlight, in your Work History section. Whether you are working on a functional or chronological resume, the place to start is by going back to your job target information *before* you review your own work experience.

Exercise:

Create a temporary "JobTarget Worksheet" one for each job you want. Start by listing the job target and the duties, requirements, experiences that are most important on this job. You should be able to get a fairly clear picture by looking at 1-2 of the Department of Labor's O*NET occupational information. If you have three job targets, then you will have three lists of important elements. There is a sample of a Job Target Worksheet in the Workbook. You can even print out those you find on O*NET or through My Next Move and work from them.

You might add to each of these, any insights you've gained from the Informational Interviews you did.

Now that you know what is important for your job targets, because you've identified key duties, experiences and requirements, you are in a better and informed position to know what to highlight in your Work History section.

Exercise:

Create a Job History Worksheet, one for each job you've held -- employer, job title, dates -- and below that list what you did. You should already be thinking about what things you did in light of the job you want and from a potential employer's perspective. List everything you can remember you did. Print that trial worksheet out (one per job target) and circle the items that are found in the target job descriptions you listed. Move key elements in your work history around to feature your skill and experience that relate to your job goals. There is a Job History Worksheet in the Workbook.

Now assemble your Work History section. Start by being all-inclusive. Put in everything you did at each employer, in the best order to support your Job Objective. You will see that some of what you did at some employers did not pertain much to the new job. That's okay. Those become easy items to delete as you work on condensing your resume to fit 1-2 pages.

Repeat the process *for each job target* since different job targets may have different or dissimilar job requirements. You will find you may eliminate different things for different job targets.

It is a bit of extra work to build your resume this way but you are building an advertising piece that will promote *you* as the best candidate for your most rewarding job. These days, using a computer makes this process fairly easy compared to the historic ways of typing or worse, handwriting and then typing a resume.

By now, you will have one, two or three resumes each more than two pages long. So what? You aren't mailing them yet. The drafts can be as long as it takes to say as much as you can. You haven't even done the embellishment step, nor put in other elements.

Take a look at those "things you did" at each employer. Especially look at the ones that pertain most to each job target. If you wrote: "Led sales strategy meetings," couldn't you say, "Led weekly sales strategy meetings and increased sales by 20 percent in one year" if it was true? If you wrote: "operate jack hammers and other construction equipment," couldn't you have said "operate backhoe, forklift truck, front-end loader, road-grader, bull-dozer, steam roller and jack hammers" if it's true?

You want to be specific and to present yourself dynamically. Here is a good example: "Prepared accurate, on-time, complex monthly reports for managed-care organizations and insurance companies, ensuring full compliance with agency requirements within extremely tight deadlines." This could be tightened up to "Prepared accurate, on-time, complex monthly reports for managed-care organizations and insurance companies".

Resume Construction Functional:

Let's break the non-traditional, functional resume down into the components. What common features do you see? These are:

- Identification
- Objective
- Profile - Major qualifications
- Skills (Summary)
- Work (Professional) experience
- Employment history (minimum data)
- Education
- References

Notice how the functional resume steps away from elaborating on job duties and details. Instead it offers you a way to describe yourself in terms of what you do (functions you have performed), your skills, and what you have done. The focus is on what you can do rather than where you worked. It offers an employer a better perception of who you are as a person, and in the workplace, than the traditional approach.

The biggest downside is that it requires you to be prepared to make the connections between this self-description and where you exercised and learned these skills, functions, and gained the experiences. Making the connections will be particularly important during an interview.

If you use a job profile from O*NET that matches your job target, you can start to create your functional resume based on the key elements from the profile. Let's look at those categories again:

- Tasks
- Tools
- Technology
- Knowledge
- Skills
- Abilities
- Work activities
- Work context (job ecology)
- Job zone
  - Title (classification)
  - Education

- Related experience
- Job training
- Credentials
- Interests (Holland Code)
- Work styles
- Work values

Now as you begin to construct your functional resume, you have material to use that helps define the job and what it takes to be successful in it. You can look to your own life experience and indicate those that best align you with your job target.

Example 1:

You are seeking a job as an Executive Assistant. You look at the work activities portion of the summary report and note that the first item listed is "Communicating with Supervisors, Peers, or Subordinates." You know you are really good at "Organizing, Planning and Prioritizing." You look at the "Knowledge" section and notice "Administration and Management," as defined are areas you are strong in along with "Customer and Personal Service."

You use that to create your Objective statement, like this:

Objective: *Executive assistant position* combining demonstrated organization, customer service, communication and project management skills.

Example 2:

You are seeking a job as a Construction Equipment Operator. You look at the Tasks and Tools & Technology, and Knowledge sections and note that the keys seem to be knowledge of Building & Construction and Mechanical Knowledge, operating specific equipment, like front-end loaders.

You use this to create your Profile Section:

MAJOR QUALIFICATIONS
- Over seven years' experience working as a general construction laborer
- Highly skilled in operating fork lift trucks and front-end loaders.
- In depth, practical knowledge of operating and maintaining general construction equipment
- Hands-on experience in tending machines that pump grout and cement

ACCOMPLISHMENTS
- Helped maintain contract by performance by always being at work, on time, and keeping all assigned equipment operating.
- Introduced and trained new construction workers to use basic construction equipment such as cement mixers and hand tools.

Example 3:

You are seeking a position as a Customer Service Representative so you look that up and see that the work activities include "Communicating with Persons Outside (the) Organization," representing the organization to customers, the public, government and other external sources. It involves Interacting With Computers and "Resolving Conflicts and Negotiating with Others." Abilities required lean heavily on oral and written communications. Important skills are active listening and a service orientation.

You use that to create your Objective: Dynamic Customer Service Representative, using successful customer-focused problem resolutions techniques and to professionally represent the company in contacts with external sources.

You also use that information in the Profile Section:

Motivated, customer service professional with successful experience in customer complaint resolution through active listening skills and a strong service orientation.

Flexible, dependable, capable representative with strong social skills, being aware of customers needs when confronted with problems that need resolution.

Then move to a **Skills Summary**:
- Strong computer proficiency
  - Excel
  - Word
  - Access
  - Sales tracking programs
  - Project management software
- Public speaking
- Call center operations
- Call center leader and motivator

There is no one "right" way to write a resume. There is no "right" approach to the task. There is a "right attitude" though. That is to invest the time and effort to create a resume that best presents you. That may be the first place you can make a good impression. Make it a dynamic selling advertising piece that works for you.

On the other hand, there are many wrong ways to write one! Your resume will almost always be screened out by a reviewer if it is sloppy, contains misspellings, poor grammar, is dirty, grimy, greasy, stained, poorly written, or is inconsistent. Show it to someone, even if you have no doubts at all that it is perfect. Better to get criticized and have time to fix it than to waste time sending out a bad representation of yourself and be screened out before you even have a shot at the job you should have!

The other item that works well with a resume is your cover letter. Again, you want to be consistent in your appearance so use the same type of paper and typeface in your cover letter as in your resume.

Resume Construction eResume:

There is a new type of resume that is becoming more common, and is evolving, the "eResume." More and more employers are attempting to automate their application process and have created an option for you to upload a resume. The best advice for this is to use a ."txt" file format as it is a format that nearly all systems can read. Whatever word processing program you use will have an option to save a file as a text file (.txt).

If you leave your file in "Word" format (.doc) or any other program format, you can pretty much count on their system not reading your file format. Use the text file format.

Some of the employers have "automated" systems that are grabbing the first 100 or so words and scanning for words that match the job descriptions they are working from. Like it or not, it is becoming a common practice. If you realize this, make sure the first two sections after your name and address, the "Objective" and the "Skills Summary" or "Work History" include some key words for the job you are seeking. That's still one more reason to use the material in O*NET or even in the description of the job you are applying for, to ensure you've used those key words.

Cover Letter

What is a "cover letter?" **Definition: a Cover Letter is a letter of introduction from you to a potential employer.** It not only introduces you to one but it is an opportunity for you to self-market and personalize your message to them.

A cover letter has three objectives:

- get the recipient to read your resume
- get an interview
- get them to want to hire you.

So, what do you put in a cover letter? You want to answer a question, the question is, "why are you contacting us?". Your answer will depend on your reason(s). If you are writing in response to an a job want ad, it will be slightly different than if you are writing "blind," i.e. not in response to a job want ad.

There are two examples of cover letters at the end of Appendix E. You should review them before you proceed.

The basic, formal, structure is:

- Your address
- Date
- Their address
- Salutation
- Body
  - Opening - statement of purpose
  - Identity
  - Enthusiasm
  - Contact
- Closing
- Enclosures.

Document the success of your efforts by keeping a copy of each cover letter you write and send.

Let's examine each element, beginning with your address. In the most formal ways of writing letters, this belongs at the top of your letter and aligned in a column on the right side of the page. You would set a tab stop, somewhere around the 5-inch mark to accomplish this. It is acceptable to simply left justify or align it or even to include it below your signature at the end of the letter.

Below your address if it is at the top, is today's date (the date of your letter). Next is the address where you are sending the letter. This should include the name and title of the person in the company that you want to receive the letter if you know their name and title. (How hard would it be to make a call and get that name and title?)

A salutation is just that line that says "Dear sir or Madam;" or "Dear Mr. White or Dear Ms. Greene" if you know their name.

Your opening paragraph indicates your purpose in writing. If you are writing in response to an ad, indicate that with a statement that references that fact and where you saw the ad. Then what position you are applying for and that your resume is included.

If you are not responding to a "help wanted ad," then you should indicate why you are writing in this opening paragraph. You might indicate that your research has led you to conclude that you would be a good fit for employment with their company in a particular job category and you are sending your resume for their consideration.

The "identity" or "who you are" paragraph follows. It should be the strongest statement you can make, in two sentences, that shows you are qualified for the job.

The next paragraph should show your enthusiasm. Indicate how much you would welcome the opportunity to discuss your qualifications with them.

The last paragraph in the body of the letter, is the "contact" or "how to reach me" statement. This should be kept to one or two sentences. You want to inform them of the best time to reach you and how they can reach you. If there are particular concerns about reaching you, you should specify them. For example, you might indicate you can be reached evenings at (555) 444-5555, or by email at my.email@internet.net anytime. You could add that you can be reached at your current place of employment during the day at (555) 555-4444 but "with discretion, please".

This last paragraph can also be more aggressively written with a "call back" closing. Here, you indicate that you will call them on a particular day and time. This is often the way to conclude your letter when you were not applying for a particular opening but rather were offering your resume because you saw the good fit between you and the company. When you call, you can ask to speak to whomever you directed your resume or think received it. You can then begin to ask them exploratory questions, like if they have an opening, what they thought of your resume and the company as a fit, if they expect to have any openings, or what you might do to be considered for the next opening that may occur.

Following this is your closure. If you right aligned your address at the top of the letter, then right align your closing. If you left aligned it at the top, left align it at the bottom. The closing is simply the standard "Sincerely," followed by your name, typed, a few lines below it.

Finally, if you are enclosing your resume, the very last line should be "Enclosure: Resume".

Get busy working on your resumes and cover letters they are keys to your future and your future success. Use them to your advantage.

Chapter 22: Applications

"The closest to perfection a person ever comes is when he fills out a job application form." — Stanley J. Randall (1908-1989) Canadian businessperson and political figure.

"A young man fills out an application for a job and does well until he gets to the last question, "Who should we notify in case of an accident?" He mulls it over and then writes, "Anybody in sight!"" — Milton Berle (1908-2002), American comedian and actor.

Background:

There was once a time that there were only a few basic varieties of paper job application forms that you would encounter. Larger employers would develop there own but still there wasn't that much variation in them. Since then, with the advent of the World Wide Web, online applications have proliferated and they are different. Quite different!

Some of those paper applications were short, running a brief one to two pages in length, to "long" versions of three, four and even six or eight pages. Now with online applications for specific jobs, they are expandable and unpredictable in length, expanding or contracting, depending on your answers.

These new on-line applications for specific jobs, are designed to be one-size-fits-all for applicants. In the "job" or "work history" section, as you complete the information for one job, you are offered the opportunity to "add another?" Some of these applications want a complete chronological (or reverse chronological) history; others will ask that you only include those where the work experience directly applies to, and supports, your application to this specific job. Other areas of the application are also expandable to match "anyone's" personal history.

It doesn't end with your straightforward job history either. Often potential employers have expanded their search and screen capabilities by adding a series of questions that you respond to as part of the process. These questions will typically state a particular task or function and then ask for more information from you related to the task or function.

Example 1:

Do you have experience analyzing financial data? In the text-box provided, please detail your experience. Include in your description where this experience was obtained. Note: consideration of the experience will only be given if the employer(s), where the experience was obtained, are currently listed on your application under 'employment history'. Failure to provide this detailed information may result in the denial of your application. Do you have this experience: Yes No.

(This is followed by a statement like the following, with an expandable "free" text box below it.) Use the space below to provide any clarification that is needed for your answer to this question.

Figure 22: Sample "free" text box which expands to contain all the text you write into it.

Example 2:

There may be a section of "Questions for Clarifying Information" in which you are again given "free" text boxes to write your answer in.

1. Please describe your experience with Excel to include your level of expertise in the various Excel functions.

2. Please describe your experience using query tools to create reports, graphs and/or financial analysis.

3. Please describe your experience in developing business requirements, technical documentation and/or procedures.

4. Please discuss your experience using technology to analyze financial data, and provide findings and/or recommendations.

The above questions are real and taken from applications for government jobs.

Needless to say, these are not "fun" to complete. They require considerable thought and effort. On the other hand they do sometimes lead to great jobs, so do not be dismayed. Plus typically these do not have to be completed in one sitting, so you can work on it one section at a time.

It is becoming commonplace for governments to use these online applications and through the magic of the internet, some of them are designed to permit your application to be re-usable. The downside to that is it is not always possible to modify the application, nor are all the jobs "the same" so it can be difficult to tailor your application to fit the specific job you are applying for.

The upside to all of your work completing these applications is the attempt by the hiring agency to be fair, unbiased and open to all applicants. A secondary benefit is that you may save considerable effort by being able to re-use your "general-form" application when re-applying at that employer or many others, particularly in the government sector.

Another feature of online applications is that you can often cut-and-paste information from a source file you've already created into the new application.

Source File

So, how do you preparer for these applications? Prepare your "Source File," a folder and or document that has your complete information in it. As you complete new applications and run into novel new questions, add them and your responses to your source file. You can call that file anything you'd like: "Me," "My Job Application Resource File," "Everything and Anything and More Than You Want To Know About Me." We chose "Source File" for simplicity. It will be your source for application information and put that information at your fingertips.

How is this different from the work you did in resume building? Your resume is a presentation about you designed to draw the interest of potential employers and motivate them to contact you. The Source File is based on application questions that you encounter. Your answers to these questions will be part of the criteria used in decision making as to include you for further consideration, for an interview for example. Many of these questions are designed to provide evidence that you possess particular skills, knowledge or experience.

Let's look at some of the specific content categories you are likely to find on all applications: 1) personal identification and contact information 2) education 3) work history 4) position applied for 5) military experience and 6)references. You may find questions about your health or your health-related restrictions, felony convictions or arrests and convictions, office or other special skills, licenses (especially drivers license) and availability for work. When you are asked for information not already in your source file, add it so that you are prepared the next time it is requested.

You may have little to say, or a lot, in response to any question but you generally do have to say something and building your source file makes the task easier.

Even before you start applying for jobs, you should prepare the information and put it into a "source file." There are two basic ways to do this. One is on paper, which has advantages, but major disadvantages, too as it does not permit cut-and-paste, and is not as flexible as an electronic word processing file.

You should use all the work you put into developing your resume in particular as source material for your Source File. You could even "dump" all your resume material into one file, and then pull out the bits and pieces you need for the Question & Answer section based on the applications encountered.

The biggest disadvantage to an electronic version is the tendency to put it together "too fast" and not fully develop the information. You can avoid this by putting each section, or even sub-sections like your work history, on a separate page within the file. Print out each one, read it, review it, think about, make corrections, add more to it, polish it. Don't overlook having a "back-up" version and lose your work. If you've never lost a file, or your work, because you over-wrote your file with an "empty" one, you are one lucky person. Always, always, always have a back-up file with a name that clearly differentiates it from your "working file."

Specific Information

All applications ask for certain information, like personal identification and contact information. You might consider putting each section on it's own sheet of paper, or own electronic page, you'll se why as you build the file.

Section 1: Identification and contact information

Name, address, phone number, email address. Easy enough. Just be careful that when you list your name as (Last, First, MI) that the application you subsequently complete uses the same order. Almost all will, except the one you really wanted, so unless you want to be forever known as Doe Jane E., instead of Jane E. Doe, pay attention!

Phones these days have strongly moved to cell phones, but if you have a landline, make sure you have both numbers in your source file. Include your email address, your most current one. If you have one used for formal things like business email, include that too. You may only want to use a "business email" address for your applications. That way if something really important, like a job offer, comes in you will see it. Make sure the addresses are current.

One other item for this section, or more properly not for this section is your social security number (SSN). It used to be commonplace for it to be on job applications but that is no longer the case. If you are asked for it, you can and probably should, decline to supply it. Explain to whoever accepts your application that in this day and age protecting your identity is very important to you. Let them know that you will be glad to supply it if you are hired. It might cost you a job you would otherwise obtain, but your personal identity and security is important. On the other hand maybe the job is very desirable and you will comply and give it. If an online application demands it, i.e. won't move past this point, consider how important it is to you to apply for this particular job and decide if you want to give it.

Section 2: Education

Start with your high school then move on to undergraduate and graduate college. If you attended any trade schools during or after high school, include them. Think of it this way: Was there an instructor or teacher involved and was it a formal training program (you had to apply for admission, be admitted, and attend classes) that resulted in some form of certification or diploma? If it did, it belongs in this section.

Start by simply listing the "schools" and then putting them in chronological order. List the school name and the dates you started and finished, a simple month and year is fine for this. You should include an address for this school, too. It would be best to have the official school address, and the address to use to obtain copies of transcripts or other administrative verification purposes. City and state are often enough, so don't lose sleep if you don't have the street number, but only the street name for your high school. You should attempt to get a full address for any education facilities you attended after high school though. Remember you can always "not use" information you have so when in doubt, get complete information.

Indicate if you graduated and when, and what degree or certificate you obtained. If you studied a particular subject and graduated with it, include that information. Examples: Graduated 1989, Certified Motorcycle Mechanic. Or Graduated 1999, BA in Psychology.

If you earned any particular honors, accomplished particular achievements, particularly if you have documentation of having done so, include these in this section. Did you graduate with "special distinction" or "recognition" in your major? Did you graduate Phi Beta Kappa? Belong to a sorority or fraternity? Take part in extra-curricular activities? Add them in.

When it comes time to use your "Source File," first make a copy of the file with a new name, like "Source File 2.0." Then work from the copy if you are going to do any editing or cutting-and-pasting. If you work from a copy you eliminate the chance that you will save or inadvertently edit a file that will no longer have all the information you started out with.

One more thing, if you are not a computer friendly person, you do have options. You can do every bit of this work on paper. There are a lot of people whose computer and technical skills are weak, soft, not too good or anyway you want to put it. You can pay people to do data entry, or perhaps you have a sympathetic family member or friend who will. You can take a class at a local community college or adult education program and get beginner level skills and sweat the work out yourself. You can buy dictation software and then dictate the information. Seriously, you are at a serious disadvantage when completing an online application if you do not have an electronic source file that you can work with. Get help if you need it. Really.

Section 3: References

You should have the full name, address and phone number for each reference you have. Indicate their relationship to you. Examples: former teacher, friend, former co-worker, brother, minister, former boss, former assistant. You might even make a note about what they could "attest to" about you, just for your own insight. Some employers will ask for only one type of reference, people familiar with your work for example. So it is a good idea to have more references listed than you "need," especially when it comes to work settings and applications.

Section 4: Work History

Let's start with what should be the obvious things. Where did you work and when? What was your job title and what did you do there? Who did you work for (your immediate supervisor). Were you doing the same job when you left as when you were hired? Why did you leave?

What you should do is plan on having one or more pages per job you've had. If you are just starting out, this may be no pages or one or two. Over time, there will be more pages. At the top of each page, start by writing down the date range you worked at employer. It is best if you have the day, month and year you began and left each employer. Some applications and some reviewers get real nit-picky about it. So try to get it as accurate as you can. Then give the employers company name and address, along with their business phone number. Next write in your entry job title. If you got promoted or transferred to a different job or location, indicate those job titles too and the dates these events occurred.

Note here that you don't have to follow this too rigorously, it is just a suggestion (and there are blank forms in the workbook). If you are more comfortable with a different arrangement of the information by all means tailor it to fit you.

For each job title you've listed, indicate who your supervisor was, including their title. Then list your duties. This is one area where you need to spend more time on really putting in everything you did. You can always re-arrange the details in order later.

Think about your major and minor accomplishments in that job. Perhaps you re-arranged the accounts receivable process and reduced average-days-collected (or "days paid" as it is often referred to) from 98 days to 56 days. That is significant and positively affects a company's cash flow, a major accomplishment.

Perhaps you arranged the first physical inventory for the employer, again a major accomplishment. Maybe you organized the customer lists from an informal on-paper system to a computerized sales contact program. Or you figured out how to move more product or store more efficiently. Maybe you increased sales 30 percent in your territory. Did you solve any major problems? What made you better at the job than someone else (that's not better than everyone else, just someone else, a more modest achievement).

How was your attendance? Was it prefect or near perfect? That sort of reliability and dependability is an asset to you and an employer. Mention it as it increases your value to an employer. Something as seemingly minor like this can be significant to an employer because it keeps work flowing. Another significant achievement easily over-looked, is if you never had any complaints about your work or a need for re-work or warranty work. Re-work or warranty work because of worker error is costly to a business. While work is being redone that employee is not making "new" money. It can even cost the company a customer if they are not satisfied with the initial quality.

After you've listed each employer and gone through and written out the job duties, wait a day and then go back and re-read the duties again. What did you forget? Keep talking about the job duties as though you were being graded on how well you remembered everything you did. How about awards you earned, maybe Employee of the Month? Did you earn any certifications or attend any workshops? Got proof?

It is easy to forget things we did. It is easy to say to ourselves, well that wasn't really important. Don't under-value it and dismiss it. Put it in. The more duties or tasks you've performed reveals your flexibility and the breadth and depth of your experience and increases your value to future employers even if it isn't for the same kind of work or industry.

Put it all in. Had to sweep and straighten out the work area or the "john"? Put it in. Had to keep track of time cards? Put it in. Had to teach newcomers the ropes? Put it in. Mentor? Put it in. Ran a large saw and cut 12' channel steel? Ground rust off sheet metal? Bussed tables and washed dishes? Trimmed hedges and removed weeds? Gave prepared speeches to homeowners on energy conservation? If you did it, own it.

Aside from just stating the facts, can you now polish up those entries and statements?

How about things like, 'steadily reduced turnover by improving interviewer skills and the selection process.' Or 'significantly reducing outstanding receivables.' Adjectives help "sell" or define success in performing your job duties and help sort you out from other applicants. It is true that not everything we do can be "sold" this way but it helps if you can make these types of statements.

Another thing to consider doing is including not only that you performed a task or duty but that you enjoyed doing it and took pride in doing it. Were you "proud of the service you took great pleasure in providing"? So much so that you were recognized as Employee of the Month? Maybe you were the "top-selling salesperson" at XCon, for the past two years and had the highest rate of repeat customers because of your "belief in being customer focused."

Yes, you can put this kind of "stuff" into this source file work history. It's where it occurred and where it will be most valuable to you again. Who says it has to be just the facts? Who decides and defines what a fact is? Fact is you are trying to separate yourself from every other person applying for that job, your competitors. Both the resume and the job application are the first things an employer is likely to see. That being the case, you want these items to present you in your most favorable light. It is one type of "first impression" and you should always want to make the best one you can.

Now, let's look at some of the other things to know about "issues" in your job history that you may have to deal with. One question that arises is "why did you leave?" or "why are you leaving?" Another is what you did during periods of apparent unemployment. For some the absence of previous employment is a concern. For others it may be the length of their work history. Still others have to cope with "frequent job change" concerns.

Potential employers review applications looking for criteria that they have established, this might include a certain amount or level or type of education. It could include certain work experiences. They also look for clues that the applicant may come to them with baggage or problems that they would like to avoid.

People who've been fired may or may not be "at fault" for their termination but if you put on your application, or in your source file that you were fired, you should be prepared to deal with it. Why were you fired? Were caught stealing, embezzling, or some other criminal act, for which you were not prosecuted? You may want to consider putting that in as favorable light as you can without lying. You may want to avoid a direct answer and think "politically" as in "being released by that employer was a favor they did for me because now I have the opportunity to find a job that better fits me, my skills, abilities and interests." Or you might realize that "the job wasn't working out and you and your boss agreed you should move on and find a better fit."

There are good reasons aside from criminal acts that can cause a person to be dismissed. Perhaps you were laid off along with others because your work was outsourced? Maybe there was a merger between your company and another and you were one of the casualties of the merger. Sometimes you and the job are not a good match and you experience relief at being let go. Why not say, "I wasn't right for that job, and it became obvious to my boss and rather than try to make it work out, I was fired."

If you indicate you were fired, then you want to look at why you were fired and try to put it in its most positive light. On the other hand, if you weren't specifically "fired" you might want to find a more accurate and less negative word. Were you "terminated?" Laid off? Maybe you were "fired" but can that be described as "released" or "no longer fit the work environment" or that "my skills were no longer necessary."

It may be that your reasons for leaving were more due to your choices. Did you quit? Why did you quit? It might have been because you couldn't tolerate one more minute working for those blankity-blank-blanks but you should consider it better to realize you were looking for employment more suitable to you and your skills. Perhaps you left to seek better pay and benefits. You may even have left for a better opportunity to advance your career, or perhaps more opportunity to grow and advance with a new employer.

You can find lots of answers to tough questions on the internet, just Google or Bing "Why were you fired from your last job?" or "Why did you leave you last job?" or "Why did you quit you last job?" There is a chapter on Interview Questions later in this book that you can refer to as well.

What you need to do is put the best answers you have for why you left each job in your source file. If you are having difficulty, ask a Career Development Facilitator at a Workforce Investment Act facility or a private counselor, or a friend or relative to assist you with this

Remember, leaving to find a better opportunity, more growth, more responsibility, to join a growing company, a dynamic company are all good reasons to move. Sooner or later most of us leave one job for another and that's fine. Your potential new employer just wants some reasonable explanation as to why you've left one so that they can decide if you would leave them for the same reason.

What about the situation where your record shows frequent job turnover? You had one job after the other, mostly doing the same kind of work. How do you explain your turnover? Some jobs are temporary in nature and if you've had those while seeking long term, steady, stable employment, say so. We all have bills to pay and people respect people who do what they have to do to survive including taking a "lesser job" while seeking a "better one."

Perhaps you worked at one place for a year or so, then left and a few weeks later got another job that lasted for two years and then you moved on. Your work history shows a pattern that may be problematic for you and an employer. If the problem is that you haven't "found" the right career for you, this is may just be you exploring your career options.

Job-hopping may not be the ideal way to "find" yourself, but it happens. If this is the case, you should realize you only have to explain your job changes one at a time to a potential employer. You should also realize that it may be time for you to examine yourself, and invest time into discovering who you are and might be, without changing jobs frequently.

Suppose your "Section 4 - Work History" is blank. You never had a job. That isn't really a problem. Everyone has to start somewhere. Everyone has to get that first job. Nothing to feel negative about or ashamed of.

It may mean it will take you more effort to land your first one, and you may want to seek suitable entry level jobs. Still, it isn't a negative to an employer, even if you think so because many job leads indicate "experience preferred." That doesn't make it so. It isn't a law of the universe after all. Everyone was inexperienced at some time in their life. You could show that you've done volunteer work, if you have. That is a great way to get experience. Or join the military, if that option is open to you. You will still have much to offer an employer, your education, your skills, you ability, and even positive worker traits and characteristics, like excellent attendance, or enthusiasm.

At the other end of a work life is the person with many years of experience. You know who you are. You've worked thirty to forty years, and have no desire, intention or reason to stop working. You love it. It gives you sustenance and all of the other rewards of work. Perhaps you've had two or three careers and seven or eight jobs. Should you list them all?

Certainly your source file should include it. After that, it is a concern. There is no doubt that age-ism exists. Just as some thought that certain people couldn't do certain jobs based on their race, some people have that prejudice in the work place against older workers. It is your job to overcome those objections. Be realistic. There are some jobs that are too difficult for some people, and that isn't just about age. If you can't lift 75 pounds, why try to get a job where you would be expected to? More typically the bias is that you may not fit, or be too slow to keep up. You should have the opportunity though.

What is typically more difficult for an older worker is simply getting the dates of employment right over their long career. Best advice is to get them as close as you can and then review your work to see if you have all the dates covered and gaps explained. Try creating a very compact outline to assist. Here is an example:

04/05/95 - 01/07/01 - Ass't Manager - BurgerWorld
01/10/01 - 11/10/10 - Manager - Buns N Suds
11/10/10 - 05/01/10 - unemployed
05/01/10 - present - Manager - Better Food Emporium.

If you think that you are being discriminated against because of your long career, you might consider omitting the oldest jobs especially if they are not relevant to your current search. You can list only the jobs you've had for the past 20 years. Some applications will even tell you not to include "old" job information that doesn't apply to the current position.

The problem of gaps in your work history is these tend to send up flags to employers who will wonder why there are such gaps. Sometimes it just takes time to get that next job after losing one. You might look at the gaps and indicate what you did during that time period that explains or helps show you did something with that time.

Did you try to start a business (whether you succeeded or not)? Did you go to school? Finish school? Get a GED? Take a training program? Travel? Try to start a new career somewhere else? Perhaps you went on a retreat? Decided just to take some time off and re-think your life? Did you volunteer? If you have done any of these things or others while you were off, by all means include it in your "Section 4 - Work History" section because you will need to be able to discuss these gaps.

Section 5 - Military Experience

Go into detail in this section, try to include your military "story," from the time you entered to your discharge (honorable or not). Each title you earned, each promotion, each assignment. Spell out your duties. Your military experience contains much that employers seek, mature, trained and trainable individuals who can both follow orders or directions and know when to get help or think for yourself. The discipline you learned in the military also translates well into employment situations. Do not understate the many valuable traits and experiences you acquired as part of your service. And by the way, thank you for your service!

Section 6 - Everything Else

You will sometimes also find questions about your health and restrictions, felony convictions or arrests and convictions, office or other special skills, availability for work.

Be prepared for questions like these as they do come up frequently. If your health is good, that is fine. If you have a health restriction, say so. For example, if you cannot lift more than 50 pounds, be prepared to say so. If that disqualifies you from a particular job, maybe that isn't a job you should be going after.

If you have a felony conviction on your record, be aware that it will be a strike against you for many jobs. You should have answers to the questions or prepared for it in an interview. People make mistakes and certainly if you were convicted of a felony, you made one of one sort or another. It will take time and effort for you to rebuild your social standing as it is similar to a financial bankruptcy which take time to overcome. Many people will react to you, and your job application, negatively. However, there are employers who are "felon friendly," i.e. are willing to give you an opportunity to rebuild your social and work life. You can also volunteer while you are seeking work. Demonstrate that you are trustworthy and safe to be around. There are incentives for employers willing to take a chance and hire you. You should seek assistance from public employment services to learn what programs are available to assist you and how they operate.

The question of "special skills" such as office equipment you can operate, often comes up. Go back through your work history and note all the special skills and equipment you can operate. Use the ones you need for that next job by being prepared to put them on the application. Don't forget to note any and all certifications you earned!

Availability for work comes up with many employers. Are they a 24-7 operation and they hire people for midnights, afternoons or start people as "relief" workers for weekends and holidays? The employer may ask how soon you can start, so be aware that it may be asked and have an answer for it.

What about illegal questions: age, race, marital status, gender, sexual orientation, handicaps, national origin, religion, etc.? Some applications still ask these questions, though most have been eliminated or modified because of lawsuits. Some employers still ask them in job interviews. There are circumstances when the "illegal" question can become "legal." For example, a towel attendant at a men's or women's locker room facility will need to state their sex. Other questions may need to be asked for data-gathering or statistical purposes and these will usually be on a separate form that indicates the purpose for which they are asked and some assurance that they have no bearing on hiring practices. How you handle it is up to you. Some of us think we should tell the interviewer that it is an illegal question. That's fine if you want to take a stand. It might cost you a job offer though. Others have no problem answering the question and get the job offers.

You might ask yourself if you want to work somewhere or for someone who doesn't know the rules or play by them. It really depends on you, your situation, and your values.

Chapter 23: Interviews, Are You Ready?

"Before job interviews, I think: What color tie best represents me as a person this company would be interested in?" — Jarod Kintz (1982-) American author, "This Book Has No Title"

"Those who do not learn from history are doomed to repeat it." — George Santayana (1863-1952) Spanish philosopher, poet, essayist, novelist.

"Find out what you like doing best and get someone to pay you for doing it." — Katherine Whitehorn (1928-), British journalist.

Background:

A job interview is a structured business meeting. It is designed with specific goals in mind. It has a business purpose. It is about business. It is not about "you." It is about the company, period, exclamation point, period. That's how you should want it too.

So, are you interview ready? Well, what does that mean, "interview ready"? Does it mean you got a call a few days ago and are meeting with an interviewer in 5 minutes to have a job interview? You made it here, you're nervous and wonder what they are going to ask? Is there more to it? Maybe.

Maybe all you needed to do to get that interview appointment was show up, and ta-da, they will be so impressed with you, overwhelmed by your answers, that they cannot help but to hire you ahead of the 10 other interviewees out of the 200 or 2,000 applicants they had. Good for you. Aside from having an interesting narcissistic complex, how'd that work out for you?

Really, you just showed up and got the job? Does your father own the company? No, who are you connected to (not that that isn't a way to get a job but it would explain your unlikely success)? Or what other magical totem got you that job? Really? Everyone would like to know how you did it. Aside from having an "in" (a special inside track that makes the vetting process unnecessary) almost no one gets more than an entry-level job that way. So it does happen, everyday. Are you ready if it does?

There are elements of preparation that most job hunters are familiar with to be considered to be "interview ready":

- Resume, be sure to take an extra copy with you, review yours to be ready to answer questions and make sure it's the same version they should already have.

- Appearance, be clean, wear freshly laundered clothing, dressed right for the job and try to have no odd or overwhelming smells from breath or body. Many people have allergies so avoid colognes and perfumes, in most situations, at least for interviews.

- Travel, plan to be a wee bit early to the interview, checking in about 15 minutes early is considered appropriate.

- Name of interviewer, make sure you know and have it with you. Sometimes you will be handed their business card. If so, place it in front of you and refer to it from time to time to make sure you know who you are talking to.

- Job title and duties, reviewed and prepared to tie in your worker characteristics into those duties.

- Expect to sell, sell, sell to get the job.

Does seem that more or less about right to you? You know where you are going, with whom you will be speaking, have reviewed the job and your resume to show where they are a match, are nicely groomed and on time. Maybe you've even rehearsed some of the likely questions you will be asked. You are <u>ready</u>! Maybe.

Maybe that will be enough. They've got to hire someone, right? Why not you? You were even smart enough or fate arranged for you to be the first or last interviewee (the best interview slot). It might be enough. Most of us have approached a job interview with exactly that and it was enough. Most of us did not get every job for which we were interviewed. Most of us got very few jobs of the jobs for which we interviewed. Face it, we're lucky if we get a job that way, the odds are against us. Unless, we possess that magical combination of having the right skills and characteristics and being in the right place at the right time.

Just as in sports, once in a while, an unlikely coalescence of the fates, luck, stars and who knows what all, a team wins a championship because everything went right and nothing went wrong for them but everything went wrong for their competition.

The competitor's star got injured, weather conditions created a sloppy field and a bad call tipped the scales. Their coach had a heart attack, a player got in a bad family situation and it distracted him just enough to miss that play, a critical practice, or crucial team meeting. On and on, bad things happen in a season and a team that should have made it to the playoffs, doesn't. And a team that "shouldn't've" does. Just like you in that interview that day. It happens.

Helpful Hint: The best interview time slots are the first, and the last interview, conducted. There are numerous psychological studies that show we tend to remember the first and last things in any sequence of events. That's why show business, and authors, like to get you hooked at the beginning and then give you the big finish. It's what you will remember later and what an interviewer will recall when making a decision.

Think about it a moment. If you are the first be to interviewed, you have the opportunity to set the stage for every subsequent applicant to have to make a better impression than you did. All of the following applicants will be compared to you as they march through the door and into the interview. The interviewer cannot help but do it, it is built into us. We naturally make comparisons.

Looking for a new car? The first one you look at will set up an automatic grading scale that the next one(s) will be compared to. That does not mean that the first always "wins," just that they have a great opportunity to make the competition measure up. You only have to hope they don't measure up in the job interview competition.

The last interview slot is also the most memorable. Everyone "in-between" becomes "grayer" and "fuzzier" in the interviewers' memory. If you can strike a winning pose in that last slot, you are in position to overshadow everyone else. Especially if everyone after the first made a good, competitive presentation. You, being last, have a built-in "easier to recall" opportunity. Again, it may not be enough but all other things being equal, which they never are, you have improved your chances of success significantly.

However, neither being first nor last to interview is as important as being truly "interview ready." That's the subject matter for the rest of the chapter.

What's a good interview worth?

If you are unemployed, you've got time, and probably the need for that next and most rewarding job. If you are underemployed, you've got less time but may still need that next and most rewarding job. If you are employed and focused on career building, you have less time but have a need to get that next and most rewarding job.

Take a look at Table 23 - 1: Lifetime Earnings on the next page:

$/hr	Hrs/wk	Wks/yr	Yrs	Total
10.00	37.5	52	44	$858,000
12.50	37.5	52	44	$1,072,500
15.00	37.5	52	44	$1,287,000
20.00	37.5	52	44	$1,716,000
30.00	37.5	52	44	$2,574,000

Table 23 - 1: Lifetime Earnings.

In your lifetime, if you average only $10.00 per hour you will earn about $858,000. Add just $5 per hour over your lifetime and you boost your revenue to $1,287,000 and you don't have to work any extra time to do it! Double or triple that to $20 or $30 per hour and you double or triple your lifetime earnings to as much $2,574,000 without working an extra minute, not one! If the difference in lifetime average earnings is just $20/hour, it will add up to an extra $1,716,000 for no extra effort!

Many jobs and careers permit you to earn that much and more. In fact, in the world of work, even $30/hour is not considered much above average. According to the U.S. Department of Labor, $25-$35/hour is about average[13]. If that is about average for an American worker, then half of the workers are making more than that. Some earn much, much more!

With all that need and time, why wouldn't you invest it in *your* future? Why wouldn't you expend some effort, invest some time to moving your lifetime average up a few dollars or more? That's only looking at the money of course, but that is part of the picture and a reason we work.

The employer in the interview:

Have you thought much about what "interviewing" is like on the interviewers side of things? You should. If you happen to watch an episode of "America's Got Talent," you should pay attention to what the judges talk about when they are interviewed. The judges talk about their initial impressions and how sometimes they were blown away by the difference between their expectations based on that first impression and the talent demonstrated.

So, what could you learn from this, aside from the fact that "America's Got Talent"? One thing you could carry away is that job interviews are a bit like auditions in that you have to show how you fit into the "show," this employer, this company and the world in which they operate, its ecology.

So how do you do it, get interview ready? Preparation, preparation, preparation. It is so important it is worth repeating, repeatedly. Preparation.

As part of your preparation effort, let's focus on the potential employer's side of things. If you have a clear picture of, and insights into, their side of the interview it will help you in your preparations. It is similar to the notion of "knowing your enemy" before you go into battle, whether in war, or games but it is different. They are not your enemy! They represent your future. They are a team you want to join. You just need to know who they want on their team and show them *you are who they want*.

So, what is it like being an interviewer? That depends on the interview situation. What's an "interview situation"? There are different interview situations although the first thing most of us will think of is the

---

13 Us Dept. of Labor, Bureau of Labor Statistics, Economic News Release, August, 1, 2014

classic setting, you, an interviewer, in an office, a cubicle or conference room. There are other settings and situations, however. Some of them are one of the following:
- Job fairs
- Phone interviews
- Group interviews
- Panel interviews
- Screening interviews
- Supervisor/peer/responds (subordinates)

Let's examine those in a bit more detail.

Job Fairs:

A Job Fair is typically day where one or more employers send representatives to a location sponsored by an organization dedicated to assisting employers and potential employees to come together. It is like Career Day, in school. Remember those? That is the first mistake you can make. It is not like Career Day back in school. The purpose then was to acquaint, you the student, to potential career paths. That is not what a Job Fair is, at all.

A Job Fair is a screening system. It is designed to surface and draw candidates for jobs within a company. These employers typically find they have to draw more applicants for a variety of reasons. The employer may be in a competitive industry and the labor pool is tight for the employees they need. Some employers offer more opportunity for new people in their company but less for promotional opportunities so they find many of their people moving to other companies for those types of opportunities. Some employers are expanding, gaining market share, and always need "new blood" to keep growing. Large employers often experience more turnover as well.

Whatever the reason, their presence should alert you to that fact that they either have a need now or anticipate it. They are not going to conduct full-on hiring interviews. If you think that they are there to just hand out information and answer your questions, you've made a mistake. They are looking for people, for candidates to join their company. It is a Job Fair not a high school career day.

You should approach a Job Fair as though you were going to an interview because you very well may be. Dress in a fashion that would match the job or job description. If they wear uniforms, dress business professional. When in doubt, dress conservatively. Bring several copies of your resume, nice clean, crisp copies.

Be prepared to answer some screening types of questions, like:
- What do you know about "Ale-Inn Breweries"?
- What do you know about "Fix'em-up Clinics"?
- What kind of work are you looking for?

You, of course, have done enough research to know what employers are going to be there, and a little about them. You know which ones you want to seek out. You are going to find them, and make enough of an impression that they will ask for your resume.

That should be your goal, for them to want to consider you. You may have to ask if they are accepting resumes and then give them one (depending on how busy their booth is). You should plan to approach them when they appear to have a lull and will have time to talk to you. Don't let yourself get lost in the crowd after all you may be the best person they could hire for the job if you help them hire you!

Helpful Hint: Never go to a Job Fair thinking it is a casual social event. Don't wear shorts and a T-shirt, even if it is 90 degrees outside. These employers are spending money to send staff to a job fair. They are working. Show them respect by acting like it. Dress right, look right, make a good impression, have a clean resume for them (make sure they get it if they don't ask for it), ask a few good questions and move on to the next booth on your list. Act like you mean business.

If you haven't done much research ahead of time, you might wander casually past the booths of interest to you and pick up their literature. Then after getting literature from each of the employers of interest to you, go have a coffee and read it. After that, go back and try to approach each one when their booth is "quiet."

Phone Interviews:

A phone interview is conducted by a screener to narrow the field of applicants down. It isn't always a smaller firm but smaller companies are often under-staffed, and don't have Human Resource Departments. A secretary often gets the job of calling 10-12 applicants and asking a few screening questions. If they "feel" like you are a good candidate, you will be offered an in-person interview.

Large companies use telephone interviews to screen applicants too, so be prepared for them, too.

The trick here is to know that you need to be prepared for a phone interview. When that phone rings, you should quiet down the environment, turn off the TV, stereo, radio, or the family. Get out or pick up your telephone call sheet, and paper and pen or pencil. (You should keep these items near the phone.) If you are out in the world, try to get to a quiet spot before you answer the phone. It is better you should get a voicemail and respond a few minutes later when you can talk in a quiet environment than to reveal you were sitting in a bar in the middle of the afternoon, or in a shopping mall.

How do you know it is a potential employer when the phone rings? You don't. If it isn't a friend on your phone, but a stranger, you should assume it is an employer. It may not be. It may be a telephone solicitor or your doctor's billing department. It is better to assume it is an employer though, and prepare yourself for their call because you are trying to get that job that you applied for, aren't you? If it isn't them, no harm no foul, nothing lost.

It might even turn out to be "not-a-screener" but someone actually setting up interviews so again it is better to be prepared than not. If you have your telephone call sheet out, then you can easily follow through. Don't have a Telephone Call Sheet? There is one in the workbook that accompanies this textbook and another in **Appendix F**.

In a pinch, remember to get the keys. The keys are vital pieces of information. Who did you talk to and when, when is your interview is scheduled with whom and where. Be sure you know the location of that person's office or workplace. *Don't forget your keys.*

If it is a telephone screening interview, you need to be prepared to answer a few specific questions about your background. Usually these will be about specific job duties in your past jobs or about specific skills or knowledge you possess. You should be prepared to discuss your background on the phone as well as you would in an interview or a job fair.

Group Interviews:

You, and a number of other candidates, are invited into a group interview. Often you will be given some of kind application, form, or test to turn in. When you've completed it, you're placed in line for what will be a series of short interviews with one or more people at a time. You may just be given numbers as you come in.

Essentially, these are screening interviews, similar to telephone interviews. If you were given a test, that may determine if you will even be subject to an interview. Sometimes the results of the test, or application or form will put you in line for "chute" interviews. You might be directed to one or more departments for an interview ("chutes") rather than exposed to all of the departments that are looking at the pool of candidates. The key to keep in mind is that it is a formal process, not likely to be a final interview but you must be prepared as well as if it was.

Panel Interviews:

Often conducted by companies, and governmental agencies, when the job requires interaction with different departments. Governments often do them with a member of the HR staff present along with someone from the hiring department to insure that all legal employment hiring practices are followed and the process is fair to all applicants.

Other employers conduct them to find people who have to interact with multiple departments on the job or if they will have to report to more than one department.

It is a straightforward process that requires you to be prepared. If you are prepared, it should not matter if one or one hundred persons ask you the questions.

Panel interviews do feel different. It is more intimidating because you are outnumbered. Someone on the panel will always seem "friendly" and someone always seems "hostile." Maybe they are, maybe they aren't but it will seem that way because you are outnumbered. You will be trying to "read" them but at a disadvantage. It is difficult to accurately gauge what anyone is thinking on the other side of the table during a panel interview. Appearances can be, and often are, deceiving. The best thing you can do is to realize it is still just one set of questions that you are prepared to answer.

Screening Interviews:

Screening interviews are what they seem to be, a job interview. You may not always know if the interview you are walking into is a screening interview, so be prepared as though it is the final interview, the one that gets you hired. If you don't, it will probably be the one that keeps you from getting hired and become the final interview.

Screening interviews are designed to narrow down the field of applicants for someone else to conduct final interviews. The final interviewer may be assumed to be someone whose time is more expensive, valuable and in demand. The screener is a "lower cost" person and may be one whose primary function is to carry out screening interviews. They may interview 20 or more candidates for a job with a goal of narrowing to the top 3-5 candidates for final interviews.

They are more apt to be looking for consistency between your application, your resume and your words in the interview. They are more apt to focus on whatever content they've been told to focus on. Typically they want to verify your skills, abilities, knowledge, traits. They may be looking to see how you will fit in based on their feelings about you. They are more likely to check your references and credentials.

Be nice to these people as you should with everyone in the process. Often people are a little judgmental and dismissive with these interviewers as though they are of lesser importance. How careless that mistake is. These screeners, along with everyone else, a secretary, a guard, a receptionist is important. They are being paid for their work. They are valuable. Sometimes a boss will eliminate someone as a candidate because he trusts the judgement of his secretary or of another screener. Don't eliminate yourself by eliminating them as important. You knew that, right? The screener may be the decision maker as to who will proceed. They are automatically important because they can exclude you from further consideration.

Employee Interviews:

It is common for your potential boss to be the final link in the hiring process. You may also be interviewed by a peer or co-worker, or even a "respond" (someone who will be subordinate to you on the organizational chart, in other words, they work for and report to you). You've overcome all the other challenges. When it is your future boss the often are the person who makes the final decision. You're ready, so it should be just a matter of follow through. This interview will require your best presentation. This is the person you will work for and they have the most to gain by a good decision and the most to lose by a bad one. This should go without saying, they are VIP's show them proper respect by being prepared.

Sometimes you will get interviewed by potential co-workers or even those who will work for you. If that happens, treat them like you would any other interviewer, with respect and courtesy and your best interview presentation. They are not going to be able to hire you but if they are there it is for a reason, that being because they will have to work with you. They can prevent you from getting a job simply by saying one of the other candidates was better in their opinion. Their opinion might matter even if they are wrong. So again, be prepared and make your best presentation with them.

That covers several types of common interview situations. Now let's talk about the interviewers themselves.

Interviewers

Who does interviews? What kind of people? All kinds of people do interviews, all kinds. It comes down to two kinds of people. There are those whose normal job functions entail interviewing people for jobs and then there is everybody else.

Seriously.

There are common themes though, in interviewers. Some have training and experience in interview skills. Some don't. So, that isn't it. They do all have to do it and do it for a purpose, a reason. The reason is that given the information available to them, within the time allotted, they have to make the best possible choice in their hiring decision from the pool of applicants and interviewees they meet.

Some people, by the nature of their job, interview lots of people and get lots of feedback on the quality of their decision making, others don't. Some get better at interviewing, some don't.

The stakes are high for every person who conducts interviews. If they are a "scout," a professional job placement person or Job Fair representative, they are judged by the quality of the candidates they pass on in the process. Especially in the case of professional recruiters, if they fail to properly screen and assess job candidates, they will lose business.

If they are a Human Resource staff person, their judgment will be called into question if they make too many bad hiring decisions.

If they are someone who interviews infrequently, like many department heads or small business owners, it will cost them in terms of non-productivity, staff turnover, incomplete work, business disruption and profit.

When you go into an interview you need to be aware of how much that interviewer has at stake. It is not only their professional judgment that is on the line, it is the cost of hiring the right person and not the wrong one.

Suppose, as a business person, you have a new job opening. Someone retired, quit, got fired, transferred, was promoted, or your business expanded. Now you have an opening to fill. How do you go about it?

One hundred years ago, and still today, one tried-and-true method has always been used: Hang out a "Help Wanted" sign. Then wait for people to see the sign, come in and apply. Enough people apply and sooner or later one of them gets hired. Seems low cost, doesn't it? Unless you think about who is doing the work. Suppose it is you, the owner, and the job is as simple as sweeping up, or busing tables. You can do it, in your busy day, you can squeeze out a little time to do it. Or you could be doing something else that would make more money. Keeping a kitchen running smooth, running a register so the wait staff can keep the food flowing. You could serve as Host or Hostess. You could be working on finding a way to save a little on your supplies and other purchases or you could be working on your books. Plus it is just plain tiring to have to do more work.

You could have someone else doing the work but the same applies, whatever time they put in doing that job, is at the cost of something else not getting done. You need the person or you wouldn't have hung up the sign, right? And either way, you find yourself spending time interviewing people. Maybe you have time for that, maybe you don't but it is at the cost of your time. If you figure your time is worth $60/hour, and it takes you 15 minutes to do an interview, it costs you $60 to interview four people.

Now suppose that you, as that small business person, decide to attract more applicants because maybe it is more urgent that you hire someone soon. Work is backing up, orders aren't getting filled, you're paying overtime and it's costing more than simply hiring someone would. Let's say it's costing you hundreds per week and it could be more in lost sales.

So, you place an ad in a newspaper for a week at a cost of $200/week and you run it for two weeks, or $400 total. From that you get anywhere from zero to 1,000 resumes flooding in, or you included your address and between 75 and 750 people showed up.

Didn't see that coming, did you? How long will it take you to just hand out and take back that many applications? How long will it take to read that many resumes or applications? That's not going to be something you do in an hour or two. Well maybe, maybe you're the sort that says, I'll just take the first ten that look like they could do the job. Some people will do just that. Pick the first ten that appear qualified, call and interview the first three. Make a decision. (Helpful Hint: Don't delay when you respond to an ad.)

Other employers will skim through the applications and resumes and do a preliminary weeding, dividing the applications and resumes into two stacks, "yes" and "no." It may take a few hours to narrow a stack of 200 resumes into a stack of 20-30 "most promising" candidates. Another 2 - 3 hours of going through those, more carefully to narrow it down to 10-15 best candidates. Interviews may then be offered to the top five and a choice made out of those interviewed, if one candidate stands out.

So, how much more did it just cost? At a minimum of three interviews of a half hour of time, at $50/hr for "owner" time, $150 then double that for a minimal resume review to a total of $700 for one hire ($400 for the ad, $150 for resume/application review, $150 for interviews). The more extensive approach doubles or triples the cost to $2,000 or more. And why would someone put in more time instead of less? Because the cost of making a bad hire costs more, much, much more than this.

Suppose you have a fairly important job to fill. They are all important of course; that's why you pay people to do them, but suppose it is a key position, maybe your Accounts Receivable Credit and Collections Clerk position. It is a fairly "background" kind of job, usually seen as a cost center in business, not a profit center, because it is in the accounting department which is a business overhead.

However, the person in the job monitors the credit extended to new customers and old. They pay attention to the company getting paid. Customers who are slow to pay cost you money equal to your cost of money, i.e. what you pay your bank for interest charges on investment loans. Customers who begin to slow down their average days paid may be signaling that they are in financial trouble and should have their credit limits reduced. When money is overdue, the A/R C&C Clerk gets involved in the collections part of their job. It is an important job. Getting the money in keeps a business solvent, keeps suppliers and labor paid and gives the business owner money to spend. Yay!

Now suppose that the "easy" interviewer hires the "easiest" to find candidate and they are in the job for two months before problems begin popping up. Their new found power to extend credit or limit it is slowing down the sales department too much, cutting into sales. Oddly, one new customer was given credit out of proportion to the normal criteria, turned out they were a friend of the new A/R C&C Clerk. They bought some goods and sold them without paying you and have ordered even more! The Clerk isn't paying attention to or doesn't like making collection calls and is avoiding it like the dickens. Several customers are letting their accounts slide into the over 90 day pay range. Others are buying more and paying less. Your costs are soaring! Plus the new clerk is argumentative and takes long lunches.

You have warned them but it is inevitable and you fire them after 90 days. Can you even calculate how much damage has been done to your business. You could, if you had the time but you don't because now you have a mess on your hands. The cost is likely in the thousands or even tens of thousands. It might have been avoided with better hiring practices.

You've learned your lesson as a business person and this time you spend $2,000-$3,000 on the hiring process and get someone who can not only do the job but clean up the mess and get your Accounts Receivable Credit and Collections in order.

Over and over again, in many ways, the costs of bad hiring decisions cost businesses money. That's not the only kind of cost either. Bad hiring decisions can cause the breakdown of morale in departments and cause worker unhappiness, and departures. They can cause work slowdowns as people respond negatively to the new hire.

Who has to deal with the bad decision the most? Often it is the person who made it, and it is no fun at all to realize you've made a bad one. You've invested your time and talent into trying to make the right decision and you are willing to back your choice, but when you make a bad one, your own thinking is called into question. Not a happy place.

The next time you go in for an interview, realize that in a few short minutes that person across from you has to make a decision about you relative to the job but that the consequences for them are quite likely to be higher for them than you. You will keep looking if you don't get the job, even if you should have. They have to live with their decision.

At the beginning of this chapter we said that the interview is a structured business meeting. It is structured because the interviewer has an agenda. They have a handful of questions they will ask. They have allocated a set amount of time, maybe a half hour per interview but only plan to use 15 minutes for each one. That way they can have a short break after each interview to make notes, get a drink and so on. They also have a few extra minutes to give to the really good, interesting interviewees.

In that brief time, they are going to try to verify that your application, your resume and your presentation all match. They will make judgments about the impression you make. They will try to sniff out hidden flaws. They will try to determine if your worker characteristics, capabilities and experience match the job opening. They will also be or should be considering you amongst your potential co-workers, supervisors, sub-ordinates, suppliers and those most precious of people, customers. All that in 15 minutes.

And yet, it is successfully done each and every day.

What do they want?

So, what are they looking for? Employers have certain common expectations for interviewees, and employees. These are:

- You want to do the job.
- You can do the job.
- You are willing to do the job.
- You will be here, reliably and dependably.
- You will be on time.
- You will show up ready to work.
- You will get along with others (customers, co-workers, supervisors and subordinates).
- You will be trustworthy.
- You will be affordable.
- You will be worth investing in
- You will stay.

As they interview you, they will be looking at your attitude and demeanor. Are you pleasant, courteous, have good posture. Do you seem to be positive, optimistic, enthusiastic? Do you seem like you will fit in? Are you a team player, a role player, a leader?

How they find these things out is by asking questions, listening to your answers. They observe you, on the way into, during and on your way out of an interview. They may check with former employers and your references.

That is not a lot to go on, is it? That is why you need to be prepared when you interview, you do not get much of a chance to show you have all those qualities.

Chapter 24: Interview Preparation: Questions

"Judge a man by his questions rather than by his answers." — Voltaire (1694-1778) French writer, historian, philosopher.

"Ask me no questions, and I'll tell you no lies." — Oliver Goldsmith (1730-1774) Irish playwright, novelist and poet.

"Questions are great, but only if you know the answers. If you ask questions and the answers surprise you, you look silly." — Laurell K. Hamilton (1963-) American fantasy and romance writer, "Burnt Offerings."

Background:

Questions, questions, and more questions. Good questions, bad ones. Stupid questions, smart ones. Illegal questions. Why do they have to ask so many questions? Where do they get those questions? How do they know which ones to ask to hit me in my weak spot? Why don't they ever ask the easy ones or the ones I want to answer? Do I get to ask any?

As you know by now, the "Interview" is an employers attempt to get to know *you*. Unfortunately, not just you but all the others who have been invited in for an interview. Each of you will have about 30 to 60 minutes per interview. After that the employer then has to make a hiring decision. It is important to them to get the right person and you want them to hire the right person even if that person is not you!

Think about it, how else could this be done? You could be given a prepared list of the questions and told to come in and do a 30 minute speech covering them all. Wouldn't that be cool for some of us, seems unlikely though doesn't it?

Given that a "Job Interview" is a structured business meeting with a specific purpose, then you simply need to prepare for that meeting. Your have two major goals for the meeting. The first is to show them who you are, why you are the best person for the job and motivate them to hire you. The second is for you to determine if you want to work there. Their goals are to find the best person for the job out of a pool of interviewees. Your goals are to best present yourself and determine if you want to work for them.

The interview will consist almost entirely of questions, or statements you are to respond to, so it may feel like an interrogation because it is. You do have some opportunity to take control of the meting and agenda. You can do this by how you answer questions and by asking your own.

Duration:

Interviews often run longer than an hour, especially with promising applicants. An interview that lasts an hour or more is not unusual, depending on the job. The necessity to explore information, validate skills, abilities, knowledge, explore inter-personal behavior, and assess or evaluate the candidate may require it. On the other hand, longer interviews are a good sign that an interviewer is truly interested in you and wants to know more about you. You will probably know which situation you are in, the need for specific information about particular skills, or the need for more information about you.

If a typical interview lasts 30 minutes, do you know how many questions are likely to be asked and answered in that time period? Even if an interview lasts 1½ hours, how many questions could be asked and answered? If the combined time for a question and an answer is one minute, then in an interview where both people spoke steadily, there would only be about 30 questions in a half hour or 90 questions in a 1½ hour interview. Both of these are high estimates by the way. You would typically only have 15-20 questions in a half hour interview and 40-50 in a 1½ hour session. Does that sound like a lot to you or not too much?

Realize that you get to ask questions, so some of those 90 questions are yours. Questions that you ask, put the other person in the "respondent" position and uses up some of those 90 questions and time. Another good reason to have some questions prepared, isn't it?

You control how long you take to answer questions. If you take ten minutes to answer one, you would only have to answer nine questions in 90 minutes. That would be a deadly mistake but we're just trying to put some limits on the situation and help reduce your anxiety at having to deal with the "interrogation."

Your average planned answer should be about 30-60 seconds in length. Some questions will take longer and a few will be shorter but use 30-60 seconds as a good ballpark figure when you are rehearsing. That would mean an upper limit of 90 questions for you to answer or ask at the upper end of a long interview.

The interviewer will be documenting the meeting, taking notes and trying to connect your answers to the job application and your resume. They are trying to visualize you in the job and that will take time too. This "time for recording" reduces the time for more questions.

Your task is to make it easy for them. You are prepared, after all. You know all about you. You've done a good job researching the employer and doing research on the job. You just need to help the interviewer see you in the job. The better they see you in it, the more likely you are to get it, if you want it.

One thing before we start looking at questions and answers. It is uncanny how interviewers, trained and untrained, skilled and unskilled, experienced, inexperienced and even those with no experience, will spot your weaknesses. Whether there is something in your resume, your job application, or about you, it seems that those weaknesses and vulnerabilities have a way of surfacing and you have to answer questions about them.

There are three things we can say about this. First, the interview is a structured business meeting with a purpose. The purpose is to get enough information to make a good decision. Therefore, they must learn all that can be learned about all the job candidates, in a short period of time, in order to have sufficient information to choose between them. This means that every candidate will be asked approximately the same questions.

Second, there really aren't that many questions you can be asked. There are maybe 100-150 or so, and many of them are variations on each other.

Third, nearly every candidate for a job will have questions that they dread, fear or just don't want to deal with. Everybody has some kind of weakness that will be surfaced during an interview. It's how the questions are handled that matters more than the fact that we are all less than perfect.

Once you realize no one is perfect, all you need is to have good answers for as many questions as you are *likely* to be asked. It is far more important to make sure the interviewer sees you in the job, that you will fit socially, handle the tasks, and be an asset to the company.

Types of Questions

Let's take a look at typical questions. There are two major types of questions that will be asked in an interview. These are questions about your ability to do the job and questions about you as a person and how well you will fit into the job environment.

Questions about your ability to do the job:
- Skills, knowledge, and abilities
- Education and training
- Strengths and weaknesses
- Work History
  - Work activities, tasks and duties
  - Tools, equipment, and technology
  - Job departures

- Salary Motivation
- How much you want and fit the job
- How well you'll do in it.

Questions about you as a person:
- Behavior
- Communication
- Competency
- Work styles
- Work values
- Your ability to work on a team, independently or with the others already in place in your work work environment
- Your leadership and your "follower" skills
- Your capacity to conform to the job environment.

Overall, they are questions designed to learn as much as quickly as possible about any given job candidate. The interviewer will try to determine what you want to do and if that is a match to their job opening. They want to determine if you can do the job. They want to know if you are motivated to do the job and work for this employer. They want to know what it will cost to hire you.

As we look at those types of questions and how to work with them, keep in mind that the questions may occur in any order, depending on the interviewer, their experience, the company, and the job involved.

Sometimes the questions will be statements that you are expected to respond to, sometimes they are actually phrased like a question. We've included some of each in the examples.

Remember that you will not be expected to answer all of these questions but you should be able to in your preparation. It is an excellent way for you to understand yourself in the workplace as well. Consider it an exercise in self-enlightenment. The questions are listed in the accompanying workbook to help you in this exercise. Develop answers to each of them. These answers should be comfortable and honest responses from you.

After you go through an interview, look to see which questions you were asked, note those as they may be more typical of the questions pertaining to the type of job you are seeking. Look at the answer you gave and decide if you could have given a better answer. You cannot fix past mistakes but you can learn and improve and do better the "next time" you are asked.

The questions are grouped, but often a question serves as an answer, or is informative, in more than one category. So don't get "hung up" on whether a question is in one category or another or which is right. That isn't really important. What is important is *your* answer to the question asked.

There are a handful of very common, basic questions that you are very likely to be asked and for which you should have answers prepared. We cover those first, along with some idea of how you should view the question and what a good answer would be.

Super-most common questions:

What is your greatest strength?

What they want to know is, what is it about you that will make you *great* at this job. Yes, you have many excellent strengths, they want one. So what it is about you that will make you great at this job?

If you've used the material in this book in your research, you should have a good idea of the one most important factor likely to make that job "yours." Time to shine. Say so and state it. If you aren't sure, pick three of your best possible answers and be ready to mention all three. Try to make sure that each is important to the job.

The best way to respond is to describe a skill and experience that directly relates to the job you are applying for.

Sample Answers:

- I meet deadlines.
- I'm organized, efficient, and take pride in the quality of my work.
- I have exceeded my sales quotas every quarter for the past three years because I love selling.
- I take pride in my customer service skills and my ability to resolve what could be difficult situations.

What is Your Greatest Weakness?

Sounds like a loaded question, right? Why should you reveal that you have a weakness? Won't they exploit it? Could it be a turn-off to an employer?

You do have to answer the question because we all have weaknesses and to deny that fact is to mean you either don't know what yours are or are trying to hide them.

The best way to answer the question is to look to yourself and your past and find an answer that shows you have self-improved, turned a negative into a positive, or that it is something unimportant to the job.

You can discuss a skill that you have improved upon during your previous job, so you can show the interviewer that you can make improvements, when necessary. Perhaps you needed better computer skills and took advantage of the company sponsored computer training programs and acquired strong MicroSoft Office skills, including Word, Access, Excel and PowerPoint.

To turn a negative into a positive, think about something that you do that maybe annoys others but actually helps you do your best work. You could something like "Even when others are pressuring me to get something done, I re-check my work for accuracy, because I believe it is better to do it right the first time than to have to do it over again. Wrong or bad information is costly."

If you analyzed the key skills and strengths required for the job you are interviewing for, you should be able to come up with an honest shortcoming that is not essential for success in that job. For example, if you are applying for a bookkeeping job, you might state that you are not particularly good at conducting group presentations.

Sample Answers:

- I recognized that my public speaking skills could use improvement and signed up for a course in it just last month.
- There are times when I get so focused on my work that I skip lunch.
- I like to double-check my work and sometimes that conflicts with the need for speed but I believe in doing things right the first time.
- I made a bad decision when I was younger and have paid for and learned from my mistake.

Tell me about yourself.

This question means who you are, professionally speaking. You should have about a one-minute answer that summarizes where you're at in your career and what you're good at, with an emphasis on your most recent job. Do not talk about your family, hobbies, friends, health, problems or where you grew up. It's about business remember?

Sample Answers:

- I am an successful, experienced operations manager in a high volume production environment interested in an opportunity to advance my career to the next level. I recently completed an advanced degree in Business Management to help facilitate this next step.

- I'm organized, efficient, and take pride in the quality of my work. I'm ready to take the next step in my career. I am recently married and looking for long term stability in my next position.
- I have exceeded my sales quotas every quarter for the past three years because I love selling. I believe it is my job to help my customer make the very best decision for their needs.
- I take pride in my customer service skills and my ability to resolve what could be difficult situations.

What interests you about this job?

We spent time talking about rewards and what rewards you want from work. This is a place you can use that knowledge. What is it about this job, this work, that ignites your passion, excites you? Sure, this work could be boring or wrong to someone else but it is your destiny. Let it flow. What is it about the substance of the role that most interests you? Interviewers want to hire people who see this as a job they'd be glad to work at every day. That means you focus on the work itself.

Sample answers:
- I enjoy challenging situations, problem solving and leading people. This job represents an opportunity for me to us those skills productively.

Do not talk about what the job can do for you, like benefits, or what you'll be able to buy or do if you get it.

Why are you thinking about leaving your job? (Or why did you leave, quit, resign, get laid off, or get fired from your last job?)

Your answer will depend on your truth. Why did you leave it? Lay-offs are commonplace, and nothing to be ashamed of, if that was it, say it and add that it is giving you the opportunity to find your next most rewarding job.

If you quit or resigned without having the next job lined up, it may show you are sometimes impulsive. You are not the only one, and sometimes work does get to a person and leaving without that next job lined seems like a "bad thing." If it got to that for you, you can state the truth, "I needed to move on as that was not the right place for me." You can always say, "The work wasn't challenging enough," or "I was under-valued and passed over for promotion" or whatever your reality is. Just think about how you want to say it, state it and move on. Do avoid bad-mouthing the employer or complaining about the work. That would make this next employer wary about hiring you. What will you say about them or their work?

Sample answers:
- I was laid off.
- I needed to move on as that was not the right type of work for me.
- I was passed over for a promotional opportunity twice because I was "too valuable in my position to promote".

Why would/should we hire you?

Here's your chance to make a case for why you'd shine in the job. It may be the single most important question you will be asked. If you don't know why, the interviewer isn't going to know, and won't bother to try to figure it out. Either you are the right person or you are not. You should have a strong answer prepared that runs about one minute and points to your skills, experience and knowledge, and ties them to the needs of the job.

Sample answer:

• I have the background, in-depth practical, successful experience to step in, take charge and keep the work focused, directed and on target.

Tell me about a time when ...

This phrase is a lead-in to a lot of other questions. When you read through the list of questions that follows this section, try to imagine them asking that question but using this lead-in. For example, "Tell me about a time when you had a problem with a co-worker." Another example: "Tell me about a time when you had to take charge." Or "Tell me about a time when you had to deal with an irate customer." Don't let yourself be thrown by this way of being asked, it's just a lead-in.

You can use the STAR technique here, to answer the question. STAR stands for Situation, Task, Action, Result. Let the interviewer's question be a prompt reminder to you of a Situation like that. What was the Task that needed to be done or what needed to be achieved or accomplished? What Action did you take to achieve that result? What was the Result.

For example, if the interviewer says, "Tell me about a time when you had to deal with an irate customer." You think a moment and recall one that you resolved quite nicely and say, "I had a customer who was irate about a 3D Blu Ray DVD player that was sold to him along with his 3D TV. He bought a warranty but it only covered the TV even though he thought it included the DVD player because he bought it as a package, and concluded the extended warranty would cover it. In reality, the DVD player was a "no charge" item given to him to close the deal. It wasn't working correctly. I knew we could lose him and as a valued customer. I didn't want that to happen. I wanted him to leave as a satisfied customer. So I said, although I cannot give you a replacement under our warranty program, let's see if I can still do something for you. I took him over to our 3D Blu Ray DVD players. I asked him what his player was doing and, although I knew it could be resolved with a software update, I also knew that it was difficult to do on his model. I told him about the top models, which were more than he needed, but that one of them, the lowest priced, was easy to do software upgrades on because it was wifi capable. I offered it at our cost if he wanted to try it. I also told him that he could try doing a software update on his own unit and how he could go about doing it. The result was he bought the wifi-enabled model because it would be easy to do upgrades and it was a relatively inexpensive unit. He called me a few days later to tell me how happy he was and that it also solved another problem he had with a streaming internet TV service he had."

What would you do in your first 90 days if you got this position?

How should you know, right? You haven't reported for work, gone through orientation or been introduced to your co-workers, your boss and your work.

You should have some idea of how you would approach being placed in a new work setting with a new job to do unless this is your first one. You will want an answer that shows you've pictured yourself in the job and have a realistic idea of what you can accomplish in that time period.

Your answer might start with the obvious. "After I meet everyone and get settled in, I like to look at the work in front of me and sort it out in order of importance and what deadlines are in place. I get organized and get busy. I check in with others to ensure I am on the track and don't wait for too much time to elapse before doing so. I am not afraid to ask for help or clarification, when it is needed, either."

What salary range are you looking for?

You should have taken a bit of time to look into wages for the job you are applying for and have prepared a ballpark range you would like that matches your experience. Try not to tip your hand to soon. Consider starting with a statement like, "I can be flexible for the right opportunity though my research says that somewhere between $ _____ and $ _____ month (or per hour) would be about right." The employer will have a range in mind for whomever they hire and try to get the most they can for the least they will have to pay. You, on the other hand, want to get as much to start with as you can because that is where you'll be starting and raises never come as fast as anyone would like. Your range should include the higher end of what they are going to offer which you should have a sense of from your research.

Example: Your research says someone with your experience can expect somewhere between $18 and $30 per hour. You say "I can be flexible for the right opportunity and I would be looking for $25 to $30 per hour based on my experience." The employer's range was $20 to $24 per hour and they are likely to say, "We can only go as high as $22, would that be acceptable to you?" Your answer, "Possibly, I normally don't ask about benefits during an interview, but what are they here?" Or you could say, "Yes." Or you could say, with a slight shake of the head, "I really think that I am worth more than that, can you bring that up to $25." Now you are negotiating. What you will "go for" is up to you but be aware that if you ask for too little, you either don't know what you are worth (not a good thing) or you might get a lower offer and be unhappy about it, leading to a job change down the road.

Incidentally, the employers range could have been, $28 to $40 per hour or more. Don't be afraid or embarrassed to ask for what you think you are worth or need to earn. If you are worth it, you will get it or something close.

There are many other common questions asked, and we'll list some of them. No list can possibly be "complete" as new questions do still occur. You should spend time with all of them. This list will provide you with a framework to create your own answers. Use the internet to aid your research. Don't forget to document which ones you are being asked in your own interviews. If you've been asked questions not listed, then add them to the list.

Some of the questions are really just variations of each other. If you prepare for one of them, you will save time by recognizing that and using your prepared answer for any of the variations with minor changes. We put them in here for you to see the different ways the same question can be phrased, as an aid for your preparation.

Common basic questions:

- Describe yourself or how would you describe yourself?
- Are you overqualified for this job?
- Are you the best person for this job? Why?
- Are you willing to relocate?
- Do you have any questions for me?
- Is there anything else I can tell you about the job and the company?
- Tell me why you want to work here.
- What are you looking for in your next position?
- What attracted you to this company?
- What can you contribute to this company?
- What can you do for this company?
- What can you do for us that other candidates can't?
- What did you like least about your last job?
- What did you like or dislike about your previous job?
- What do you know about our company?
- What do you know about this industry?
- What interests you about this job?
- What's your ideal company?
- When were you most satisfied in your job?
- Why do you want this job?
- Why should we hire you?

Work history
- What relevant experience do you have?
- What was the last project you headed up, and what was its outcome?
- What were the responsibilities of your last position?

Achievements & accomplishments
- Give me some examples of ideas you've had implemented.
- Give me an example of a time that you felt you went above and beyond the call of duty at work.
- Tell me about your proudest achievement.
- What are you most proud of?
- What is your greatest achievement outside of work?
- What major challenges have you handled?
- What was your biggest accomplishment (failure) in your last position?

What are you like to work with (how do you fit in)?
- Can you describe a time when your work was criticized?
- Describe a difficult experience at work and how you handled it.
- Describe a difficult work situation/project and how you overcame it.
- Describe how you would handle a situation if you were required to finish multiple tasks by the end of the day, and there was no conceivable way that you could finish them.
- Do you take work home with you?
- Have you ever been on a team where someone was not pulling their own weight? How did you handle it?
- Have you ever had difficulty working with a manager?
- Have you gotten angry at work? What happened?
- How do you feel about taking no for an answer?
- How do you handle pressure?
- How do you handle stress and pressure?
- How would you feel about working for someone who knows less than you?
- How would you feel about working for a woman?
- How would you feel about working for a foreigner?
- How would you feel about working for a man?
- How would you handle it if your boss was wrong?
- If I were your supervisor and asked you to do something that you disagreed with, what would you do?
- If you found out your company was doing something against the law, like fraud, what would you do?
- If you were at a business lunch and you ordered a rare steak and they brought it to you well done, what would you do?
- Tell me about a time when you had to give someone difficult feedback. How did you handle it?
- Tell me about a time where you had to deal with conflict on the job.
- What assignment was too difficult for you, and how did you resolve the issue?
- What irritates you about other people, and how do you deal with it?
- What is your greatest failure, and what did you learn from it?
- What problems have you encountered at work?
- What was the most difficult period in your life, and how did you deal with it?

- What's the most difficult decision you've made in the last two years and how did you come to that decision?
- How do you think I rate as an interviewer?

Goals

- How do you want to improve yourself in the next year?
- If I were to ask your last supervisor to provide you additional training or exposure, what would she suggest?
- What are you looking for in terms of career development?
- What kind of goals would you have in mind if you got this job?
- Describe your career goals.
- What do you ultimately want to become?
- How long do you expect to work for this company?
- What are your goals for the future?
- What are your career goals for the future?
- Where would you like to be in your career five years from now?

Culture & values -- Who are you?

- Describe your best boss and your worst boss.
- Give me an example of a time you did something wrong. How did you handle it?
- How do you evaluate success?
- How do you measure success?
- If you were interviewing someone for this position, what traits would you look for?
- What negative thing would your last boss say about you?
- Do you think a leader should be feared or liked?
- List five words that describe your character.
- Tell me one thing about yourself you wouldn't want me to know.
- Tell me the difference between good and exceptional.
- Was there a person in your career who really made a difference?
- What are the qualities of a bad leader?
- What are the qualities of a good leader?
- What are three things your last boss would say about you?
- What are you passionate about?
- What challenges are you looking for in your next job?
- What do you do in your spare time?
- What do you expect from a supervisor?
- What do you like to do for fun?
- What do you like to do?
- What do you look for in terms of corporate culture?
- What do you think of your previous boss?
- What is your personal mission statement?
- What kind of personality do you work best with and why?
- What three character traits would your friends use to describe you?
- What was most (least) rewarding about your job?
- What will you do if you don't get a job offer?
- What will you miss about your present/last job?
- What's the most important thing you learned in school?

- Who was your best boss and who was the worst?
- Who has impacted you most in your career and how?
- What is your greatest fear?
- What is your biggest regret and why?
- Who was your favorite manager and why?
- Why did you choose your major?
- If the people who know you were asked why you should be hired, what would they say?

Performance & evaluation -- what can we expect from you?
- How long will it take for you to make a significant contribution?
- How would you go about establishing your credibility quickly with the team?
- If selected for this position, can you describe your strategy for the first 90 days?
- What do you see yourself doing within the first 30 days of this job?

Salary
- How much do you expect to get paid?
- What are your salary requirements?
- What were your starting and final levels of compensation?
- If I were to give you this salary you requested but let you write your job description for the next year, what would it say?
- What salary are you seeking?
- What's your salary history?

Work context
- Do you prefer to work alone or on a team?
- Give some examples of your work as a team member or leader.
- Is there a type of work environment you prefer?
- What techniques and tools do you use to keep yourself organized?
- What would be your ideal working environment?
- Describe your use and competence with computer technology.

Work styles
- Describe your work style.
- How would you describe the pace at which you work?
- How would you describe your work style?
- If you had to choose one, would you consider yourself a big-picture person or a detail-oriented person?

Once they have completed asking you their questions, it is officially your turn. The following are questions you should ask because they will help you decide if they are an employer you want to work for and if this job is right for you.

That is not to say that you should not ask questions along the way. If you prepare yourself, you can ask a question after you've answered one of theirs.

For example, if they ask, "What interests you about this job?" After you've completed your answer, you could ask, "What does a typical day look like?" or "Can I see where I would be working?" or "Do you have specific examples of the type of work I would be responsible for?" (which you would just happen to love doing and be great at, right?)

Questions you should ask

Here are some questions that you might ask in an interview. They do not all fit or apply to every job or job situation that you might be applying for. In the workbook, they are all listed, with the suggestion that you highlight or write down the ones that seem most appropriate to you. Then list those questions in your "Source Book" as questions you are comfortable asking *because you want to know the answers*. Add you own, it's about *you* after all.

The Job - Try to get as clear a picture as you can about the day-to-day duties of the job, the work you will be doing.

- What does a typical day look like?
- What are the most immediate projects that need to be addressed?
- Can you show me examples of projects I'd be working on?
- What are the skills and experiences you're looking for in an ideal candidate?
- What attributes does someone need to have in order to be really successful in this position?
- What type of skills is the team missing that you're looking to fill with a new hire?
- What are the biggest challenges that someone in this position would face?
- What sort of budget would I be working with?
- Is this a new role that has been created?
- Do you expect the main responsibilities for this position to change in the next six months to a year?
- Are you most interested in a candidate who works independently, on a team, cross- functionally, or through a combination of them all? Can you give me an example?
- How much travel is expected?
- How has this position evolved since it was created?
- How do you see this position contributing to the success of the organization?
- Is this a new position, or did someone leave? If someone left, why did they leave or what did they go on to do?
- What would you say are the three most important skills needed to excel in this position?
- What specific qualities and skills are you looking for in the job candidate?
- What are the duties and responsibilities of the position?
- What are some challenges that will face the person filling this position?
- What is the single largest problem facing your staff, and would I be in a position to help you solve this problem?

Training and professional development - You are on a path to obtain your next Most Rewarding Job and Career. Will this job help you get there?

- How will I be trained?
- What training programs are available to your employees?
- Are there opportunities for advancement or professional development?
- Would I be able to represent the company at industry conferences?
- Is this a new job or did someone leave?
- If someone left, why did they leave or what did they go on to do?
- Where have successful employees in this position progressed to?
- Does the company offer continued education and professional training?
- What is the typical career trajectory for a person in this position?

- What are the prospects for growth and advancement?
- Am I going to be a mentor or will I be mentored?

Your performance
- How will they measure your performance on the job?
- What goals are in place that you will be measured against and your performance evaluated?
- What are the most important things you'd like to see someone accomplish in the first 30, 60, and 90 days on the job?
- What are the performance expectations of this position over the first 12 months?
- What is the performance review process here? How often will I be formally reviewed?
- What metrics or goals will my performance be evaluated against?
- How will you judge my success?
- What will have happened six months from now that will demonstrate that I have met your expectations?
- What would success look like?
- What have past employees done to succeed in this position?
- What is the top priority for the person in this position over the next three months?
- What particular achievements would equate to success at this job?
- What are the qualities of successful managers in this company?

Interviewer - That person across from you; he or she is important and they count. You could be the only person who makes them feel that way today; do it.

- How long have you been with the company?
- Has your role changed since you've been here?
- What did you do before this?
- Why did you come to this company?
- What have you like most about working here?
- What do you like about working here?

The company -- Who do you work for? The company. You work for the company, not one boss, one department, but the company.

- I've read about the company's founding, but can you tell me more about the history?
- Where do you see this company in the next few years?
- What can you tell me about your new products or plans for growth?
- What are the current goals that the company is focused on, and how does this team work to support hitting those goals?
- What excites you most about the company's future?
- What do you think distinguishes this company from its competitors, both from a public and employee perspective?
- What is the company's management style?
- Is relocation to another company location a possibility?

The team -- Who will you work with? It can make all the difference in your happiness and job satisfaction.

- Can you tell me about the team I'll be working with?

- Who will I work with most closely?
- Who will I report to directly? Can I meet him or her?
- Who will report to me?
- What are their strengths and the team's biggest challenges?
- Do you expect to hire more people in this department in the next six months?
- Which other departments work most closely with this one?
- How many people work in this office/department?
- What kinds of processes are in place to help me work collaboratively?
- How can I best contribute to the department?

The culture -- What kind of environment is it, what is the ecology? Conservative, wild, competitive, exciting, calm, cut-throat, cooperative? What kind of place are you stepping into, and is it what you will find a rewarding environment

- What is the company and team culture like?
- How would you describe the work environment here, collaborative or more independent?
- Can you tell me about the last team event you did together?
- What's your favorite office tradition?
- What do you and the team usually do for lunch?
- Does anyone on the team get together outside the office?
- Do you ever do companywide events?
- What's different about working here than anywhere else you've worked?
- How has the company changed since you joined?
- How would you describe the company's culture and leadership philosophy?
- Can you give me some examples of the most desirable aspects of the company's culture?

Next Steps -- Make sure you leave no questions about you in the interviewer's mind and that you're clear on the next steps by asking questions.

- How do you see me as a candidate for the job in comparison with an ideal candidate?
- Now that we've talked about my qualifications and the job, do you have any concerns about my being successful in this position?
- Do you have any remaining questions about my qualifications?
- What are the next steps in the interview process?
- Is there anything else I can provide you with that would be helpful?
- Can I answer any final questions for you?
- Would you like a list of references?
- When do you think you will be making a decision?
- When can I expect to hear from you?
- If I am extended a job offer, how soon would you like me to start?
- This job sounds like something I'd really like to do. Do you see a fit here, too?

As always, if there are other questions you want answers to, and they would leave a favorable or at least neutral, impression on the interviewer, add those to your list and your Source File.

It is possible that you might want to ask one of the following questions but don't. They are bad questions. You should have done a little research so you know the answer to some. The others are just questions that annoy or scare interviewers. Don't do it!

Interview questions NOT to ask (These are dumb questions! Yes there really are dumb questions no matter what else you may have heard. This is a JOB interview not a classroom.)

·   What does this company do?
·   What's the company mission statement?
·   If I get the job when can I take time off for vacation?
·   Can I change my schedule if I get the job?
·   Did I get the job?
·   Do you do background checks?
·   Do you monitor e-mail or internet usage.

Do you see why these are dumb questions to ask in an interview? The first two indicate you are clueless about the company, bad start. The next two are presumptions and say to the interviewer "I'm way more important than this job". The fifth doesn't need to be asked, you'll know. The sixth makes the interviewer think you have something to hide and is right up there with "do you do drug testing.". Why would you want an interviewer to be concerned about you? The last implies you will be doing something illegal or illicit or doing something "personal" on company time. Don't create problems for yourself.

When all is said and done, interviews seldom last as long as a movie or TV show. You will not know what the "right" answer is to some of the questions asked, as you will not know what has happened behind the scenes within the company recently. We've covered more than you are likely to have to deal with in order to help you prepare, to survive and thrive in the challenging "Job Interview". There are other things to be aware of in interviews and we cover them in other chapters. Do some research, put some time in, you'll do fine. Good luck to you in your next one.

Chapter 25: Interviews: do's and don'ts

"Whenever you are asked if you can do a job, tell 'em, 'Certainly I can!' Then get busy and find out how to do it." — Theodore Roosevelt (1858-1919) American president, statesman, politician, author, naturalist, explorer, and historian.

"Opportunities don't often come along. So, when they do, you have to grab them." — Audrey Hepburn (1929-1993) British actress.

Let's start with things you should not do before moving on to a well-prepared approach, and follow through to after the interview.

Don't do this!

You wrote a resume that you are comfortable with, sent it along with a cover letter and got a call for an interview.

The day of the interview arrived. You woke up late, so you skipped the shower and shave (a day's growth is so stylish these days anyway isn't it?) so you'd be on time. Can't be late! You tossed on your clothes and took off fast. You got the address right, but were just a few minutes late, as you didn't anticipate the traffic, nor the parking problems. You finished your cigarette on the way in, and tossed it on the ground as you hustled inside.

You got annoyed with the guard because he slowed you down and made you sign in even though you told him who you were there to see, and it was someone way more important than a guard. When you finally got inside and to the interviewers' office you were only ten minutes late. What's 10 minutes after what you went through to get there? "I would've been on time, but that guard slowed me down" is what you told the interviewer when they asked why you were late.

The interviewer began asking you questions. Some of them were just plain annoying. Like why do they need to know why I really left that last job? They act like nobody ever stretched the truth on a resume. I almost graduated from that school. I only had a year left and was close to flunking out, so I took a little break. Still you could've finished, it's not like that last year would have made a big difference, would it?

I told them what I thought of that last boss too. She was always riding my butt, singled me out from day one. I tried to do everything she wanted but some women are just like my mom, never satisfied.

I can do this job, how hard can it be? Okay, I never really did that specific job but it's just working with numbers, right? My friend told me he got a job as a bookkeeper and it's a piece of cake. You just put numbers into the computer and it does the real work.

I probably shouldn't have been on my phone during the interview but I had to follow-up with that text from one of my buds, right? Not like I lost track of what that boring dork was saying. She sure droned on and on and on. I thought she would never finish asking me questions.

When she asked me if I had any questions, I had some for her all right. How much does it pay? When do I get a vacation? When can I start? How long until I'm promoted?

Then I told her that I was pretty sure I was the best candidate they'd get so I look forward to hearing back from them soon, 'cause I want to get started right away. I need the money for a new car and to get outta my parent's house. I'm 29 and still living in their basement and that's getting old.

She thanked me for coming in, of course. I went out whistling a happy tune. I stopped in the john and couldn't believe it when I looked in the mirror: My zipper was all the way down. Oh well, hope she didn't notice. I probably shoulda brushed my teeth. I did have a piece of that breakfast burrito stuck in there. They probably didn't notice that either, they were so focused on that sheet in front of them, with all the questions on it.

I high-fived the guard on the way out, no hard feelings right? Besides I'll be starting soon and he was just doing his job. I lit up again on the way to the car, hopped in and took off, looking good.

So, now it's a few days later, and I wonder why they haven't called? I'll call them next week if I haven't heard by them. Meanwhile, this new videogame is awesome ...

Okay, so nobody is that oblivious in the interview process right?

Do you think people don't arrive late? Lie or stretch the truth on their resumes? Smell of smoke, of all sorts, on the way in? Forget to check their zipper, let alone show up being showered, shaved, and looking sharp? Have a bad attitude throughout the process? Play with their phones during an interview? Be overconfident and under-qualified? Have expectations out of proportion to their worth? Arrogant? Don't follow up properly?

You haven't interviewed people then.

Preparation

There are basically three ways people go into interviews: the wrong way, an okay way or a prepared and dynamic way. What's the difference, aside from preparation and time, and the most favorable of outcomes? Not much.

The wrong way of going into an interview is going in unprepared, poorly prepared, unaware, and unfocused. This is your future, your earnings, your rewards, and you should put as much effort into getting your next most rewarding job as you will in it. An okay way is to have a resume, and just go into interviews with it and a sense of what your skills, etc are and hope they will see something in you that moves them to hire you. The best way, a prepared and dynamic way, is to approach this opportunity with the kind of effort your employer would want to see on the job. It is a competition and to the victor go the spoils.

Interview Process

Let's review the sequence for a standard job interview.

- Identify potential jobs to seek.
- Identify potential employers for those jobs.
- Prepare resume.
- Make contacts designed to get interview
  - job application,
  - informational interview,
  - network,
  - job development
- Get interview
- Conduct interview
- Follow-up
- Get hired
  - job offered
  - job accepted
  - given start date and details.

That is the basic sequence.

Where are you in the process?

Do you have a target job? Have you identified potential employers? if not, you can look elsewhere in this book for ways to develop both of those.

Do you have a resume? Probably. A resume is almost always the first thing we think of when we start a job search, right? Need a job better prepare a resume because everyone wants one. True enough. If you don't happen to have one, there is a chapter in the book about them. But notice that it wasn't the first thing on the list? Why do you suppose that is? It is because you first need to identify what you can and want to do. After that, when you are looking for a particular job at a particular employer you can construct the resume to best represent you for that job and employer.

There is another chapter about resumes in this book but if you have your resume already written, why not write a version for your target market, that is the employer with the job you want?

You possess some characteristics, abilities, interests, values and work style. You have skills, knowledge, education or worker requirements or qualifications. Along with those characteristics, and qualifications, you have experience, training and skills.

How you package yourself in your resume can and should be directed toward your particular job and employer target. You also can put some of what you want to advertise about yourself in a cover letter, so it is not necessary to try to cram it all in on a one page resume.

If you have done your research, you should have a sense of the company values, its culture, its style. You'll know how they see themselves and where they are going, as well as where they are and where they've been. Why not package your resume to match them?

For example, suppose you have a job goal that is found in two different employers. One is an "old" firm in business for over a hundred years. They have and have had a solid business during that time. They are a market leader and innovative in creating new markets. Everybody knows who they are and they are worldwide. They not only have a dominant position in the marketplace they are known for -- a soft drink -- but they are also invested in other markets, like chain restaurants and snack foods. The other potential employer is a new entrant in the market place with one product. This one product is a hit, and it is literally flying off the shelves.

Do you think they are looking for the same type of person to fit into their company and do they offer the same opportunities? Yes and no. It may depend on the particular job as much as "who" the company is and their culture.

You might think of one as more traditional and structured and the other as more flexible and nimble. Consider writing your resume to feature different aspects of you as a worker. For the one you are a team player ready to fit into a position where you can contribute to the continued success of the organization. In the other you are an optimistic, flexible person eager for an exciting career opportunity in a challenging, growing and dynamic company with an opportunity for personal growth.

Another point about resumes before we move on: Be honest. Do not claim education you do not possess. Do not make false claims about your work experience. Don't try to cover gaps in your work history by "adjusting" the dates. It is okay to "round off" dates to the years you worked in a company but you should be prepared to give month and year on any application you complete. Since that is always required, always, you may want to put the month and year on the resume and be prepared to account for those time periods when you may have been unemployed or otherwise out of the work force.

It is permissible to fluff or exaggerate your experiences and put them in their best light, just don't claim you did something when you didn't. You may have been a janitor or a sanitation engineer. You may have been responsible for a million dollar inventory, or an inventory. You may have been a top producing sales executive for a company or simply a sales representative. Just describe what you were, where you were, *in the best way you can present yourself*. Just don't lie about it. If you do, you may still get the job, even if they vet (investigate) you thoroughly. You may not get the job if they do because you lied and were caught. If they are counting on you to deliver what you've promised, and you can't because you lied about your experience it will be to your detriment and your employers. It very often leads to termination.

Do not claim education and training you never received. Sometimes employers fail to follow through and check this information, so you might not get caught. Then again, you might during the the background check process or even after being hired only to be fired because of it.

After you have written a job and employer targeted resume, you then need to get that resume into the right hands. You can hand carry it to the potential employer and ask to complete an application. You can write a cover letter and send it to the right person. You can use your Personal Network to find the right person to send it to. You can make contact by using your Informational Interview skills. You could wait until they post an opening, too.

The best course of action is to place your resume in the hands of someone who can do something with it and about it. If it is in the hands of a person who is in a position to hire you and they suggest that you fill out an application, you have tremendously increased your potential to get the job. They may have created an opening for you or they can direct HR to be sure to include you in the group being interviewed. What a great reference!

Now that your resume is in the hands of someone who can do something about it, and you've completed an application (possibly the day of the interview) it is time for more preparation. You should keep a telephone contact summary by your phone or with you (there is a blank form in your workbook) so that you are prepared for their call.

You have a checklist of things to review before you leave for that interview. You have made yourself interview ready. You will have answers to questions prepared and a list of questions you want to ask. You have your presentation based on your Marketing Plan ready. We cover "Your Marketing Plan" and "Interview Questions" in other chapters.

A Before-you-go Checklist

Appearance
- Hair clean and in place.
- Men facial hair trimmed or shaven?
- Clothes clean, pressed, and job appropriate
- Women: too much cleavage, skirt too short, too much make-up
- Perfume or aftershave - none
- Piercings removed, tattoos covered?
- Teeth, brushed, mouth rinsed
- Smoke (cigar, cigarette, pipe, other) - don't.
- Gum chewing
- Fidgety
- Shoes shined.

A few words about appearance. Consider what people look like where you are applying. If you were applying to work in a motorcycle shop with retail sales and a service, department, you can present yourself differently than you might at a banking facility. In a motorcycle sales and service shop, men with tattoos, beards and long hair are part of the culture and women with tight, revealing clothes, tattoos and piercings will be welcomed. (I know those are also generalizations but as I said, go look.) What both of these businesses will expect is competency and professionalism at work even though the appearance standard is different.

When it comes to scents, no scent is common sense, except for a clean scent. Many people have sensitivities and allergies to colognes and perfumes. In any large group of co-workers, someone is almost guaranteed to have them. To these folks, almost any scent is too much. Some of us seem to have no sense of smell and just dollop on the cologne and perfume. Trust me, the rest of us try not to make fun of you for doing so but we all wish you wouldn't. It might smell great to you, and help mask the way world smells to you, but to us, you are offensive.

One more set of smells not to share with others are those of smoke, of any sort. It may be that you have an addiction to tobacco. Or you just like smoking. That's okay. It is your life, no value judgment about that. However, if you go into an interview smelling of smoke you may find it overwhelms anything and everything else and *can keep you from getting a job*.

Most employers no longer permit smoking on their premises. Some will not hire smokers because of insurance reasons. Some won't like you because it stinks. Don't smoke the day of an interview until the interview is over. If you are like most smokers, that's difficult to do, so go for an early morning appointment if you can. Short of not smoking at all, try having one before you shower and bathe and then wait. If you can't go that long, try standing outside for a good 30 minutes before the interview, spray yourself with a "scent remover" and hope you don't smell too strongly during the interview. Definitely don't have one on the way in.

The exception to the "no scent" rule is the "good scent" rule: shower or bathe, use deodorant, brush your teeth and rinse your mouth. A clean, fresh, soap scent about you is what most of us prefer. You should even consider a mouth freshener to use before you go into the building for that interview. It is good to smell clean.

Gum chewing is a habit and pleasure for many people. Some even use it as a breath freshener. Don't chew gum during an interview, it just sends negative impressions of nervousness (if you chew fast or change your pace when asked certain questions) or docility if you chew slow and steady. Enjoy a stick on the way home but ditch it on the way in (and not under the interviewer's desk).

Try not to fidget even though you may be nervous and eager. Practice at home. Sit straight, cross your legs at the ankle or sit with legs parallel, and fold your hands and rest them in your lap. Sit Up!

Practice interviewing with family, friends, employment professionals. Practice being comfortable while being interviewed. It is a set of skills and you can become better at them, especially if you get feedback. Ask your interview partner to focus on one or two aspects at time, like your appearance and answers to questions.

Actors rehearse their parts before going on-stage, singers and dancers as well. That's why it looks so easy when they do it. They practice until they have it "letter perfect" because they want to give a good performance and their jobs and livelihoods -- and that of the rest of the cast and crew, producers and directors -- depend on it. Aren't you dependent upon a good performance in job interviews?

Details and Additional Preparation:

- Resume
  - Two clean extra copies in a "protected" folder
  - Read and re-read so you know it cold
- Pre-completed generic job application sheet
- Interview details

It is advisable for you to carry two extra copies of your resume with you. One of these is for you to review one last time before the interview. You cannot know if the interviewer may want another one nor if you will need to attach one to a job application that you are asked to complete before an interview. It would seem unusual to have to complete an application for a job that you are being interviewed but it is not. You may be called in based on a cover letter and a resume, that you sent. You could be called in on the strength of a inside reference who alerted Human Resources to bring you in.

If you have to complete a job application on the spot, bring a completed generic one in with you and you can rapidly and accurately complete it. Plus the job application information will match the information on your resume. You have the benefit of not having to rely on your memory for data nor leave sections incomplete because you don't recall or have specific data at your fingertips. Ever try to recall your references' phone numbers of addresses? Or the exact dates you worked somewhere, twelve years ago?

Interview details are the date and time of your appointment, the exact location, and with whom you are meeting. They include directions from your home to the interview site. Not only should you know how to get there but you should know how long it will take to get there and if there are obstructions to work around. If you drive, what will traffic be like? If you are taking a bus, how precise are they in their stops and how long will that take? If you have to rely on others or take a cab, include time for them to pick you up.

Not only should you know the name and title of the person who will interview you but also the name of the person who scheduled the appointment, and the date and time they made it. Sounds silly until you walk into an interview only to find that no one knew you were coming because of an internal error. Things happen, but if you can say you are here because you spoke with Ms. X, or Mr. J on Wednesday July 8 at 10:00 am and they said to be here "to meet with Ms or Mr Big, on July 10, at 11:00 am", the employer will do what they can to rectify the mistake. It may mean they go ahead and interview you (good thing you have the extra resume, huh?) . Maybe they'll find that it was recorded on another day and time and ask that you return then. You should ask if they could interview you now if there was some extra effort for you to come in (like you live 100 or more miles away).

It is also possible that they just didn't mark you down in their records and weren't even going to interview you because of that error. By having sufficient detail to help "jog" their corporate memory, you may save the day and get interviewed (again, nice to have the resume although they should have a record about you somewhere if they intended to interview but lost track of the appointment).

Those are some of the things you should check before you leave for an interview. How about when you get there?

Onsite Checklist Items:

- On the way in
  - Be on time (15 minutes early)
  - Smile
  - Mind your manners
    - Don't sit until invited.
    - Don't remain seated when an interviewer enters the room if they weren't there when you were brought in.
    - Greet everyone with a pleasant greeting.
    - Say please and thank you.
  - Turn off your cell phone before you enter the building (or at least silence it).
  - Calm yourself.
  - Remind yourself to listen and answer the question asked, and to slow down.

Plan to go into the building and be at the interview location 15 minutes early, even if it takes you an extra hour to do it. At a really large industrial facility it might take you 15-30 minutes to find a parking spot, walk to the entrance, be admitted and then walk to the actual interview site. It is usually closer than this but still allow for it.

Don't show up at the interview site or meeting point more than 15 minutes early. For one thing, it will make you look more desperate than eager, and for another there are likely to be other interviewees waiting, especially if the interviewer falls behind. You don't really want to be part of a congested waiting area nor begin to compare yourself to others. Plus it annoys business people who have other jobs besides interviewing, when people arrive too early. That time may be reserved for a quick bathroom break, a coffee break, a quick call, a piece of work to complete, whatever. They tend to see it as disruptive if you are too early, immediately giving you a negative mark and you haven't even been seen!

You will often be made to wait even if you are on time. Some interviewers do it to keep you off balance and to see how you handle it (They may have the secretary or receptionist keep an eye on you to see how you handle it, so handle it with grace, calmness and dignity). Some are just busy and run late. The interviewer before you may be getting extra time because they too are an outstanding candidate and the interviewer wanted a more in-depth interview or the interviewee asked the good questions you should be asking and so they are running late. There is no point in you adding to your wait by being more than 15 minutes early.

If you are more than 15 minutes early, stop at a restroom and check yourself out one more time. No bird splatters to clean up, zippers up and in place, hair and appearance good? If you are so early that a five minute restroom stop won't use up the time, try sitting in your car for a while, bring a book or find something to do that helps keep you calm and centered.

In general, you should smile at everyone you encounter on the way into and then in the interview (not to mention on the way out -- be consistent). These folks may all become your co-workers and you never know whom you may encounter. Some business owners walk around in everyday street clothes and not all "businessed up" (suit clothes). They own the place and don't have to. They like to manage by walking around and some areas will be messy. They also see their informality as a way to be "nearer to" their employees. So that guy that looks like nobody could be the company owner. Smiles are inexpensive, alway wear well and are a sign of happy person (not necessarily true but it is the appearance that counts). Who doesn't want to work with a happy person? There are some jobs where smiling may not be in your best interests, like for a prison guard, so again pay attention to the environment for cues as to whether you should not smile.

Be on your best behavior. Mind your manners, it is a sign of respect. Turn off your cell phone. Get up from your chair when someone enters a room. Do not sit until you are invited to. Use the words "please" and "thank you." These are all simple ways to show respect. You want respect? Why not show some. Not showing respect is a good way to make a unfavorable impression and not get a job.

Making a favorable first impression is very important. That is worth repeating, the first impression you make is very important. If you make a bad or poor first impression, it can be overcome but it takes a lot of work. You do not get a second chance to make a good first impression.

As you walk through the building and into the interview, you are constantly sending a message out to the world about you. You should want that message to say, "I belong here," when you are going to a job interview. You will only have one chance to make a favorable first impression. One chance. Don't squander it. Interviewers do make allowances for people just having one of those days. We've all had them, the ones where it seems like every little thing, and big thing, just goes wrong. So, if you are having one of them, you might share that with the interviewer if your interview is really unlike you. If you are late but are typical punctual, but a truck over-turned on the freeway and it was shut down while you were on it on your way to the interview. Tell them but you probably should have called from your car.

The moment the interviewer sees you they will have conscious and subconscious responses to you. That's part of being human. Based on those response they will react to you. A subconscious response may be based on someone they knew when they were a child and still categorize people as "nice/not nice" based on those experiences. Not much we can do about those kind of instant, reactions.

Within 30 seconds the interviewer will have "taken you in." They will have done a more thorough, though quick, evaluation of you. From your greeting, the warmth and dryness of your extended hand and the firmness of your grip, to the tiny things like waiting for them to sit and appearing calm while waiting for the first question. Everything about you in those first seconds helps form an impression of you in the interviewer's mind.

Try to make those first moments work for you. The first impression is not the "moment" they see you but rather those first few seconds and minutes.

Interview checklist items

- Answer the question asked, and use the rule of 30:60:90.
- Know why you want the job
- Jokes? No jokes. No joking.
- No badmouthing anyone anywhere

- Pre-defined presentation "pitch."
- Have good questions to ask.
- Don't lie or make up answers.
- Don't forget to say "please, and thank you."
- Use a call-back closing.
- Speak with positive body language.

The interview is a structured business meeting, remember? The interviewer has goals, objectives and an agenda. Their goals are to hire the best person by unearthing sufficient information to be used in their decision-making process. They want to explore what you have to offer and mentally compare it to the job's requirements. They want to explore you as a person to see if you will fit in with everyone else (more or less important depending on the job and the company). They want to verify your information across your resume, application and verbally in the interview. They want to see if and how your goals and history line up with the company culture. Their agenda includes finding someone whose hiring will be a plus on their record, not a minus. They will attempt to do this in a 15-30 minute interview. They will plan for longer interviews, but these in-depth interviews are usually second interviews and for specific jobs that require more intensive interview exploration.

Is it often a good sign if your interview extends past 30 minutes and not a good sign if it is no more than 15 minutes unless it is a simple screening interview.

Plan to use the 30:60:90 rule to answer questions. Thirty seconds to answer most questions asked. Sixty seconds for some questions will make sense. Sixty seconds is a long time in an interview but there are times when a question will need a longer answer. If you don't believe it, write out your answer to some, or all to be thoroughly prepared, of the interview questions in the workbook. See how long it takes you to give a good, clear and concise, answer to each question.

TV commercials seldom run more than sixty seconds. If they can sell a car, a credit card, a cell phone, a cell phone carrier, a breakfast, lunch or dinner, a house, an insurance company, well you get the idea, in sixty seconds or less, you should be able to answer a question in that time. If you are bumping into 90 seconds, you might need to work on answering that question before the next time you run into it.

If you find yourself rambling when answering a question, stop yourself as soon as you can and smile and say something like, "That question really got me thinking," then shut up. Some people can talk for hours about nothing. An interview is not that place. It sends a message to an interviewer that you think their time is yours. It demonstrates a lack of understanding of what the interview is and what the interviewer is trying to accomplish. It cuts into the short time you have to actually sell yourself or answer really important questions.

If you wander off topic or give too much information or irrelevant information you may find you've talked yourself out of a job.

At the extreme opposite end of this, is the one or two word answers that some people think are sufficient for any question asked. The interviewer wants and needs you to talk. Life isn't just yes, no, maybe, true or false. Some questions can be answered that way but some that could would be bettered answered with a short statement.

Example:

Interviewer: "It says here (on your resume) that you worked as a sales executive at Bolton Aerodyne."

Interviewee: "Yes" or

Interviewee: "Yes, I worked there seven years, starting as a sales assistant making inside cold calls and working my way up to the midwest territory sales executive."

Which was a better answer to you? This kind of question is often followed up with "Why did you leave there?" or "Why are you leaving them?"

You should have a rational answer for that question and be prepared for it. Look at some of the answers in Chapter 24: Questions and the answers you've developed. This is a good time to interject why you want to join their company and using your "pitch" can come in handy. You can reveal that you know why you are applying for this job at this company because it represents the next logical step in your career plan while what you bring to the table dynamically fits their needs and why you are right for the job. All that instead a simple, "I got laid off" or any other negative reason. Even a simple "I am leaving there because I would like to work here", can be used.

If you find yourself really comfortable with the interviewer, maybe they said something funny, and the rapport between you seems great. Resist the temptation to tell that joke you heard last night, or that favorite one you tell your friends, or the sure-fire ice-breaker. There is no time to waste in an interview doing stand-up comedy, unless you are applying for a job as a stand-up comedian or comic. It wastes precious time. It might be misconstrued or properly construed but offensive to the interviewer. Just. Don't. Do. It.

That bad boss you had or that terrible company you got out of, before you went postal, and they really were the worst boss ever or the most malicious employers who violated every rule of decency along with as many laws as they could? No matter how real those things are and were, this is not the place to set that baggage down. It's not a counseling session.

The interviewer won't know how much is truth and how much isn't. Truth is sometimes different between parties and generally lies somewhere in-between, hence the reason for courts, lawyers and resolution programs. Truth and facts aren't always the same thing, and "facts" aren't always what they seem to be. A tactful interviewer might try to explore distasteful information with you, but is more likely to see this as an attitudinal problem that you have. How unjust.

It is likely that the interviewer will think, "If that's what they say about SmedCo (or your ex-boss) what will he say about us, if and when he leaves?" You may be the kindest, "hard-working-est", most talented contributor, best employee ever and who really did have a dreadful boss or employer. Keep it to yourself. It may be that you have nothing but good things to say about every other boss and every other job. Say those things. Just don't "dis," disrespect or bad-mouth the bad ones. It is possible, not likely though, but just maybe possible, that you were in the wrong, too. Not much of a chance, but you should allow for it. The smart money is on keeping the bad to yourself.

"If you can't say something nice, don't say anything at all".

Uh-oh, you just got a question that you don't have a good answer for and didn't see coming, now what? Lie? Make up an answer? You could but it wouldn't be smart. Make sure you understand the question, sometimes if you ask the interviewer to clarify the question you will find that the re-phrased version is one you are prepared for, you just didn't recognize it.

Sometimes though, you just won't have a good answer. Perhaps they ask you to explain why it took six years to get your undergraduate degree or why there was a one-year gap in your work history. You should have anticipated those questions but if you hadn't, what should you say.

Don't lie and say something like, "I joined the Peace Corps," when what you did was just enjoy campus life a little too much. Or try to conceal that you were incarcerated for a felony conviction. On the other hand, you can try to put as positive spin on your answer as you can.

"It took me six years to earn my undergraduate degree because I really enjoyed campus life and learning and I changed major twice before completing my studies. I did support myself during that time period, too and that sometimes got in the way of having a full time class schedule as work and school schedules conflicted. I was a bit immature and uncertain about what I wanted. It took me longer to grow up."

"I made a bad decision back then and had to deal with it." (If you had a jail sentence for a felony for example).

During the interview, speak to the interviewer with positive body language and attitude. What's positive body language and attitude? Open, warm, friendly, confident, and positive.

Maintain good posture, not necessarily ramrod straight in the chair but upright, and open, in other words don't cross your arms or fold them across your chest. Be open, shoulders down and back. Positive expression on your face. Nice clear voice when speaking. No defensiveness. No arguing with the interviewer. No sighs, or eye rolling, or "tsk-ing," head shaking. Don't say or imply that a question you were just asked was stupid. Maybe it was or even illegal, but how you handle it may be what the interviewer is looking for. Maybe they meant to ask an illegal question and want to hear your answer. Read the Interview Questions chapter for insights before your next interview.

Before the interview is concluded, you will be almost asked, "Do you have any questions for me?" You better have some questions prepared. Have a "go-to" list of up to 5-6 questions and a few specific questions for the interviewer. These questions should all be selected by you to help you decide if you want to work for this employer and do this job. See the Interview Questions Chapter for some examples.

What you do not want to ask is a "dumb" interviewee question. Yes, there really are dumb questions, despite the platitude, "there are no dumb questions except the ones not asked." This does not, repeat, does not apply to interviews.

Do not ask "What does the job pay?", "When do I get a vacation?", "What are the benefits that go with this job?" and "What days do we get off?."

Finally, you reach the end of the interview. The interviewer stands up and that's a cue that let's you know you're at the end. You should say something like, "I really want to thank you for the opportunity to interview with you today Ms. or Mr. J. I really think working for LandMore Marketing as a customer service representative would be an excellent career step for me and that I would be an asset to the company. When do you plan to make your hiring decision? May I call you back then?"

The truth is, interviewers mostly don't want to have you call them back. If you got the job, they'll call you. If you didn't, well it makes them uncomfortable to know that you'll be calling them back. They'll probably suggest you not do that. But they'll remember you might and there could be the tiniest bit of a push for them to pick you instead of one other final choice.

After the interview checklist:

- Be polite and friendly with everyone on the way out.
- When you get home, review your performance.
- Prepare your thank you letter and send it out that day or the next.

Be polite and friendly with everyone on the way out. You still may be being evaluated for consistency.

When you get home, review your performance. Make notes about how it went. Were there questions you didn't anticipate? Answers you gave that you didn't like? What could you have done better. It is pretty commonplace to have more than one interview with more than one employer when seeking a new job. Why not learn from your own experience? You can take these notes to a professional Career Development Facilitator for their insights and input.

Prepare your thank you letter and send it out that day or the next. In the letter try to say a bit more than the usual "thank you for meeting me on July 8th. I look forward to the opportunity to join your winning team." Perhaps you learned something about the company from the interviewer and could mention it, like "I didn't realize how much the company gives back to the community until we discussed MedRed's Community Commitment Program that you head. I was very impressed by that." Or "I didn't know that LandMore Marketing had such an extensive commitment to its employees until you told me about the Employee Childcare Program. Thank you for telling me about it."

On the day their decision is anticipated, call and ask if you can speak to the interviewer. Ask if they have made their decision. It you weren't called, it may be bad news. Even if you weren't the person chosen, make sure that they are aware of your interest in their company and your availability for that job or any similar position that might open up. You may have been the runner-up to an internal candidate who gets first shot at the job, and they may not work out. If they did move into it, they moved out of a job and perhaps you can fill that one. Ask about the job they vacated and when they will be hiring for it.

If you weren't chosen, remember everyone doesn't work out in every job and they employer ma be looking again in 1-2 months. They might get other openings too. You want them to feel your positive acceptance to a disappointment. That is one more way you can make a positive impression.

This is also a good time to ask if there are any other openings now or if they anticipate any other openings to develop in the near future. Then pitch your open-mindedness about other jobs in a company for which you would like to work.

Tests

One more set of things happen as part of the interviewing and screening process: tests. You may be given an aptitude tests. You may be given a personality test. You may be told to go somewhere for a physical or a drug test.

Test of one sort or anther are part of the hiring process, so be open to taking them and prepared to pass or fail. There isn't much you can do to prepare for the aptitude and personality tests. You just take them. Though sometimes you can "psych" them out and try to answer the way you think a successful employee should answer them. Consider though whether you want the job if you cannot be yourself and instead have to conform to a standard you are not comfortable with. As far as the drug tests are concerned, if you can't pass one, maybe you need to do something about that while you are looking for work. Not judging you, just sayin'.

Chapter 26: Networking

"Sometimes, idealistic people are put off the whole business of networking as something tainted by flattery and the pursuit of selfish advantage. But virtue in obscurity is rewarded only in Heaven. To succeed in this world you have to be known to people." — Sonia Sotomayor (1954-) Supreme Court Justice.

"Social networking helps reach people easier and quicker." — Bill Cosby (1937-) American comedian, actor, author, television producer, educator, musician and activist.

"You can make more friends in two months by becoming interested in other people than you can in two years by trying to get other people interested in you." — Dale Carnegie (1888-1955) American writer and lecturer.

Background:

What is networking? Everybody talks about it these days, especially "social networking" with LinkedIn and Facebook and similar online social networks available to everyone.

What is it? It is a means of being connected to other people. Who are you connected to? Who do you know? Who knows the people you know and who do they know? How do you locate your network? You look to your resources.

Start with your address book, the good old-fashioned paper kind or the modern electronic kind, that have names and phone numbers in it. That is your starting network of contacts available to you. If you have some old address books to go back to, you can dig up more people that you can still reach.

Do you have a collection of business cards you've received? Maybe just bound with rubber bands stashed in a drawer or your wallet or purse or neatly put into a book? One way or another they have done business with you and they are more contacts in your network that you can use. They are business cards aren't they?

Your relatives, your friends, members of clubs and associations you belong to or you once have belonged to are part of your network. People who know you from school, church, civic, and business organizations, are all part of your network.

Thinking bigger than that and by joining one of the online social networks, you are literally connected to thousand and then millions of people; in theory, everyone on earth.

Your network's starting point, though, is everyone you've ever been in contact with and could contact again.

Deep Background:

A degree of separation is a link between any two people - you and a friend for example, are two links in a short chain. Two degrees of separation are two links apart. All of the people any friend of yours is friends with, that aren't directly known or linked to you, are at two degrees of separation. Three degrees are three links between you, your friend, and their friends' friends. So think of each link as a "friend of a friend."

In 1929 an Hungarian author, Frigyes Karinthy, wrote a short story entitled, "Chain-Links," in which a group of friends create a game where it is suggested that any person picked at random, anywhere on earth, could be contacted through a friendship network and that the most direct set of person to person, or friend to friend links would only be at six links or degrees of separation.

A game, "The Six Degrees of Kevin Bacon" is based on Karinthy's theory. The website LinkedIn (LinkedIn.org), a professional networking site, applies the theory as way professionals can make contact with one another. This is useful if you are trying to make contact with someone in a specific organization. Suppose you want to do an Informational Interview with someone in a nearby company or one much farther away, like across the country or overseas. You may only need to turn to your "LinkedIn" network to make such a contact.

Unfortunately, not all of us would really be considered "professionals" nor would we use or care to join LinkedIn. What if you are a baker, a side order cook, a skilled trades worker or physical laborer? You might not join LinkedIn. You might sign up for Facebook though and connect through that network.

Does it really matter if we are all within "Six Degrees of Separation," whether from Kevin Bacon or anyone else? Not really. For one thing, there are people who live in remote places, deep in jungles, out in the wilderness or at the edges of civilization. They might not be possible to reach, but then again, if you are looking for your next most rewarding job or building a career, why would you need to? Unless that job is writing about, photographing, doing scientific research, out in those remote areas.

What is more important is that you be aware of Your Network and then have some idea of how to tap into it.

Notice that people in your network are not the same as "references," those folks listed on your resume. They are most assuredly in your network, but there is the added notion that these "references" will vouch for you. Not everyone in your network can or would be appropriate to use in that manner.

However, they can vouch for you enough to let you talk to or connect with someone in their network. That is what and how you can utilize people in Your Network.

Suppose you want to make contact with someone inside a hospital, a manufacturing plant, or a warehouse company and that you do not know anyone in that company at this time. One way you could try to make that contact is to call each person, one at a time, in your phone directory, and ask them if they know of someone in that place. If they do, ask if they would put you in touch with that person. Then ask them if they would contact anyone they know who might know someone inside, for you too.

Obviously if you know someone working in one of those places, you could just ask them. Your doctor might be a contact for a hospital for example. Your cousin who works for a manufacturer would be an inside contact there.

There are problems with this phone networking approach. It is tedious. You will use valuable time just making "networking" phone calls. Depending on what you are saying or asking for, you then have to rely upon them following up and making calls too. That isn't going to happen. Some people will make calls on your behalf, but how many really will? The plus side of it is that it should be nice to speak with people you know. Don't forget to be sociable while making these calls.

Still, it does work.

A Missing Piece

There are jobs that never get posted, listed, or advertised and yet get filled. How does this happen? Networking.

When there are job openings, people know about them. They don't occur in a vacuum. As soon as the grapevine hears about an opening, word goes out. If someone "knows someone" that is looking for a job, the word will go out, "tell them to get in here and apply on Monday at 8:00 am" or "bring your resume to me today or tomorrow." Often the next thing that happens is they get the job. They have the skill set necessary and get hired without most job hunters even aware the opening existed.

The Telephone Approach

The key to the telephone approach is to know who you are and what you want or are looking for. Use this script as a basis to develop your own:

"Hi, this is (your name), remember me? (Wait for their response or remind them of who you are)

Have you got a minute to talk? (If they don't, ask when a good time to call would be.)

Good, here's why I'm calling. I am looking for a job as a chief executive officer (or dishwasher, insurance salesperson, photographer, or whatever your job goal is). Do you know of any openings for one? (Wait for their response. If they do, follow up on it immediately after you complete this call.)

If they do not know of any openings, ask if they know of any openings for someone with your skills (then state your top three, the three you would like to use in your next job) or similar jobs. (If they do, follow up on it immediately after you complete this call.)

If they do not know of any openings, ask if they know of anyone else who might be able to assist you in finding similar openings.

Be sure:
- to ask if you have their okay to use their name as you follow up on any contacts they give you
- to get the names and phone numbers of anyone they refer you to.
- to thank them for their time.
- to ask them to let you know if they hear of any openings similar to those you asked about.
- to give them your phone number.

This method does work. Practice it with family members or close friends first. Get your own comfortable approach, your own script worked out. Plan on spending a few hours each week using this approach. You should create your own based on finding a contact inside a particular company.

The eMail Approach

You may be better off writing an email and sending it to everyone in your email directory. It is fast, it is easy and your contacts are likely to forward your email to friends and contacts of theirs. Still, you will not get 100% cooperation from everyone. If you get creative with your email and can offer something to those who do, or for the one who gets you that contact, your odds of cooperation increase.

Example 1:

"Hello World, this is an email from me, (your name here). I am looking for a job as an executive chef (or your job choice). Do you know of any openings for one or a similar job? Do you know of someone else who might? Would you let me know who I should contact and their phone number? May I use your name when I make the contact? I will do the same for you any time in the future. Thank you so very much."

Example 2:

"Hello World, this is an email from me, (your name here). I am looking for a job using my skills and experience as a data analyst and accountant. Do you know of any openings for one using those or similar skills? Do you have questions about those skills?

Do you know of someone else who might know of any similar openings? If you do, would you let me know who I should contact and their phone number? May I use your name when I make the contact? I will do the same for you any time in the future. Thank you so very much."

Example 3:

"Hello World, this is an email from me, (your name here). I would like to contact someone, anyone who works for XCorp or their suppliers or customers. If you do, would you please contact me at: (your email address here)? it is really important to me and I can only offer you my thanks and appreciation for you helping me this way. If I can ever be of help to you, please let me know. If you do not know anyone at XCorp or their suppliers or customers, would you send this email to people in your directory? I will be glad to do this for you any time in the future. Thank you so very much."

Now, any of those, or a better one that you create, may not get you that sought after contact but it isn't going to take more than a few minutes of your time to find out. You could even try to do this to see if you can contact someone you've always wanted to meet.

When you develop a contact through your network, you have the added advantage of now coming in with a "reference", a "friend-of-a-friend". You have been recommended by someone and that provides extra social value. Who doesn't want to help a friend or friend-of-a-friend? You may be in a position to return that favor someday after all.

Alternative Approaches

There are other ways of developing a contact in a company instead of using your network. Try reading about the company in a business newspaper, likes Crain's Detroit (Business) or through online research into the company. Look for news or press releases for the names of people who work there. Once you have their names, and titles if you can get them, and locations, use your phone and make a call. Write a letter to them. Ask if you can meet them. This is a more direct way to approach those companies and more likely to get you in the door.

One more networking approach is to find their network. Look for trade papers, journals, magazines, newsletters, and dig in. Go to the library and get help identifying what organizations that company might belong to. Often, the organizations and trade papers post job openings or leads for members. Are you a member of one of those organizations? If you were a member could it help you got a job in the industry. Look into industrywide organizations, statewide, and nationwide. One way to unearth them is to google/bing something like "state mental health associations," or "state mental health board associations" or "state mental health professional associations." Look at the top 10-20 results you get and search for the one that actually has job postings and follow-up with them or try to arrange an Informational Interview.

Part 6: Survival

"It is not the strongest or the most intelligent who will survive but those who can best manage change." — Charles Darwin (1809-1882) English naturalist and geologist.

"Survival can be summed up in three words -- never give up. That's the heart of it really. Just keep trying." — Bear Grylls (1974-) British adventurer, writer and TV presenter.

This book is about survival in a modern world. It is not just about survival, but how you can thrive in your future. So, don't just survive, thrive. Don't settle for less!

There have been times in America's past when unemployment reached 50 percent and more. The breadlines of the Great Depression of the 1930s have given way to the War on Poverty and Bridgecards. But poverty still exists. It is still possible for a job seeker to go more than a year without a job in America.

Depressions and recessions. Global economies. The rise of China as a major economic powerhouse. Computerization. Robotics. All of these things lead to uncertainty and instability for the American worker.

When you look around you, do you see others as competitors? For the last 30 years, at least, schools have trended toward making children grow up thinking competition is "evil" and something to be frowned upon and not healthy.

Here is a cold, hard reality, *everyone is not a winner*. That is simply not true. Substitute the notion that "everyone is a winner" for "competition strengthens". Here in America we work from the premise that all people are created equal. We have enacted legislation to provide for equal opportunity free from prejudice. Somewhere along the way the notion that competition is not a good thing got mixed in. That is unfortunate because there are "natural laws" that tell otherwise.

The first law of nature is "eat or be eaten." The second is "only the strong survive." We humans thrive on competition, it makes us stronger, faster, smarter, quicker. As a species, we are at the top of the food chain because we are so competitive. You should want to be "King of the Hill", to be the king of your hill, king of your castle (or queen, or any pc way you want to look at it).

Our nation grew and flourished based on competition in industry and labor. Along with that we have worked toward equal opportunity, giving everyone a fair chance to "pursue life, liberty and happiness."

Take another look around you at others in the work place. Look at those seeking employment. Look even at those who have given up trying to find a job. Look at those nations, and businesses who are trying to take your work away, away from your company, your community, from you. The competition for resources, for money, for food, is fierce.

Your survival depends upon you giving yourself as much opportunity to thrive as you can. You have to realize that those others applicants and job seekers have as much right to that job and that work as you do. Only one of you will get it. Will it be you?

Will you grab a seat when the music stops? Will you be able to move from job to job if and when you need or want? Will you work up to your potential? Will you enhance your value in the market place by knowing it? Will you see to it that your spouse, your children have more of everything they need to be prepared for their future?

If you work for food, literally for a bag of groceries, who do you want to have those groceries? Who do you want to see eat? You and your family? Your neighbor and his? A stranger and his family? I hope you answer, those are my groceries, they belong to me and mine. If you don't hunger for them, someone else does.

It will take effort. Do not think for a minute that your survival is not dependent on you being as competitive as you can be. You can have a better future. You can do better than settling for what comes along. What if nothing comes along? Will you be one of those who just gives up? Not if you take action. Use as much of the material in this book as you can, and other books too, and work for your own best future.

Winner or loser, the choice is yours!

Chapter 27: Job Loss & Grief

"In three words I can sum up everything I've learned about life: it goes on." — Robert Frost, (1874-1963) American Poet.

"You must make a decision that you are going to move on. It won't happen automatically. You will have to rise up and say, 'I don't care how hard this is, I don't care how disappointed I am, I'm not going to let this get the best of me. I'm moving on with my life." — Joel Osteen, (1963 -) American Preacher, minister, author of "Your Best Life Now: 7 Steps to Living at Your Full Potential"

"Recession is when a neighbor loses his job. Depression is when you lose yours." — Ronald Reagan (1911-2004) American President, actor.

"Grief is the price we pay for love." — Queen Elizabeth II (1926-) Queen, British monarch.

"Grief is in two parts. The first is loss. The second is the remaking of life." — Anne Roiphe (1935-) American journalist and writer.

You lost your job.

How does it feel? It hurts right? Whatever the reason, it's hard to not take it personally. It was your job and now you've lost it. It's gone. For good.

How'd it happen? Were you laid off alone or with dozens or even hundreds of others in a plant closing? Maybe you were the only one let go because you had committed one too many an infraction on the job. Perhaps you were part of group let go after a merger. It could be that your employer lost funding for your socially important project and so *your* department was shut down. Did you tell the boss off after not getting a raise or promotion or some workplace injustice? Quit, fired, terminated, laid off, down-sized, riffed. There are many ways to lose a job. How did you lose yours?

Whatever the cause, the reality is that it's gone. You're unemployed. Yesterday you had a job, today you don't.

How's that feel? What are you feeling, not just thinking, but feeling? Write those things down.

A little numb? Shocked? Stunned? How could it happen? After all those years you worked there. Every day, rain, snow, sleet, ice storms, heat and humidity, every day you were there, on time. All those years of loyalty, gone.

It wasn't just the paycheck either. Heck, you liked that job. It might not have been the best one anyone ever had but it was your job. Banker, accountant, line worker, machinist, nurse, teacher, unskilled laborer, or highly skilled technician. You were needed and they could depend on you, right? They did, too, didn't they?

Gone, like you didn't even matter. Nobody offered to negotiate anything with you; you would've taken a pay cut to keep your job. Your best friend Ralph got the ax, too. What's he going to do? He's got five kids, the oldest in college, the youngest in fourth grade. It's all either of you have done since you started there -- 20 years ago for you and 22 for Ralph. Probably won't see him again; you live on opposite sides of the county but you sure had some good times on the job, didn't you? Betting sports, talkin' politics and world affairs. Not that anyone was as close to you and knew what you went through better than Ralph. You shared your jobs and your sorrows. You were there for him when he lost his mom to cancer and he was there for you when your brother died from it.

How about the others at work? There were Janet, and Jessie, Bob, Mike, Laura, Leo and the others you hung out with at lunch. Gonna miss that gang. You got awards for the quality of your work, and made the company some extra money from your ideas.

Don't even mention the overtime that always came in handy, but between the ten hour days plus eight on Saturday, that was a big piece of your life. Built a nice home for the wife and kids. It ain't right. Dang it. They just shut the whole place down and kicked you out like you were nobody just so they could move the work overseas and save money.

Maybe you were one of the ones who got cut in a "trimming the fat" movement at work. You knew that bringing around that "efficiency expert" meant someone was going to lose their job. Hard to believe they picked you, though. There was a Reduction In Force (RIF) and you got "riffed"

You worked your butt off for them. Okay, so maybe you weren't the swiftest guy in the parts department but you knew parts and the inventory like the back of your hand and you always took care of the customers didn't you?

Or, yesterday was the last straw. You watched the boss' girlfriend do it for the last time. She showed up late, again, and went right into his office like she owned the place. She struts out and ten minutes later he comes out and tells you, you've got to take on some more of her work. What's left for her to do? You're already doing most of her job. So you sit and stew awhile and then get up and march in there and tell him off. You tell him what you think of how he treats his employees and that "girlfriend" of his. You even threaten to tell his wife. Next thing you know, you're being escorted out with "you're fired" ringing in your ears.

Though maybe you're the one they always counted on to ...

... whatever. Now you're out on the street.

Grieving a Loss

For every job loss there is a story though the stories are not the same. The sudden end, even when you knew it was coming, is a shock and the loss is felt. The feelings you go through are real and painful.

It is more common to think of grief and grieving as something we go through when someone dies, especially when that someone is close to us or important to us in some way. We tend to first feel stunned at the news and then react in disbelief, denial.

"I hate to tell you this but Joe just passed away." "No," is your first response, "I don't believe it. I just saw him an hour ago (or yesterday or last week)". Then it hits you and you just feel shocked and stunned, your emotions seem lost to you, you don't know what you're feeling. It hurts though. The pain sweeps over you.

"How'd it happen?" you ask. You start thinking about how it happened and what could've been done to prevent it. You think, "If only I'd have ..." or if he'd "gone to the doctor" or "if he'd turned right instead of left." You get angry. Angry with him for not taking better care of himself. Angry with the doctors for not diagnosing him quickly enough or for providing the wrong treatment and delaying the right treatment for too long. Angry with him for not telling you and not giving you a last chance to talk with him.

Gradually though, you come to accept it, and then prepare yourself for the follow through. Visitation at the funeral home, then the funeral. The group of friends and relatives gathered to pay their respects and share their grief. You share memories and try to be of comfort to each other, to those closest to him. The burial and the wake afterward to celebrate his life and begin the moving on process. Dealing with the grief and getting on with life.

We go through similar feelings at times of calamities too. A tornado rips through your town and your house is destroyed along with those of your neighbors. A "never-ending" rainstorm that causes a river to overflow its banks and your town is washed away. A nearby forest burst into flames, threatens and then consumes thousands of acres, including your home.

On a more personal level, maybe your home is lost to a gas explosion but no one was hurt. Your brand new car is hit by an inattentive driver, more intent on their darned cellphone and texting than on driving a two-ton truck. Wham, totaled.

At first we are shocked and stunned. Then we get angry and vent. Gradually we take care of our business, accept the events for what they are. We grieve, begin to accept and then move on. Not all at once.

We feel the pain over again when we think about it, as we inevitably do. As time goes by, we cope with it better, hurt a little less, and heal as best we can.

Grieving A Lost Job

We don't often think about "grieving" for a lost job. In some ways, it is more difficult to cope with than the loss of a loved one or something of material value. We invest ourselves and our time in our jobs. They occupy such a large part of our lives, that the loss is often devastating.

We don't have support groups to help us deal with it. We don't have funerals for lost jobs. Friends and families don't rush to us in our hour of need and crisis, to lend us support. We have no ritual of support for sharing the pain of the loss.

More often it is the case that we hear platitudes such as "you'll get another one, don't worry" or "you'll do better with the next one" or even "suck it up, man up and get over it." Not a lot of sympathy out there for the folks who lose a job, is there? It's almost as though you were careless and somehow misplaced it or lost it somewhere. It does seem to get trivialized by others around us.

What happens when you do want to talk about it? When you want to talk about how you feel about losing your job? People don't want to hear it, do they? They let you "whine and cry" about it a little while. They let you "vent" but then they want you to "shut up about it already" and "get over it" and tell you "everything happens for a reason."

Almost from the moment of the loss, the thoughts start flooding in.

What are you going to do? Yeah, you can get unemployment, but you might have a waiting period because of how you were terminated. Doesn't matter though, it isn't enough, it will barely cover the bills, how you gonna eat? The kids go back to school in a month, and now you won't have enough for new clothes for them. You'll find a way though.

It's almost Christmas, you're still looking, six months later, and it is looking bleak this year. Now it's the middle of winter and you are having trouble keeping heat and lights on. How long since you've had a job? When will you get another?

You're angry, hurt, frustrated, worried.

Anatomy of Job Loss Grief

Let's talk about it. Let's see what is going on with you. Let's talk about what you're feeling inside. Then how to accept it and use it to turn your life around. How to use it to motivate you and get moving again.

Why does losing a job hurt so much? You lost you livelihood, your income and the source of your benefits. The more you liked your job, the more it hurts and the more frightening the thought of maybe never having one that good again becomes.

A large portion of your life is dedicated to your job. There are 168 hours in a calendar week. In a typical, eight hour a day, five day a week job, we actually spend not just 40 hours at work but an additional 2-5 hours at lunch per week, usually with colleagues. That doesn't include the time spent before work and the water cooler time we spend socializing, sharing our lives, stories and mutual interests. Our job is a big part of our social life.

We will spend another 7 - 10 hours going to and from work each week. Another 7 hours getting ready for work each week. Conservatively we spend another 16 to 22 hours in work related activities, for a total of 56 to 62 hours in work and work related activities *each week*. That's the equivalent of all day Monday, Tuesday and some big chunk of Wednesday, all on work. And many jobs and occupations require far more than 40 hours a week.

Thirty-five percent and more of our lives are spent at work or on work related activity. Many of us spend even more time that way what with overtime, Saturday or Sunday work, and longer commutes. Still at 35 percent we are spending more than one-third of our life on work. One-third!

That's a lot of time suddenly on your hands.

So what else did you lose? How about your identity? You used to be Somebody. When someone asked, "What do you do (for a living)?" you answered "I'm a reporter for the Daily Times." Or if they asked, "Where do you work?, you said, "at So-AndSo (insert name of your former employer here)." Was that TWA, PanAm, Gateway Computer, Packard, Mercury, Pontiac, Farmer Jack, Hudsons, Marshall Fields? Those names provided identity.

People knew something about you immediately. Now, who are you? Just an unemployed person. You hang your head down a little when you say it, when being asked, don't you? They treat you like you've got something contagious, don't they, or does it just seem that way?

Part of that identity was that you belonged to something, something identifiable. Your membership in that employer group told people something about you. Now that you've been kicked out of your group, you may be feeling isolated and shamed. by the loss. "It's a shame, ain't it?"

Not only that, but you lost your social support group. Those people you talked with every day, who you listened to and who listened to you. Maybe it was at the water-cooler or coffee pot, or lunch or at breaks. You cared about them.They cared about you. What you did, how the family is, where you're going for vacation, the gossip, the joys and sorrows of your lives. They were like family to you and now they're gone. The very people you'd like to share your burden and grieve with you over your job loss, are out of your life. Sure, some of them may be out on the street too and if you get together you can commiserate about your misfortunes but you probably won't even be looking for them or them for you. Others are still working and won't have much time for you. They may be too embarrassed to even want to talk with you anymore, or it seems like it.

You lost the personal meaning of your work life and what you do in it. Was it a great and important job, like being the Wizard in Oz? Was it something small and humble like a housekeeper in a nursing home? No matter, it was important because they paid you and you did it, with pride too. It gave your life meaning. It was your means of being productive. On your job you solved problems or helped people or built things, or maybe put in a transmission. You helped others. It was what you did. And now you don't. You were part of a team and now you are not.

How about the lost opportunities for more training, awards, and recognition for what you did?

How about all the things associated with your success as an employee? The things you bought or were buying? The recognition and esteem of others? What about your social standing? Your pride as someone who earns and pays their own way?

That is a lot of "loss" isn't it? You might think society recognizing the need to help people cope with that much of a loss would have support groups for the unemployed but it seems to be a need that is over-looked.

There are job clubs and programs that will help you recover, by helping you find your next job, but there are very few support groups to help you heal, to deal with and accept your grief and make it easier to move on. It is difficult for many of us to cope with that loss, and we seem almost ashamed to admit we are unemployed and that we have "feelings" about it. Yet it is almost a certainty that each of us will someday lose a job. That is the way of today's world. Jobs come and go.

By all means, you should use every tool and service available to you to get working again, but there are things you can and should do as part of dealing with the feelings of losing a job, and the vast emptiness and negativity that accompany it.

Coping With Job Loss

The very first thing you should do is simply accept the fact that you are unemployed. It means swallowing your anger, frustration, depression, even despondency and then saying to yourself, "Yeah, so what? It is what it is, despite whatever else I might want it to be." It isn't likely to be fair but then you won't be the only person to whom something unfair has happened. If you haven't heard, life is grossly unfair.

Remind yourself that whatever else happens, you are now working on the next chapter in your life. You can choose to let your self-pity immobilize you but that does not lead to resolving anything. You can be caught up in the anger but that won't resolve anything either.

You will pass through the grief stages to acceptance and move on with your life. It may happen faster than from catastrophic losses, faster than the loss of someone near and dear to you. It is tragic, hurts and it *is* personal. You may have to work even harder to overcome it. The pain may go on for years but with time it will subside.

There *is* hope. You have an opportunity in front of you. You can pick a new direction for yourself, not that you may have wanted that choice. That opportunity can be in the form of an even better job than the one you had. It happens. It really does. You can do things that improve the chances of that happening. You can replace a lot of what you lost when you lost your job because it wasn't just the money.

If you do things to replace some of what you lost, you will feel better about yourself, even feel good again. You can do that even before you get your next rewarding job.

Give yourself a little time, a week or two, to sort things out and to heal. You need to apply for unemployment, work through your budget. Don't forget to pamper yourself a little, be nice to you. It may not be easy, but then what is? Life is filled with upsets, and events that go against us. It's at times of adversity that we build character and become better, stronger people.

Here is a summary of what is lost when you lose a job:
• Money and the things money can buy or pay for
• Socialization and belonging
• Identity
• Utility or purpose
• Time-bound activities
• Self-esteem and the esteem of others
• Health
    • Physical
    • Emotional
    • Mental

Now, what can you do about them?

Take Action

You can work on your budget and start to cut out the extravagances, the excess. Businesses call this trimming the fat. (Were you part of the fat that got trimmed? Isn't that annoying?) You may be able to re-arrange some of your debt. Review your resources and prepare yourself for life on a lean budget until you get your next job and back on your feet again.

You should working on a plan. What are the first things you could and should do?

Clearly, getting another job is going to be at or near the top of your list. Realistically, how many hours a week are you going to spend working on it? You spent 60 hours a week on work related activities when you worked. Will you spend that much on job seeking? Probably not, though you could.

Why not plan to invest half of that on finding your future, your next most rewarding job, building your career? That's only thirty (30) hours a week. More would be better -- and depending on your circumstances and motivation maybe you will. There is enough material in this book to give you ample resources for things to do. From meeting with the local Workforce Investment Act facility to engaging in your own work research using O*NET and DoL, to preparing resumes, cover letters, a source file, thank you letters, and doing informational interviews, you can put in a lot of time. Once your job hunt is in full swing, you will be busy.

In the meantime, you need to feel productive and useful. One way is with your job seeking efforts. Another is doing things that you had put off because you didn't have the time. Another important way is by volunteering.

When you volunteer, you get the immediate benefit of being of value to someone. Help a child or a senior and see the thanks in their eyes. Visit and read to children in a hospital, or talk with a wounded veteran in a VA hospital, and let him or her know the gratitude of all of us for his or her sacrifice.

Doing things like this will reward you and make you feel useful because you are. Plan on using four hours or more of those "extra" hours you now have each week. You might even keep it up after you get working again.

Volunteering is a great way to learn new skills or use the ones you have to the benefit of others, serving them and their need. It will help you forget your troubles and help you put them into perspective.

Being a volunteer sends a very powerful message to interviewers. When you are being interviewed, if you can state that while you were off, you did volunteer work. It shows motivation, and a social conscience. If the interviewer also volunteers with the same volunteer organization or another, and many do, it will be a big plus for you. On the job as a volunteer, you will make contacts with people who become part of your network. Sometimes they are people who are in a position to create jobs or hire others. Many corporations sponsor volunteer programs as a way to give back to their community and expect employees to participate. You would not be the first person to find themselves working next to a vice-president in a company you might want to work in.

Get out and spend time in recreational activities. It is one way you can refill some of the lost socialization. Go to the local recreation center or community center and join in. There is always room for another person. Maybe you can teach something, maybe learn something, maybe just play. It is good for your mind, body and spirit.

Plan to work on yourself physically. Why not take a one-hour walk each day? Is that too far to start? How about a half-hour and build up to an hour. It's hard to find time to do this when you are working but you have the time now and the benefits are tremendous. You not only find you improve your physical health but as you get in tune with nature, you'll find you adjust to the seasons and the weather better. You'll notice sights and sounds you'd long since stopped seeing and hearing. The pace of walking is natural and relaxing. You may make acquaintances with others who are out doing the same thing. This will make you feel like you belong and are part of the community because you are! It re-unites you with your community.

As you spend a portion of your time on developing your job future, maintaining positive contacts with family and friends, investing time in volunteer work, time in recreation and physical health, you will find that you recover better, faster and quicker from your loss.

This improved sense of well-being that you've earned, is not only directly rewarding but will pay off in your interview presentations. That's because you will feel better about yourself, and are a better person, with all you've accomplished. You will look better in an interview to an employer.

An Action List

Don't know what to do? Here's a starter list for *you*:
• Job Seeking
   • Visit public Workforce Investment Act sites
   • Visit private employment services
   • Research using O*NET, My Next Move, and the Department of Labor's Occupational Outlook Handbook
   • Prepare a great resume
   • Prepare a wonderful letter of introduction (Cover Letter)
   • Prepare a Source File and Job Application Cheat Sheet
   • Practice interviewing
   • Research potential job alternatives

- Research potential employers
- Write a generic thank you letter
- Informational interviewing
- Volunteer Work
  - VA
  - Feed the hungry
  - Clean water
  - Political campaigns
  - Multi-cultural sensitivity
  - Fight crime
  - Fight poverty
  - Help youth
  - Help senior citizens
  - Help the disabled
  - Look around you and see what needs to be done, and do it
  - Look around, what needs to be changed? Help change it.
- Exercise
- Read
- Self-help activities
- Develop and use your personal network
- Learn new things
- Meditate
- Take care of yourself, your family, your home
- Create a support group for the unemployed
- Develop a work plan and then work your plan
- Go to a community center and join in and get involved
- Go to a recreation center and join in
  - Play volleyball
  - Swim
  - Play baseball
  - Play cards
  - Knit, needlepoint, sew
  - Play chess with an oldster or youngster
  - Learn to play chess from a youngster or an oldster
- Go the library and check out books and tapes
  - Job hunting
  - Self-improvement
  - Entertainment
- Join a group
- Help a neighbor
- Write letters
- Join
  - Fraternal organizations
  - Community groups
  - Veterans groups
  - Alumni associations
- Call and visit friends and relatives.

What else can you come up with? Plenty. Write them down and do them.

Do not do the following:

- Sleep in
- Watch more television
- Play pointless video games
- Waste time "web-surfing" and on "web-porn"
- Increase your drinking, gambling, drug taking
- Be an abusive jerk
- Stewing and obsessing and being angry over the loss.

What else should you avoid? Probably a few more things. Write them down and avoid them too.

Remember that what you are going through is a shared experience. It isn't just something unique to you. Millions of people have experienced it throughout history, and are going through it just like you are now. It is something to talk about with your family and friends, but don't overwhelm them with your self-pity; instead ask them to talk about other things, the things you used to talk about. The next time they ask, "What have you been doing?" tell them and smile while do.ing so.

Chapter 28: Stress

"To achieve great things, two things are needed: a plan and not quite enough time." — Leonard Bernstein (1918-1990) American composer, conductor, author, lecturer, and pianist.

"If the problem can be solved why worry? If the problem cannot be solved worrying will do you no good." — Śāntideva, 8th century Buddhist Monk.

"Reality is the leading cause of stress amongst those in touch with it." — Jane Wagner (1935-) American writer, director, and producer.

Stress Defined

What is stress? Stress is tension. It is tension between two or more forces on some body, or someone. It is a natural part of our physical universe. It is part of life and can strengthen us, if incorporated properly. If not, it can temporarily or permanently damage us. Distress is when there is too much stress. Too much stress and we become distended, bent out of shape.

It is a concern for both long-term and short-term unemployed people, because not having a job is distressing. Being in the wrong job is distressing. Not having functional job and career goals can cause us distress, too. We need to be aware of the effect of stress and distress in our lives. We need to have techniques, tools, and methods of coping with it to remain healthy and have happy , productive lives.

Suppose you have a job but are miserable in it. It pays enough and the benefits are good enough. You have some friends there. You're good at what you do. Still, you are miserable. You are secure in the job. You have a family that depends on you to keep the money, and the benefits, flowing. They are a kind and loving family and you want to support them like you do.

Is this a stressful situation? Sure. Should you do something about it? Maybe. It depends on what you have in mind. How do you handle the stress of long-term job unhappiness? Does it mean changing jobs or careers? Possibly.

Suppose you have been unemployed for 15 months. Your unemployment ran out long ago but your spouse works and after you made adjustments to your spending, you are "getting by." Is that a stressful situation? Yes. Should you do something about it? Probably.

Now consider the situation where you just lost your job of 15 years. It was the second job you ever had and it was a darn good one. It paid well. You enjoyed, or tolerated the work. The benefits were great. You have a young family. Your wife is a stay-at-home mom for your three kids, two of whom are in school, one is still at home. The company closed its doors and everyone was laid off in one fell swoop. Two hundred and fifty people out of work, just like that. They were the big employer in the area and there are no jobs like that to be found. Is that stressful? Oh yeah, very. Should you do something about the stress? Definitely.

Types of Stress

Let's talk more about stress before we move on. Stress for us as people tends to be either "event driven" or chronic in nature. Short term or "acute" stress is unwelcome, and is experienced to a severe and/or intense degree. Long term stress or chronic stress is usually less intense but is extensive and is more wearing, draining and fatiguing over the long term.

Long term misery in a job, and long term unemployment are both examples of the less intense long term stressful situations. Recent job loss is an acute, painful, intensely distressful event.

The Need for Stress

Stress is not only a natural phenomenon but is a necessary component for making us stronger under ordinary circumstances.

Watch an infant as it grows into a toddler and strengthens its muscles before it learns to walk. The young infant wiggles, struggles, and squirms as it begins to acquire the muscles and coordination it will need. The baby crawls, then grasps things as it struggles to stand. They hold on and bounce up and down as the gain strength and motor control. They learn to walk by hanging onto things as supports to begin to take those first steps. Then finally, success! The baby is now a toddler. The child learns, grows and develops using the stress and tension between their muscles and gravity.

Fast forward a few years, and watch the child struggle with a set of weights. They want to be big and strong but aren't yet. They pick up a barbell or dumbbells and begin to work out. They challenge their muscles and their bodies respond. Their muscles grow in size and capability. They soon require heavier weights to continue to make progress. If they add too much weight though, they can suffer physical consequences. Perhaps their joints and tendons aren't prepared for the weight. Perhaps they aren't lifting correctly. Suddenly, something bad happens, a muscle tears, a ligament, tendon or joint fails and there is damage. An acute and distressful event.

Controllable versus Non-Controllable

Events and situations in our lives tend to fall broadly into two kinds. Things we can directly do something about and things we cannot directly do something about.

There are tragedies that occur in our lives. A flood, a fire, the death of a loved one, an automobile accident. There are good things that are stressful too, like buying a new house for one, the birth of a child for another.

These things happen. They may be repeated or not, but they are events that happen.

Other situations exist that we can do something about. An unhappy marriage can end in divorce, a separation can be resolved by reconciliation. A miserable job situation can be resolved by finding a better one.

Stress is part of our lives. Even as children we learned ways of coping with it. Perhaps we learned to take things on, be assertive, confront the challenges. Maybe we learned to withdraw and retreat from negative situations. Certainly we all found our "own little worlds" that we withdrew to and rested. We used the relaxation and recreation to restore, rejuvenate, and to recharge our batteries. We played baseball, or soccer, read science fiction or played with dolls, joined one social group or another, and all the other things that "kids do." Sometimes we just cried in our room to release the pent up emotions of the childhood traumas that afflicted us. Certainly some of what we learned or did to cope with stress was good, functional and healthy, some of it was not. Did you bully or ridicule someone else because you felt weak, insecure or bad about yourself? Not really a good response to your own stressful, bad situation.

Some of these negative ways of coping with stress we carry into our adult lives, just as we do the healthy things we learned.

We learned and developed responses to stress in our childhood. We can continue to learn new ways to cope with it, too. We've encountered and coped with stress all of our lives. What about now and how does it apply to our work or out-of-work situation?

Let's begin that discussion by realizing that we are typically always under some form of stress. It takes effort to overcome or deal with the normal, routine, activities of daily life. It would be easier to stay in bed than get up, get dressed and ready to go, then go and fight traffic and weather just to get to our job. Then we must do our job in an environment that may or may not be comfortable for us, survive it, and get home, fighting new traffic and weather conditions once again. Once home we are assailed by things gone bad with spouse, kids, parents, and what-all befalls us that evening. Life's little stresses.

Some days, all the bad things happen and yet you still pass through them, deal with them as though they were nothing. Then one day, a few minor things happen and wham, you are blowing a gasket!

How does that happen?

It is a combination of factors that cause that cataclysmic eruption. Sometimes we become aware of something "building up" inside of us. Enough little annoyances, enough little things going wrong, enough little unhappiness, and we feel the pressure building. Accompanying that and adding to it, is some reduction in the restorative aspects of our lives. We don't play as much as we should. We wait too long to take a vacation. We're not putting anything or enough back into our reserves.

Then a short while ago, one of those extra bad and sad events drained us even more. Maybe our dog died or a parent, a close uncle or even someone we "grew up with" a friend or a role model.

And now, today, someone said or did the one wrong thing that pushed us over the edge. A minor accident, hardly more than a ding and not even a real dent and we come out screaming at the "careless, stupid, moron ..." that bumped us. (Even if they were.) Our spouse says something and we "jump down their throat." Our boss says something and we've "had enough and tell them to take their job and shove it."

Yes, it has happened to most of us in one form or another. Why? Because stress is a background element in our lives and is always there. It is necessary to maintain our strength, but too much of it becomes distress, distention and damage, sometimes irreparable damage.

So, what can we do? We can self-monitor to be better prepared to recognize the signs and symptoms of distress. We can have plans in place to help insure we do things to help us cope with both event-driven and chronic stresses. We can reduce or eliminate some sources of stress. We can learn to accept some stressful events as part of life that can only be accepted with time. We can even learn to see some stressful things as things we can change our response to rather than be "stressed out" about it.

On the next two pages are two stressful checklists. The first checklist is of acute, stressful, events. The second checklist is of chronic stress-inducing events, situations and conditions. As an exercise, check the ones that have popped up in your life. (They are all in the Workbook too, along with blank spaces for you to add your own stress-inducing events and situations).

	Stressful Events (check any that have occurred in the past year)		
	Death of a spouse		Foreclosure of mortgage or loan
	Divorce		Child leaving home
	Marital separation		Outstanding personal achievement
	Death of a close family member		Spouse starts or stops work
	Personal injury or illness		Begin or end of school year
	Wedding		Revision of personal habits
	Dismissal from work		Obtaining minor loan
	Marital reconciliation		Buying a car
	Retirement		Taking a vacation
	Change in health of family member		Christmas, shopping and holidays
	Pregnancy		Minor violation of law
	Sexual difficulties		Flat tire on car
	Gain a new family member		House destroyed in a calamity
	Business readjustment		Floods
	Sudden change in financial state		Fires
	Obtaining major mortgage		Death of a pet

	Chronic, long term situations and conditions (check any that apply)		
	Marital problems		Change in working hours or conditions
	Problems with children		Change in residence
	Problems with parents		Change in schools
	Problems with co-workers		Change in recreation
	Problems with business partners		Change in church activities
	Long term business problems		Change in social activities
	Change in sleeping habits		Change in eating habits
	Imprisonment		Mental health issues
	Personal injury or illness		Recurrent car trouble
	Adjusting to marriage		Transportation problems
	Retirement		Job dissatisfaction
	Pregnancy		Too much to do
	Business readjustments		Money problems
	Change in responsibilities at work		Drug and alcohol abuse
	Problems with in-laws		Gambling addiction
	Change in living conditions		Cellphone, video game addiction
	Revision of personal habits		Problems with friends & relationships
	Problems with a boss		Problems with significant others

Some of the "events" may occur at a point in time but the repercussions continue, sometimes for only day, sometimes throughout the rest of our lives. Some of the items listed as chronic conditions may seem like they are only a point-in-time event but often that is just the start of continuing, long term problems.

Resources

Now that you have identified a number of stress inducing events and circumstances in your life, how do you cope and deal with them? What resources do you have available to you

For some events like the death of someone in your life, and the grief that accompanies it, you may benefit from individual grief counseling or from grief support groups. Sometimes we turn to our family and friends help us. Sometimes we simply have to let the wound heal with time.

You can benefit from counseling or therapy for other things, like child, parent and spouse problems, drug and alcohol abuse or other addictions. If you are having problems with issues like these, why not get help?

Are you feeling stressed? Look at your lists and see that you've checked more than just a few items, try treating your "stressful situation" as a goal-oriented, problem-solving opportunity.

Stress management problem solving

List of all the things that are causing you stress from the two checklists. Next to each item, write down what the problem is. Try sorting out the problems into two broad categories, thing you can't change and things you can. Can you prioritize the problems you can do something about? How sure are you that the things you can't change, can't be dealt with?

For example, suppose your car needs a brake job, you are having problems with a co-worker, you have a health issue that you need to follow up on and a close relative has passed away. They are all stress inducing events, which do you solve first?

What actions can you take to resolve these items promptly? You resolve to make a doctor appointment tomorrow (and do it), you make arrangement to drop your car off for a brake job (drop off on the way to work and arrange alternate transportation to and from work and the service center). You consider and decide to join a "grief therapy group" when you get your car back.

This leaves your co-worker issues. One of the simplest things you can do to resolve problems with another person is talk to them. You could write down those things and then get together and say something like "some things are bothering me between us, I figure it's part me and part you, and I don't want cause problems but I want to solve them so we're both happy." Then tell them you'd like to either read everything on your list, or have them do it, or just do it one thing at a time. At least this gives you an opportunity to "clear the air." It may turn out that they had no idea that some of that stuff was bothering you. They may get angry or defensive, it is a risk. But try to bring the conversation back to your first points: that these things are bothering you and you don't want to cause problems, but just solve them.

The other person is likely to introduce new issues into the discussion, things that are bothering them. You should expect that and accept it. It would be hard to believe only one of you isn't happy but it could happen. So, accept what they are saying and then take your two-person list of problems and see what you can do together to solve them. You don't have to solve all your problems at once. It may turn out that only a few of them are the real issues and once you solve them, things are much better between you.

It could turn out that your issues are unresolvable though. It may be time to consider parting ways with this person or changing your relationship with them. We have all walked away from people in our lives because we had to move on or move in a different or new direction in our lives. We have all had people leave us for the same reasons. There are times when you have to ask yourself if it is better to leave this person or try to make things work out better. You have to honestly examine yourself and them and their behavior to try to answer that question but it is an option, especially when the relationship is detrimental to you.

As you resolve your problems, you will increase you control over your life and that is a powerful antidote to stress.

Coping:

There are other ways of coping too. How long since you took a vacation? Went to a baseball game, a party or a concert or a museum or whatever form of entertainment it takes to make you feel good?

Don't overlook the power of a well-timed vacation, or a regular night at the movies, alone or with others. Walking daily for your physical and mental health is an inexpensive way to help keep yourself calm and deal with stress. Time alone with your thoughts can help you sort them out. It can also be a time when you don't think about your problems, or your families, or the problems with today's world.

Have you done any volunteer work? Helping others can make you feel better too.

The following are some suggestions and ideas for coping with stress.

Self awareness -- It starts with you recognizing you are feeling excess stress, distressed. How do you know when you are feeling stressed? Think about it and write it down. Document it. What are your signs?

Identify the problems -- If you're feeling distressed it is almost always more than one thing that is impacting you in a short span of time. Take a few minutes and write down as many of those things as you can Use the checklists for some ideas but don't stop there. There are probably others. Don't forget to write down things that you've had to put aside or give up for a while, the things that give you pleasure. Not having them in your life, even for a short while, is a problem because not having a pleasure, a reward, a "rest and relaxation" thing in your life is a stressor too! Can you put any of those things back in your life?

Break each problem down into its parts.

Solve the problems you can solve:
- Are there parts that you can do something about?
  - Parts you can delay?
  - Parts that are so far in the future you can forget about them for now?
- Sometimes you need to cope with stress by having an adult conversation with others. It isn't easy. Give it a try though.
- Live with some problems, by themselves they aren't a big deal.
- Live with other problems, they are big deals but not within your control to do anything about. Usually these are "facts of life" like you bought a house, or a family member passed away. Acceptance of some events as unhappy, or happy, is something we do. Consider short term counseling, grief counseling, or talking with your doctor.
- Make changes -- in yourself, your relationships, your lifestyle. Helpful Hint: It's easier to change yourself than to change someone else and changing yourself is tough enough, isn't it? Still ...

Review your successes

Reflect on what you've done. The problem solving action steps you took and the results you've achieved. Doing something is the best tonic. Is your stress level back to normal? If not, repeat and keep working on it. It's not that you failed, you're just not done yet.

More ways to reduce stress:

- Get a new job.
- Lower your expectations, take the pressure off yourself.
- Maintain emotionally supportive relationships or get some.
- Learn and practice calming techniques.
- Take up yoga.
- Listen to plain chants (Gregorian chants).
- Learn and practice relaxation training.
- Change your lifestyle.
- Exercise daily.
- Improve your eating habits.
- Drop bad habits.
- Be honest with yourself.
- Take a long walk outdoors.
- Catch your breath - step out of what's happening for a few minutes.
- Practice "calming, breathing techniques."
- Play a team sport.
- Get a massage.

- Give a massage.
- Do something about your physical health:
    - See a doctor
    - Talk to someone about your problems
    - Get advice and follow it
    - Work on it
    - Eat right
    - Get enough sleep
    - Exercise
    - Relax
- Not enough money? Trim your budget.
    - Drop cable TV.
    - Eliminate or reduce phone costs.
    - Cut out extras.
    - Use the library instead of buying books, music, etc.

Be proactive and work on reducing and eliminating excess stress. Treat stress management as an exercise in problem solving and then solve them.

Long term stress can wear us down and leaves us feeling depressed, and helpless. It can lead to serious physical health problems, including; heart disease, asthma, obesity, diabetes, headaches, depression, anxiety, accelerated aging, nausea, diarrhea, constipation, chest pains, loss of sex drive, even cause premature death and development of nervous habits, like tics, heart palpitations, nail biting, hair loss.

Don't be a victim of stress, learn to cope and deal with it. You can! Be proactive, and create your own custom-made long term stress reduction program and stick to it.

Chapter 29: Hiring Yourself

"The critical ingredient is getting off your butt and doing something. It's as simple as that. A lot of people have ideas, but there are few who decide to do something about them now. Not tomorrow. Not next week. But today. The true entrepreneur is a doer, not a dreamer." — Nolan Bushnell (1943-) Entrepreneur, founded Atari and Chuck E. Cheese's Pizza.

"If you're going through hell, keep going." — Winston Churchill (1874-1965), British prime minister and politician.

"The way to get started is to quit talking and start doing." — Walt Disney (1901-1966) co-founder, The Walt Disney Company.

"A pessimist sees the difficulty in every opportunity; an optimist sees the opportunity in every difficulty." — Winston Churchill, British Prime Minister.

Introduction:

Why not hire yourself? If no one else has snapped you up, you can always work for you You can start as small as, well, you, part time. You can do this formally or informally. Your hours can be as flexible as you want them to be.

This is a chapter on self-employment and starting your own business

Should you or shouldn't you start your own business? Yes! No! Yes and no?

What are the risks? What are the rewards? When is it the right time to start one? How do you even do it? Could _you_ start one? What kind could you start?

The answer to "should you or shouldn't you?" is maybe. There is a lot to consider about starting a business and there is no definitive answer. If someone says "you should" or "you shouldn't", you should take that advice very carefully and with a grain of salt. Other people should not make your decision for you as to whether you should or shouldn't start a business. You must make that decision. Nobody else.

People have their own agendas, biases, notions, ideas about "starting a business." They hear how many people go broke trying. They hear about friendships and marriages breaking apart because of it. They may be "risk averse" and can't imagine doing something this bold. Friends may encourage you even if they think you might fail or want you to fail. They might be so excited by your prospects that they encourage you to start it without laying a foundation for success.

You can get free advice from professionals, like the advisers with SBA and SCORE, and they can be wrong, too. They could imply you have a good concept and a good likelihood of success and be wrong. They could suggest you drop the idea as impractical and be wrong. They can also be right. That's why it is _your_ decision.

Listen to your head and your heart, when it comes to finally making the decision to start one or not.

If you have a great idea, surefire, can't miss, it's time to slow yourself down. Starting your own business is EXCITING! You can be so overwhelmed by that excitement, that you leap in without stopping to analyze the situation and make a business decision, that being whether to start it or not.

"Your own business." Think of it. No one else telling you what to do. You set your own schedule, work your own hours. And all that money you're going to make. It's a great idea. It's hard to believe no one else thought of it. Maybe it is and maybe it isn't, maybe someone else did, maybe not.

Some people do start their own business and succeed. They are everywhere. Look around and you'll see them. Do you recall the ones that used to be around and aren't?

Before we talk about the type of business you could start, or discuss reasons why you should, or even how to go about doing starting one, the best place to start is to talk about risk.

Risky Business

In business we talk about risk. It is expected that you will be rewarded for taking risk(s). We can attach numbers to it, to quantify it, before we make business decisions, financial decisions, operational decisions, and so on.

"Risk" is also how we refer to the chance something will work out or not. You've heard the expression "what's the risk?" Riskier things have more chance of failure. Low risk things have less chance of failure. That does not mean that low risk things may not fail. It does not mean that highly risky things won't succeed. It does mean there is doubt about the outcome. That "doubt about the outcome" should concern you. A lot. A whole lot.

No one starts a business expecting to fail. No one. It takes work and effort and good decision making, timing and a dose of good luck, which never hurts. Even if you put in the time, the effort, make good decisions, have good timing, and a bit of luck, you can still fail. You can do it all wrong and still succeed.

Before you even think about starting a business, think about the risk and why you would take the risk instead of getting a rewarding job and career. Think about who else is directly impacted by your risk taking, like your family.

There are three groups of people who start businesses: young people, old people, and everyone else. Funny, right? No, really, it's true, but they have different reasons for doing it and different situations to work with.

Young people often get great ideas and jump in with both feet. They take their great idea and run with it. They typically aren't "beholden" to anyone else and can take all the risk themselves. They may be over-confident and over-eager.

Older people, late in their career lives, often find it difficult to secure a job and turn to starting their own business as almost a "default" opportunity or an act of desperation. They often have a spouse to consider and are usually more cautious in their approach to getting one going. They will often "start small" and try to grow from there.

The "in-betweens," or everyone else, are people who may be tired of working for others, seeing them "make all the money" and think they can do it better. They sometimes have a really good idea and develop it while still working, gradually making a transition from working for someone else to their own business. They generally have a spouse, and kids.

These are rather broad generalizations but there were some concepts presented that you need to consider.

The first is, who suffers if you fail? What happens if you lose your life savings? What if you are left with debt and no income? Are you risking just yourself or others? Will you have time to recover if you fail? If you are young, you probably have lots of time to try and can accept the failure, learn from it and move on with your life. If you are over 55, should you take the same risk? What about the impact on your spouse and children? If you are in the "everyone else" category, who shares your risk?

Most of those who attempt to start a business are excited! Excited about their product or service. Excited about their prospects, the opportunities. Excited about the reward(s) they think, believe and expect to get. Most of them don't know enough to pull it off but some do.

Some people find the way to make it work. They make mistakes and make adjustments. They overcome their flaws and the risks and succeed. Some don't. What is the cost for failure?

Success or failure, it all comes down to you and you making the commitment to start and succeed in business, and then taking action.

If you succeed, despite the risk, the rewards can be generous and there is really no limit to what you can achieve. Just realize that most people who start one, fail. If that happens to you, you can always try again.

Starting Up

For some people, self-employment is a business form that is perfect. They have a skill or skill set that is in sufficient demand and the barriers to entry are low enough, that they can be self-employed. There are many skilled trades workers who work for someone else "by day" and for themselves at night and they gradually transition to self-employment and then develop it into a formal business. People who have "side jobs", and you probably know someone who does this, have a full time job but do odd jobs or contract jobs on the side. Maybe you have a friend who "hangs siding" on the side. Perhaps you know an accountant who does tax work on the side. These folks are self-employed and have a path into full time self-employment if they want it. Can you do the same thing with your business idea? If you can, that is an excellent way to transition before you strike out on your on. You can use this method to develop a business idea into a business even if you don't have "side job skills."

Suppose you have a great idea. It is the next hot product or a great new service. At least you think so. You can do a lot while you continue working. As they say "don't quit your day job" especially if you have others who depend on you. Instead, work on a plan to develop the product or service business plan.

Instead of asking yourself, "should I start a business?", ask yourself "what should I know in order to start a business?". The first question has no right or wrong answer. The second is a lot easier to answer and worth spending your time on, even though there is a lot to it.

One of the first questions you should ask yourself is "What do I know about business?" When we examined your potential jobs, one of the elements we discussed was "knowledge." This applies to starting a business, too. It is helpful if you have some knowledge of business, such as accounting, finance, marketing, operations, and management. You are going to be doing all of them as the owner.

Next consider what *type* of business to start. You probably have a good idea of what *kind* of business you want to start. A restaurant, a flower shop, an auto repair shop, a bookkeeping business? A pizzeria, a coffee shop, a furniture store, a robotic repair facility? A computer support service facility? A telephone supplier, a website designer, a taco stand, a food truck, a fruit and vegetable market? There is almost, and may be, no limit to the different kinds of businesses people can start and operate. The question of "type of business" though, is a legal issue with financial ramifications.

You can go into business without registering your "company" as a business. You can operate it that way. You will still owe taxes on the net income your company makes. Eventually, you do need to declare your business officially, i.e. register it with your county (or parish if you're in Louisiana) and possibly with your state.

Notice: This is not legal advice and cannot and should not be relied upon as such. You should consult with an attorney even before you start a business and if not then, before you register one. Repeat, this is not legal advice, got that?

Now then, there are several formal types of business. You can own a business as a sole proprietor. You can own a business with one or more partners in a partnership. You can form several different types of corporations, each with its own unique advantages and disadvantages, with stock holders as the owner(s), such as an LLC, a Sub-Chapter S, and a general Corporation. You can own and operate a franchise with or without partners. You can start a non-profit corporation. You cannot own a non-profit but you can be the sole employee.

There are many books on the types or forms of businesses. Resources such as the Small Business Administration (SBA) (www.sba.gov) and SCORE (Senior Core Of Retired Executives) can help you understand these forms in detail. You should see your own attorney and most definitely talk with an accountant, preferably one who seems successful. Use the internet to learn more about business types.

In a nutshell, these forms of business define who owns what, who will get to make decisions, who will get what share of any proceeds (profit or loss) from that year's work and earnings, who owes what taxes and who has what liability. Again, see an attorney to work through the details.

Here are some considerations to make in your decision making process. First, it is simplest to own and operate a sole proprietorship. You generally register these at your county clerk's office for a small fee, around $15 - $20. Call your Clerk's Office for the actual amount. The other thing you need to do is apply for Federal Identification, which provides you with your Federal Tax Identification Number or TIN. You do those two things and you've handled the minimum necessary to formally establish your business. Notice I said "formally" because you do not even have to do that much when you work for yourself. You can simply do your own record-keeping and pay taxes based on the profit or loss from your self-employment. **Notice: This is Not Legal Advice!** Talk to your own lawyer for that.

The reason that this sole proprietorship is the simplest to own and operate is that you as the owner: own it, make all the decisions, make the profit or take the loss, owe the taxes and carry the liability for your company. You can buy insurance to help limit your liability for many aspects of your business and its operations. That insurance is part of your cost of doing business. All of your costs of doing business are called "expenses" and they reduce your "revenue" (sales usually) so that what is left is "net income" (which is sometimes a loss).

Accounting for Your Success

If you do not understand the basics of bookkeeping and accounting, it would be well worth your time to take an entry level class on the subject, talk with a CPA, take an online tutorial, and learn all you can about it.

There is an accounting formula that describes your business income, Revenue - Expenses = Net Income. That's one of two important accounting concepts. The other is Assets - Liabilities = Owners Equity. The first formula basically tells you how to keep track of how much money you are making during a period of time. Typically you want to know this by the month and by the fiscal year (a legal year of business, which doesn't necessarily coincide with a calendar year). The second formula states who owns how much of your business, you (Owner's Equity) or your creditors (Liabilities).

It gets very complicated after that. That's why you need to find an accountant who is good and with whom you are comfortable. Let them work with you to help you understand the income formula. They might help you set up your books. You could also purchase a program, like QuickBooks (this is not a recommendation, there are others out there). Set up a test company on whatever program you choose and pretend you are buying and selling stuff. You will get the hang of it or you won't. Work with a bookkeeper or an accountant to help you set up and get the hang of recording what goes where, or to do it for you if you find you can't or don't want to do it yourself.

This is real important, this whole bookkeeping and accounting aspect to owning your business. Real important. Why? First, it gives you the information you need to pay your taxes. Second, when it is done right, it helps you make sound business decisions. Third, as you grow, you may need financing, as from a bank and good record-keeping will help you to know when you should get financing and help you obtain it.

That first item, "pay taxes," is a big area you should be concerned with and again your accountant will help you with this. As a sole proprietor it is your responsibility to know what taxes you are liable for and when to pay them and how much to pay. It is not your accountant's responsibility but they will help you. It is not the government's responsibility, but they will be glad to accept your payments and do what government's do when you don't pay them, even if you didn't know you owed them!

That's right, you may owe taxes you don't even know about! As a private citizen, you should know about paying your personal income tax. As a sole proprietor, your business proceeds are taxable to you as income (or deductible as a loss). However you could also owe other taxes, like diesel taxes, use taxes, personal property taxes, and payroll taxes (Federal Income Tax (withholding), Social Security, Medicare, and Federal Unemployment Taxes (FUTA)) and more! Whoa, that got complicated fast, didn't it? You might, and probably will, have state taxes as part of the picture, too.

Did I mention, see your accountant? The whole tax concept is tricky and a normal part of business is avoiding, not evading them. Make sure you have a good accountant to work with. If your company grows big enough, hire the best one you can find, they are worth it. Again, not legal advice, just a business suggestion.

As long as we're looking at your business and its initial design, we should look at whether you need to operate as an "official" business or not. You can be self-employed, work, earn money, keep records and not register as a business. Or you can register as an official business. Either way, you will be expected to pay taxes. You will be subject to income tax on your earnings. You also have to add in payments to Social Security, and Medicare, plus state income taxes. You can deduct all of your legitimate business expenses either way. So, what's the difference? Why register as a business?

Sole Proprietor

What's the difference between being self-employed and owning a business? Usually, "self-employed" means you work for yourself. You might have a "helper," but that's about it. If you operate a business, you will typically have others working for you. Another difference is that if you are self-employed, you do not have a company "name." If you start a business, you get to name it. Naming your business creates an image that is very different from "self-employed." You could do the same work for the same income but having a business name creates a new entity and a new image for you to use.

Among the first things you do when you elect to officially register your business, is complete the form that lets you identify your business name, "doing business as." You can take that form to the bank and get a checking account in the company name. You can apply for your Federal Taxpayer Identification Number. You are in business!

Either way, self-employed or registered business, if you decide to expand your business and hire people, there are different ways you can go about it. You can hire people as independent sub-contractors. You can hire people part time and you can hire them full time. You get to decide what you are going to pay them and what they to do for the pay. You can even decide how long they will work for you. That is all dependent on them agreeing to it, of course.

Be very careful about who you plan to hire as a subcontractor. It is outside the scope of this book to try to define who is and who isn't a subcontractor. Ask your attorney and or your accountant for clear, current information.

Your major benefit of hiring a subcontractor is that you can issue them a "1099" at the end of the year, and indicate what you paid them. No need to withhold taxes for them. No need to pay for overtime (unless it's in a contract you sign with them). No other employer-employee employment laws will enter the picture. Again, **this is not legal advice**, seek a lawyer for their opinion and advice. You can also speak with an accountant as they deal with these distinctions too. Be sure to ask them about the having the sub-contractor provide their own insurance coverage for any work hazards or damages they may encounter or the cause.

If you do plan to use someone for say, 20 hours per week, on a routine basis and you define their hours and their work, you've pretty well hired yourself an employee. Now that they work for you, you have obligations. You must withhold from their pay their contributions to Federal Income Taxes, Social Security (FICA) and Medicare *as well as your own obligations for them*. You will likely want insurance to protect them on the job, and to protect you, your business and your customers. The reason you are hiring them is because you cannot do all the work that needs to be done, so you need someone to help. Part of your cost is not just their wage but their benefits. You may offer as little in the way of benefits as possible but there are some like Medicare, that you have to provide. They pay a share and you pay a share. On the other hand, you hired them to do work you can't do, so you should find you make more money by hiring them than it costs you. It works out.

It is simpler if you are going to hire employees, even one part-timer, if you have formed and registered as a business. It is easy to do and doesn't cost much. When it is time to start buying business insurance, or paying payroll taxes, it is easier and simpler to do it when you are a registered business.

Multiple Partners

Life is more complicated when you have partners, though it is often necessary if none of you can or wants to start the business alone. Two or more people will be sharing risk, doing the work, making the decisions, and sharing in the rewards.

The best advice is to be careful, many friendships end over becoming business partners. Seek legal counsel. Seek financial counsel. Seek business advice.

Warning: if your partner makes deals, takes out loans, etc. in the "name of the business", your partner is putting you at risk and if they "disappear" you could be responsible for the debt they rung up. Again, **this is not legal advice**, see a lawyer or attorney for legal advice.

That may seem a little extreme but the reality of a partnership is that it can be and usually is, a very difficult business type to enter into and then to be successful. The best of friends, the closest of relatives, have a great deal of difficulty working together as business partners. You should consider working with a lawyer to create a legal contract and define who is responsible for what, who does what when, who makes which decision, who gets what rewards for what work and then make the contract "recognizable in court."

Why? Although some people who take the time and effort to do this still end up in court, a good agreement can ward off many potential interpersonal conflicts that would end up there. Lots of people who don't take the time and effort to set up a "partnership agreement," as these contracts are called, end up in court and one partner or the other gets a lot less or a lot more than they bargained for.

Yes, the reality is that many partnerships don't work out, even when the business succeeds! Many things that can go wrong. Suppose you look at the work you are doing and the work your partner is doing. Your partner want half the money that is coming in, after expenses, but you don't think they've earned their half. How will you resolve that or what could you have done to avoid it?

Your partner wants to re-invest a percentage of this quarter's (three months) net income back into the business, you want to just split it because you need the income and they don't because their spouse is working.

You bought a new computer without consulting with your partner. They went out and bought a TV and game console for the office. You don't like talking to customers, your partner does. You do the work that is coming in, but, in your opinion, they aren't marketing enough and bringing in enough business,. They think you can't keep up already. They brought their dog to work, you think there's no place for the dog in the office.They bought a car by taking out a loan through the company and didn't talk to you about it. They expected you to do their job when they had to go away for a week. You don't even know how to do it. They didn't seem to care enough about the customers. They didn't seem to know how to sell and bring in more business.

You realize you're type "A" and they're type "Lay-Z." They disappeared with the money in the bank and you're left holding the bag for debts and a legal judgment that you just found out about.

There are many horror stories about business partnerships. A contract that spells out who does what, who makes which kind of decisions, etc. helps you get through those difficulties.

Even when you are both bright, caring, mature individuals, little things can make it difficult to work together. Try talking things out. Try to envision all the things that will likely happen in your day-to-day business and then how you want those things handled. Communicate your concerns.

Two or more partners? You can have as many partners in your co-partnerships as you want. More partners make things more complex in some ways but simplifies some things too. With an odd number of partners, you can always "take a vote and let the majority win." Usually more partners means the work is more divided up and more clearly structured. Again, a partnership agreement is a great way to handle and prevent many business problems that are owner problems rather than the business' problem.

You and your partner(s) can work out your own "partnership agreement," but you should seriously consider enlisting an attorney to assist you in creating it. They have experience and knowledge that you don't and they can help ensure that you cover issues and concerns that you may overlook. One more time: **This is not legal advice**.

Corporations

Creating a corporation is more difficult, time consuming, and truly something you want to get professional help to create. The new corporation has its own legal standing, and offers advantages to the stockholders that a proprietorship does not. It is outside the scope of this book to provide more information and insight on forming corporations. One thing that can be stated is that funds can be raised by selling shares (of ownership) and so it is a way to start a bigger company quicker than might be done by an individual or by a partnership.

The remaining basic type of business is that of a non-profit corporation. Again, just as with any corporate form, you should seek both legal and accounting help in creating the new entity. One strikingly different feature of a non-profit company is that no one owns it, it owns its own self. In a "for-profit" corporation, one person can own it if they own all the stock. Two people can each own half the stock of a "for-profit" corporation. No one can own the stock of a non-profit corporation; it owns itself. There is no net income in a non-profit and therefore it is "exempt" from paying taxes on earnings. As long as all the rules are followed, of course.

So, why would you start a non-profit if you are not going to make any money doing so? Non-profit corporations make money, not profit. They are usually started by someone to do something of socially redeeming value and not for "the money." You can be the principal employee of a non-profit, that you start, and direct how the funds earned are to be spent.

Other business types

There are other types of businesses you can start or buy into as well: co-operatives and franchises to name two. You should take time to do research into starting your own company to determine the right type for you. Learn all your options and what the impact of making those choices is likely to be. Your local library can help provide you with this information, as can the SBA and SCORE, and lawyers and accountants. If you won't put effort into this part of starting a business, you should realize this is an indicator that you should not do it.

Are you business ready?

What do you know about the business you plan to go into? Do you have a business plan? There are countless stories about people who had a little money to invest in a business they knew something about and then went broke trying.

Do you know who will or would be likely to buy your product or service? Where will you locate your product or service? What will it cost to start your business? What will it cost to operate it for six months?

Do you know the difference between fixed and variable expenses?

Let's say you want to start a company that is going to require a good location in a storefront. How much will that storefront cost you to rent? How long a lease must you sign or commit to? If it is $1,000 per month for a two-year lease, you are committing $24,000 just to have a place to do your business. How much of your product or your service will you have to sell to make a $1,000 per month? If it was a pizza business, and you sell your pizza for $15 each and $5 of that was variable cost (the cost of creating the pizza), then you would have a contribution of $10 per pizza. At that rate, you would only have to sell 100 pizzas ($1,000/$10).

The storefront is overhead and a fixed cost. You also will have to buy (or lease) some equipment (fixed cost) and probably have to make payments on it. Add that to your fixed cost stack.

You want to try to identify your fixed costs because they represent your costs even if you make no sale, not one penny in revenue. That's big. Of course, you plan to make sales. Sales of what, at what price? Your price has to include covering the direct cost of the sale. For a pizza, it is the cost of the ingredients. You can put your labor, as a sole proprietor with no employees, out of the picture for now. You'll get your money as net income. You do want net income don't you?

How about the sales side of the picture. Even if you get the cost stuff right, you can easily fail if you don't handle the sales side. This is often referred to as marketing. It is more difficult to find good marketing help than say accounting or legal help. In part this is because although there are marketers out there, they are not as defined a group as accountants or lawyers.

Even if you do find a marketer, they are more likely to want to do your marketing, which is beneficial to you but it is a cost that you may not be prepared to bear that early in your project. Still, it can't hurt to locate and talk to one or more. You might consider going to the closest business school in your area and seeing if you can meet with someone, an educator, who might be able to help you figure out who your customers might be and estimate the size of the market for your product.

This can work but what if your product or service is new or unique. You might not be able to get a good handle on this aspect.

Let's suppose you had a new product, and without you knowing it, you could sell 1,000 of them a week at $20 each. Your task is to try to find out how many you could sell per week at $20 if that represented a fair price and covered your variable costs, fixed costs and left a profit.

Sometimes when you start to look at it, you begin to realize that you have a good or a bad shot at success with the product. For example, if you do some math of your fixed costs plus your variable costs and decided that 15 percent should be left over to put into growth and profit, and that all of that resulted in you needing to sell one "Whatsis" at $1,000,000 per unit per year, should you go for it? Maybe. What if you could make and sell five or ten a year. You'd do well, probably. What if you didn't sell one?

What if you needed to sell a million "Whatsis" at $1 each, should you go for it? Again, maybe. What if there was only a market for 500,000 units at best. You lose. But if there was a market for 3,000,000 you'd be doing well, probably.

The idea here is that you need to have some idea of what your cost to produce "Whatsis" is, some idea of what you can sell them for, and how many of them you can expect to sell.

Did that all sound confusing or complicated to you? Especially because all you want to do is sell cupcakes, or ice cream or pizza. What we're getting at here is, you need to know, or should know, or should want to know, things about business before you start up yours running on your enthusiasm and money, alone. Get with an accountant can help you identify your costs. Some research online can help. Read a book or two. Get free help from government organizations. Get all the help you can. Or you can just jump in and open your restaurant and hope you picked the right location, make good food at the right price and build your market.

One more thought to consider is, how easy are you making it for yourself to get out of the business you got into, no matter what form your business takes or what happens.

Should you own a business?

Here are some of the traits or characteristics of successful business starters, entrepreneurs. Ask yourself, "Is this me?". Try to be honest since your future and that of your family depends on it.

Self-motivated -- Do I really want to do this? Will I push myself to overcome setbacks, barriers and obstacles? Am I motivated?

Persistent -- Will I keep at it? Will I keep at it through the hard times?

Creative -- Can I solve problems I've never seen before? Do I know when to get help and be willing to get it?

Risk taker -- How big a chance am I taking, for myself and my family? Will I get cold feet?

Independent -- Can I control myself and my business?

Flexible -- How quickly can I "read the writing on the wall" and make adjustments?

Realistic -- Do I have a practical plan?

Pressure -- Can I take it, if it is all on me, because it will be?

If your answers to those questions about yourself, are "yep," "sure," "I can do it!" then good luck to you. A couple of other points for you to ponder: Nearly half of all new businesses fail in the first five years, ninety percent within ten.

There is no patented guaranteed way of starting and succeeding in business. Yet thousands if not millions of people own their own businesses worldwide and succeed. You can too.

Some people begin very small, doing "odd jobs" for friends and family. Maybe you make pies, or have handyman skills, or know how to prepare taxes. As you do these for a few people, word spreads and you pick up more jobs. Perhaps you decide you can cut grass, pull weeds, use an edger, a weed whacker and a leaf blower, so you decide to knock on doors, maybe create a flier and distribute them in your neighborhood. These are some of the ways people have turned a set of skills into full-time work.

Some of the large fruit markets we see around us today started out as "peddler's carts" years ago. Literally. One man got up early and went down to the commercial warehouse, picked out a selection of fruit and vegetables and toted them back to his cart and stood on a street corner and sold his produce. As he flourished, he added a truck that roamed through our neighborhoods. He grew and saved until he could get his first permanent stand, a small storefront and grew and grew.

There is nothing wrong with starting small and growing a business. We wish you all the success you deserve if you start one this way and succeed. Good luck to you.

Appendices

Appendix A: The O*NET Content Model

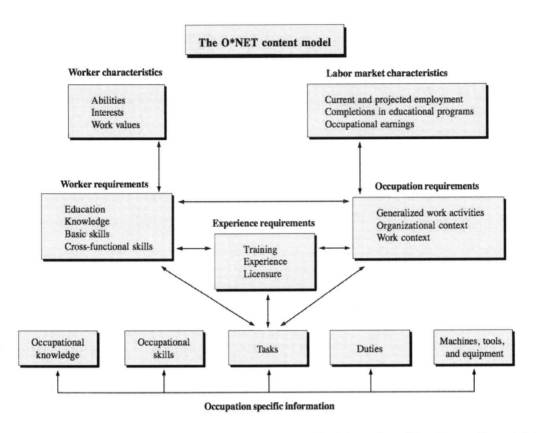

U. S. Department of Labor, Employment and Training Administration, "Replace with a database: O*NET replaces the Dictionary of Occupational Titles", Occupational Outlook Quarterly, March 1999 (web address: http://www.bls.gov/careeroutlook/1999/home.htm).

Appendix B: Informational Interviewing

"Set the Stage" letters

Example 1:

Michael T. McMurray, Sales Manager
MedRed, Inc
1234 Fifth Street
Fiction City, MI 48999

Dear Mr. McMurray;

I am writing to you because of my interest in the development of new markets for medical devices. My research revealed that MedRed is an international leader in creating new markets for medical devices and that you are a key individual in their success.

I am sure you have a very busy schedule but I would like to arrange a brief meeting with you to discuss your personal growth and development to become the leader you are. I can meet with you at any time that would be convenient for you.

I plan to call you on Tuesday, between 1:00 pm and 2:00 pm, to make arrangements with you or you may feel free to call me at 555-333-2424 anytime.

Thank you so very much and I look forward to meeting you.

Sincerely

James Jeffries

Example 2:

Lee Atwood, Manager
Televideo Productions
47 South Main Street
Wet Lake, MI 48999

Dear Ms. Atwood;

I am writing to you because of my interest in the production of Graphic Novel narratives. I have been watching Televideo Productions as far back as I can recall and enjoyed nearly all of your Graphic Novel Adaptations. I know that you are a key individual in their production.

I am sure you have a very busy schedule but I would like to arrange a brief meeting with you to discuss how you got to the position you are in as manager with Televideo. I can meet with you at any time that would be convenient for you.

I plan to call you on Thursday, between 10:00 am and 11:00 am, to make arrangements with you or you may feel free to call me at 555-333-2424 anytime.

Thank you so very much and I look forward to meeting you.

Sincerely

Louise Burton

Example 3:

Ms. Virginia McGraw, Vice President
Professional Accounting Services
1600 Park Place
W. Bloomfield, MI 48999

Dear Ms. McGraw;

I am writing to you because of my interest in corporate mergers and acquisitions. I have been in contact with Judy Jones who suggested I talk with you as you are the most knowledgeable and successful strategist she knows.

Ms. Jones told me you have a very busy schedule, but that you might be willing to talk with me because of our shared commitment to children. I would like to arrange a brief meeting with you to discuss your career development and rise to your position. I can meet with you at any time that would be convenient for you. We can also talk about the Challenge the Community for Children program I lead too.

I plan to call you on Wednesday, between 4:00 p.m. and 5:00 p.m., to make arrangements with you or you may feel free to call me at 555-333-2424 anytime.

Thank you so very much and I look forward to meeting you.

Sincerely

Malcolm Williams

"Set the Stage" Telephone Scripts

Example 1:

You: "Good morning, my name is Sandy Hills, and I'm calling to speak to Ms. Detloff. She's expecting my call."

Them: "I'll connect you," "This is Ms. Detloff."

You: "Good afternoon Ms. Detloff, this is Sandy Hills, I wrote to you a few days ago to tell you I'd call you now and request a brief interview with you. Did you have a chance to read my letter?"

Ms. D: "Yes, I did and I'd be happy to meet with you. Can you be here tomorrow at 2:00 p.m.?"

You: "Yes I can absolutely be there at 2 o'clock. Thank you very much for being willing to talk with me. I look forward to learning from you."

Ms. D: "You're welcome and I'll see you tomorrow then. Good-bye"

You: "Good-bye."

Example 2:

You: "Good morning, my name is Benjamin Barthold, and I'm calling to speak to Mr. Seals. He's expecting my call."

Them: "I'll connect you," "This is Jim Seals, sorry I can't take your call, please leave your name and number and a brief message and I'll call you just as soon as I can."

You: "Good afternoon Mr. Seals, this is Benjamin Barthold, I wrote to you a few days ago to tell you I'd call you now and request a brief interview with you. Did you have a chance to read my letter? I hope that you have and that you will call me back as soon as is convenient for you. My number is 555-888-2233. Thank you very much."

He calls back later:

You: "Hello"

Mr. Seals: "This is Jim Seals and I'm returning your phone call. I did receive and read your letter and thank you for your kind comments. I'd be happy to meet with you. Can you be here Friday at 10:00 am?"

You: "Yes I can absolutely be there at 10 o'clock. Thank you very much for being willing to talk with me. I look forward to learning from you and thank you for calling me back. I do appreciate it."

Mr. Seals: "You're welcome and I'll see you tomorrow then. Good-bye"

You: "Good-bye."

Example 3:

You: "Good morning, my name is Michelle Thompson, and I'm calling to speak to Mr. Jones. He's expecting my call."

Them: "I'll connect you," "This is Bob Jones."

You: "Good afternoon Mr. Jones, this is Michelle Thompson, I wrote to you a few days ago to tell you I'd call you now and request a brief interview with you. Did you have a chance to read my letter? When will you be able to meet with me?"

Mr. Jones: "I did not receive your letter (or did not have a chance to read it). Can you tell me what this is about?"

You: "Yes I can. I wrote to ask you if I can arrange a brief interview with you because you are a recognized leader in drone technology and I'm completing a program in micro-electronics. I'd like to learn from you and how you've become the leader in drone technology. Would you be willing to meet with me?"

Mr. Jones: "I don't know, couldn't you just ask me your questions now?"

You: "I could ask you a few questions now but I'd really like a chance to meet you as well as talk with you. I won't take long I promise. Please?"

Mr. Jones: "Oh all right, when do you want to meet?"

You: "When is a good time for you? Mornings, afternoons? I am flexible. After all you are doing me the favor."

Mr. Jones: "Well, anytime after 4 is best for me. How's Monday or Tuesday look for you?"

You: "Monday would be perfect Mr. Jones. I will plan on being there at 4 o'clock. Is that good for you?"

Mr. Jones: "Monday at 4 it is. I look forward to seeing you then. What did you say your name was again?"

You: "Michelle Thompson and you should have a letter from me there somewhere, too. Thank you again for being willing to meet with me, I'll see you Monday. Good-bye."

Mr. Jones: "I'll see you then and I'll look for your letter in the meantime."

Appendix C: My Marketing Plan

Unique Selling Proposition (25 words or less): _____

_____

_____

_____

_____

Phase 1: Preparation

Goals:

1. Personally rewarding factors:
   1. _____
   2. _____
   3. _____
   4. _____

2. Job Targets
   1. Target 1: _____
      1. Requirements for that job at your current Job Zone level:
         1. Knowledge:
            1. Knowledge required:

               _____

               _____

            2. Your knowledge and where did you acquire it:

               _____

               _____

         2. Skills
            1. Skills required:

               _____

               _____

            2. Your skills:

               _____

               _____

         3. Abilities
            1. Abilities required:

               _____

               _____

            2. Your abilities:

               _____

               _____

         4. Personality
            1. Personality factors involved:

               _____

               _____

            2. Your personality factors:

               _____

               _____

         5. Technology

1. Technology involved:

   _____
   _____

2. Technology you possess:

   _____
   _____

6. Education
   1. Educational requirements:

      _____
      _____

   2. Your education:

      _____
      _____

2. Target 2: _____
   1. Requirements for that job at your current Job Zone level:
      1. Knowledge:
         1. Knowledge required:

            _____
            _____

         2. Your knowledge and where did you acquire it:

            _____
            _____

      2. Skills
         1. Skills required:

            _____
            _____

         2. Your skills:

            _____
            _____

      3. Abilities
         1. Abilities required:

            _____
            _____

         2. Your abilities:

            _____
            _____

      4. Personality
         1. Personality factors involved:

            _____
            _____

         2. Your personality factors:

            _____
            _____

      5. Technology
         1. Technology involved:

            _____
            _____

    2. Technology you possess:

    _____
    _____

6. Education

    1. Educational requirements:

    _____
    _____

    2. Your education:

    _____
    _____
    _____

3. Target 3:_____

    1. Requirements for that job at your current Job Zone level:

        1. Knowledge:

            1. Knowledge required:

            _____
            _____

            2. Your knowledge and where did you acquire it:

            _____
            _____

        2. Skills

            1. Skills required:

            _____
            _____

            2. Your skills:

            _____
            _____

        3. Abilities

            1. Abilities required:

            _____
            _____

            2. Your abilities:

            _____
            _____

        4. Personality

            1. Personality factors involved:

            _____
            _____

            2. Your personality factors:

            _____
            _____

        5. Technology

            1. Technology involved:

            _____
            _____

            2. Technology you possess:

            _____
            _____

6. Education

1. Educational requirements:

_____

_____

2. Your education:

_____

_____

_____

4. Target 4: _____
   1. Requirements for that job at your current Job Zone level:
      1. Knowledge:
         1. Knowledge required:

            _____
            _____

         2. Your knowledge and where did you acquire it:

            _____
            _____

      2. Skills
         1. Skills required:

            _____
            _____

         2. Your skills:

            _____
            _____

      3. Abilities
         1. Abilities required:

            _____
            _____

         2. Your abilities:

            _____
            _____

      4. Personality
         1. Personality factors involved:

            _____
            _____

         2. Your personality factors:

            _____
            _____

      5. Technology
         1. Technology involved:

            _____
            _____

         2. Technology you possess:

            _____
            _____

      6. Education
         1. Educational requirements:

            _____
            _____

         2. Your education:

            _____
            _____

2. Where do you want to live? _____
   a. Are you willing to re-locate? _____

b. How far from home are you willing to travel? _____

c. How much are you willing to travel away from home for the job? _____

3. What kind of company do you want to work for?
    3. Your prioritized preferences
        1. First choice: _____
        2. Second: _____
        3. Third: _____

4. How much am I willing to work for? _____

5. Pre-search Preparation:
    1. Resumes Prepared (and error free): Generic, Chronological, Functional.
        1. Generic: Yes/No
        2. Chronological: Yes/No
        3. Functional: Yes/No

1. References
    a. Reference 1: _____
    b. Reference 2: _____
    c. Reference 3: _____
    d. Reference 4: _____
    e. Reference 5: _____
    f. Reference 6: _____

2. Cover letter, do you have one you are comfortable with to use as a model? Yes/No

3. Commercial - your Unique Selling Proposition.

4. Phone Preparation. Phone response record pad

5. Online Preparation
    a. Social media presence reviewed? Acceptable? Yes/No
    b. Email address (Don't forget to check your spam folder)? Yes/No

6. Tracking System. Some sort of calendar system that works for you, ready? Yes/No

7. Documentation all prepared?
    1. Letters of Reference. Yes/No
    2. Training Certificates. Yes/No
    3. Diplomas. Yes/No
    4. Driver's License. Yes/No
    5. Proof of Insurance. Yes/No
    6. Trade Certification. Yes/No
    7. If you are going to be asked to "prove it," do you have proof? Some applications will require you to arrange to have it sent directly, like college diplomas. Do you have the address to contact to make those arrangements? If not, get it. Prepare, remember?

1. Interviews. Practiced, comfortable? Yes/No

2. Job leads and contacts:
   a. List of potential employers of interest
   b. Job Postings/Recruitment Advertising
   c. Job Fairs
   d. Cold Calls
   e. Using Your Network
   f. Job-hunting on the Web
   g. University Career Centers Job Postings(they aren't limited to students as a rule)
   h. Alumni Offices of schools if you went there
   i. Headhunters & Recruiters at Executive Search Firms
   j. Public & Private /Employment Agencies

Phase 2: Action

Nothing is accomplished without action being taken. Nothing. You have to activate your plan. Use it to guide your actions. Review this list frequently!

1. Apply for jobs.
   a. Vary your approach
   b. Start with your target list
   c. Do it!
   d. Keep track of where and when you applied.
   e. On applications, follow the directions completely.
   f. Organize your job hunting for efficiency.
   g. Try to engage the hiring manager.
   h. How did you get each interview?
   i. How did you handle any telephone interviews?
   j. Did you rehearse telephone interviews?
   k. Did you being your "cheat sheet" with you to make filling out an application easier?

2. Interviews.
   a. Dressed "right"
   b. Brought supporting materials (resumes, references, copies of transcripts, certifications, etc.)?
   c. Used Interview Checklist?
   d. Prepared, practiced, have USP, STARs, and ready for tough, embarrassing questions.
   e. Relaxed yet eager for the opportunity?

3. Post Interview:
   a. Sent a hand-signed thank you letter or note.
   b. Followed up as you committed?
   c. Called back and re-pitched.
   d. If offered job, prepared to negotiate?
   e. If job obtained, informed and thanked everyone who helped.

Remember to Evaluate Daily, Weekly and Monthly.

Strengths, Weaknesses, Opportunities, Threats (SWOT) Analysis:

As a person and as an employee:
My strengths: _____

_____

_____

_____

_____

_____

My weaknesses are: _____

_____

_____

_____

My opportunities are: _____

_____

_____

_____

My threats are: _____

_____

_____

_____

Appendix D: Sample Resumes

There are five examples of chronological resumes, followed by five examples of functional resumes. Feel free to use these as models and adapt them for your own use.

Mary A. Lamb
1624 Wilson, Macomb, MI 48043
(555) 456-8765, ma.lamb@somenet.net

Job Objective
Customer Service Representative for a major bank, lending, or financial institution, using leadership, financial and inter-personal skills.

Summary of Qualifications
- Adept in financial transactions.
- Proficient in the use of computers and other office equipment.
- Trained in Microsoft Word, Access, Excel.
- Excellent written and oral skills.

Professional Experience

Bookkeeper/Administrative Assistant, Johnson Construction, Chesterfield, MI, 2004 - present
- Maintained company financial records.
- Managed accounts receivable, payables, payroll and invoicing.
- Produce monthly, quarterly, and annual financial reports.
- Periodically handled telephone order desk, inside and outside sales.
- Operate and upgrade computerized bookkeeping system

Lead Sales Associate, Hometown Department Store, New Haven, MI, 1999-2004
- Provided customer service to over 200 customers daily.
- Received inventory, stocked shelves, maintained inventory records.
- Operate HP electronic register system.
- Maintained department daily closing procedures.

Bookkeeper, Herm's Lumber, Mt Clemens, MI, 1998-1999
- Maintained company financial records.
- Managed Accounts receivable, payables, payroll and invoicing.
- Prepared financial reports.
- Operate computerized bookkeeping system

Education

Associate Degree, 1998 – Macomb Community College, Warren, MI

Additional

- Financed education through part-time and summer work while maintaining 3.8/4.0 GPA.
- Fluent in Spanish
- References available upon request.

Peter Piper
10490 Fanciful Lane, Sunshine, FL 98765
cell: 555-999-3333 email: pp10490@one.net

Energetic, motivating leader. Proven ability to effectively manage personnel and projects. Self starter and strong independent worker. Excel at analyzing procedures to generate new ideas to improve efficiency and production quality. Highly adaptable and flexible. Contributing member on any team developing and executing strategic business plans.

PROFESSIONAL EXPERIENCE

ComfortYou, Inc., 2005 - present - Manager
Managed daily operations of a $15 million foam fabrication company.
Developed an effective marketing campaign and restructured product pricing/discounts resulting in an 82% bid acceptance rate.
Implemented new bidding process utilizing Excel spreadsheets to formulate more accurate bids. Spreadsheets facilitated tracking individual job costs and provided crew efficiency to control and reduce waste and labor hours.
Developed sales team's knowledge in the areas of product quality, features, benefits, flexibility and production capabilities in order to provide customers with the information to successfully plan for and utilize foam product.

United States Coast Guard Rescue Officer, 1985-2005 - Manager (2003 - 2005)
Data System Network Manager — Managed command and control data network used to generate and display video of geographic area surrounding ship. Team consisted of 48 individuals from four departments, operating 24 - 7 - 365 while deployed.
Assistant Command Duty Officer - Directed daily routine of a duty section of 600 personnel from 12 different departments.
Aviation Instructor (1997-2003)
Standardization Officer, Assistant Operations Officer, Flight Commander, Instructor Pilot, Mission Commander, Squadron Scheduler, Program Manager, Training Officer

EDUCATION AND TRAINING
MBA - Finance, University of Miami, Florida,
B.A. - Business Economics - University of Miami, Florida
Aviator - Advanced Flight Training, United States Flight Patrol
Integrated Project Team - United States Flight Patrol Project Management College

AWARDS AND COMMENDATIONS
Navy Marine Corps Commendation Medal (2), Navy Marine Corps Achievement Medal, Humanitarian Service Medal, Global War on Terrorism Service Medal

Joseph Murray
1312 Wilson, Mt Clemens, MI 48043
(555) 999-4545, jmurray@internet.net

Job Objective
Retail salesperson, using my demonstrated successful customer service skills, excellent communication and math ability.

Employment Experience

2001 - present: Product sales representative, MedRed Inc., Eastpointe, MI 48333. Handled telephone order desk, inside and outside sales, cold calls, and tracking customer orders.

1986 - 2001: Sales Associate, Metro Auto Parts, Harrison Twp, MI 48444. Assisted sales staff with parts stocking, ordering, inventory and customer service. Helped maintain a 99.9 percent inventory accuracy.

Education and Training

2001 – B.S. Marketing, Wayne State University, Detroit, MI
1999 – Associate in Business Administration, Macomb Community College, Clinton Township, MI

Skills

Customer Service, Accounting, Sales Contact Database, Public Speaking, Inventory Control

References

Betty Lou Johnson (supervisor), 234 Sycamore Lane, Mt Clemens, MI 48043, 586-555-3456
George Porgie (relative), 17751 Hamburg, Macomb Twp, MI 48046, 313-555-8822
Helen Denby (co-worker), 42445 32 Mile Road, Princeton, Mi 48222, 517-555-7823

Amy S. Black

1312 Main, Mt Clemens, MI 48043

(555) 876-4545, jlblack@internet.net

Job Objective

A sales position that will utilize my excellent, clear communication skills and organizational abilities.

Work History

2001 – present – Sales Representative, MedRed, Inc, Eastpointe, MI 48333.
- Serviced Great Lakes sales region.
- Averaged two new accounts per month.
- Increased sales revenue, over 125%.
- Periodically handled telephone order desk, inside and outside sales.

1994 - 2001 – Sales Associate, MetroMed, Harrison Twp, MI 48444.
- Provided service to customer base of 1,800 individuals.
- Managed all product requests and orders.
- Served as liaison for customers between sales and service departments.

1989 - 1993 – Student Intern, University of Michigan, Ann Arbor, MI 49333
- Assigned to local businesses to provide accounting support.
- Assigned to regional businesses to provide marketing support.

Education and Training

1996 – MBA, Wayne State University, Detroit, MI

1993 – B.S. Business Management, University of Michigan, Ann Arbor, MI

Skills

- Supplier award for largest sales increase by a salesperson in one year.
- Proficient in computerized inventory control and sales contact database.
- Trained in customer service methods.
- Skilled in public speaking.
- Trained in conflict resolution.

References

Jason Proudholm – Internship Supervisor, University of Michigan, (555) 888-4567

Martha Jones – Supervisor, MetroMed, Harrison Township, MI (555) 654-1289

Bill Wilson – Supervisor, MedRed, Eastpointe, MI (555) 987-6321

Jane Cranston
1010 Summit Place, Davison, MI 48999
(555) 222-3456 • jane.cranston@anymail.com

OBJECTIVE: obtain full time employment as Sheet Metal Worker. Over 18 years experience working in Sheet Metal Manufacturing. Sheet Metal Apprenticeship Certificate. Forklift Driver's Certification. Propane Installation Training. Bridge and Gantry Crane Certification. J.I.T. Team Concept Training. Operated CNC equipment, brake presses, punch presses, drill presses, shears, forklifts, overhead cranes, pneumatic and power tools. Read and interpreted blueprints, performed machine set-ups, and produced custom parts. Physically fit, lift heavy loads and perform repetitive tasks. Ready, willing and able to work long hours,

WORK HISTORY
1984 - 1995 – Brake Press / Set-up Operator, McDonnell Douglas Ontario, CA
Operated a brake press, produced custom parts for the aerospace industry. Frequently performed set-ups for small quantity runs. Adhered to stringent quality standards.
1995 - 2001 – Brake Press Operator, SuperSheet, Troy, MI
Operated brake press in the manufacture of electrical lighting fixtures. Read and interpreted blueprints, prioritized work orders, met specified deadlines and production standards. Pulled and loaded stainless steel on to shear for cutting using bridge crane.
2001 - 2003 – Machine Operator, AAA Tooling Industries, Madison Heights, MI
Operated punch presses in a fast-paced production facility producing parts for the automotive industry.
2003 - 2006 - Brake Press / Set up Operator, CMF Custom Metal Fabricators, Inc., Ferndale, MI
Operated brake presses, cranes, forklift trucks and other equipment. Produced stainless steel hospital equipment, formed panels for electrical cabinets, formed light fixtures from mirror finished aluminum.
2006 - 2014 – Brake Press Operator, ATS Automation Tooling Systems, Troy, Mi
Set up and operated a CNC brake press in a manufacturing environment. Produced small quantity batches for robotic machinery. Operated forklifts, transported and organized skids.

EDUCATION AND TRAINING
2006 Forklift Driver's Certificate, ATS Automation Tooling Systems, Troy, MI
2006 Propane Installation Training, ATS Automation Tooling Systems, Troy, MI
2007 Bridge Crane Certificate, ATS Automation Tooling Systems, Troy, MI
1990 J.I.T. Team Concept Training, McDonnell Douglas Canada, Ontario, CA
1984 Sheet Metal Apprenticeship Certificate, Central Technical College, Ontario, CA
(Accumulated 10,000 hours of apprenticeship training over five years). Completed Shop Practice, Blueprint Reading and Development, Trade Theory, and Math courses

References:
Supplied Upon Request

MaryAnne Jones

567 Rosewood Lane
Waterford, MI 48207
(313) 555-1212
m-a.jones@somedomain.com

OBJECTIVE

Executive Administrative position requiring demonstrated organization, customer service, communication and project management skills proven by 17 years of successful employment.

PROFILE

Motivated, personable business professional with multiple college degrees and a successful 17-year track record of business management. Talent for quickly mastering technology. Diplomatic and tactful with professionals and nonprofessionals at all levels. Accustomed to handling sensitive, confidential records. Demonstrated history of producing accurate, timely reports meeting stringent HIPAA and Managed Care and insurance guidelines.

Flexible and versatile. Poised and competent with demonstrated ability to easily transcend cultural differences. Thrive in deadline-driven environments. Excellent team-building skills.

SKILLS SUMMARY

- Project Management
- Report Preparation
- Written Correspondence

- Computer Savvy
- Customer Service
- Scheduling
- Marketing & Sales
- Team Leadership

- Insurance Billing
- Accounting/Bookkeeping
- Front-Office Operations
- Professional Presentations

PROFESSIONAL EXPERIENCE

Team Leadership:
- Directed the activities of 22 staff: 14 – Accounts Payable/Accounts Receivable, 6 – Information Technologists, 2 – Clerical.
- Represented department in administrative capacity, internally and externally; Chair and member of several inter-departmental committees.

Communication: Reports/Presentations/Technology
- Prepare complex reports for managed-care organizations and insurance companies, ensuring full compliance with HIPAA, internal and external agency requirements and tight deadlines.
- Responsible for professional correspondence to customers and vendors.
- Design and deliver series of classes for local businesses and associations, providing information on using services of Oakland Tech Services.
- Conduct small-group sessions on billing and claims submission.
- Communicate billing concepts to consumers using layman's terms to facilitate understanding.
- Rapidly learn and master many computer programs; recently completed Microsoft Advanced SQL Server certificate course.

Customer Service/Marketing/Problem Solving
- Oversee front-office operations and provide impeccable customer service:
- Develop and implement strategic operations plan for business: Launched a new managed care information system, on-time and on-budget.
- Made presentations to hospital, insurance and regulatory groups on Oakland Tech Services

Detail Mastery & Organization
Manage all aspects of day-to-day operations of Oakland Tech Service:
- Facilities maintenance and upgrades.
- Finances: accounts payable/receivable, invoicing, insurance billing, budgeting.
- Supervision of a total of 22 staff
- Compliance with all healthcare facility, HMO and insurance requirements.

EMPLOYMENT HISTORY

Oakland Tech Service -- Pontiac, MI 48999, manager, 1997 to Present
Lakeview Restaurant -- Minneapolis, MN, manager, 1994 to 1997

EDUCATION

University of Minnesota – Minneapolis, MN, MBA, 1997, GPA: 3.89/4.0
University of Minnesota – Minneapolis, MN, BA - Business Management, 1994, GPA: 3.89/4.0
Hennepin County Community College – Minneapolis, MN, Associates Degree, 1992, GP 4.0/4.0

COMPUTER SKILLS

- Microsoft Word
- Microsoft Excel
- Microsoft Access
- Microsoft PowerPoint
- Microsoft SQL Server
- Medisoft (Insurance Billing Software)

Mary Beth Johnson
132 Riverside, Mt Clemens, MI 48043
(555) 456-7777, mbj@company.net

Professional Objective
An administrative position with a social services agency that can utilize my exceptional organizational and communication skills, and involves, staff training and personnel management.

Areas of Expertise

Organization:
- Coordinate a Child Protection Service (CPS) department serving 500+ clients.
- Managed Annual budget of $400,000.
- Directed program activities of staff.

Communication:
- Presented monthly department reports to county commissioners.
- Represented CPS at state and national conventions.
- Maintained private counseling practice for 12 years.

Leadership & Training
- Supervised staff of 18 case workers.
- Led professional development program.
- Led workshops in parenting, conflict resolution, social service program management and more.
- Coordinated activities of organization with Diocesan programs and projects.

Experience:
- Associate Director, Religious Family Service, Macomb, MI, 2000 - present.
- Area Manager, CPS Department, Mt Clemens, MI, 1990 - 2000
- Counselor, private practice, Sterling Heights, MI, 1986 - 1988

Education & Licenses:
- MSW, Wayne State University
- BS, Psychology, University of Michigan
- LCSW, State of Michigan

References available upon request.

Jonathan Shaheen
9009 South 34th Street, Grand Rapids, MI 49888
(555) 912-9009, Email: JonSha@newmail.com

OBJECTIVE: A Construction Worker position using manual dexterity, knowledge of commercial construction and construction equipment to provide excellent construction services.

MAJOR QUALIFICATIONS
• Over nine years' experience working as a construction laborer
• Highly skilled and experienced in demolition
• Skilled in preparing layouts and erecting frameworks
• In depth knowledge of operating general construction equipment
• Hands-on experience in tending machines that pump grout and cement

ACCOMPLISHMENTS
• Constructed a multistory building in record time without compromising on building quality
• Trained new construction workers to use construction equipment such as cement mixers, hand tools, and laser levels.

PROFESSIONAL EXPERIENCE
August 2005 - present: BetterBilt Constructions – Grand Rapids, MI
Construction worker
• Mop, brush and spread paints and epoxy sealant
• Operate jackhammers, front end loaders, backhoes
• Position and seal structural components
• Use cement mixer, and pour and spread concrete.
• Tend various construction pumping machines

EDUCATION
2004 - Grand Rapids High School, Diploma

ADDITIONAL SKILLS
• Excellent manual dexterity
• Basic maths skills
• Ability to handle heavy material
• Ability to understand written and oral instructions
• Excellent communication and interpersonal skills

Jonathan Welch
5678 Canfield Drive, Ferndale, MI 48777
Phone: 555.123.4567, Email: jwelch@email.com

SUMMARY
I am looking to put my experience to good use in an entry-level management position in a customer service setting. I am a strong leader and plan to gain employment with a company that will benefit from my experience and passion.

EDUCATION
2004 to 2008 Oakland University, Bachelor of Science, Business Administration, Grade Point Average: 3.2

MANAGEMENT EXPERIENCE

Team Leader - Cellular Network, Warren, MI, November 2012 to December 2014
Worked as a senior sales representative for a cellular phone provider. Trained and coached new employees. Led sales strategy meetings. Consistently exceeded sales goals. Supervised store employees during periods of management absence.

Assistant Manager - Hamburger Haven, Ferndale, MI, June 2006 to August 2010
Promoted to Assistant Manager. Acted as manager in his absence. Supervised employee shifts. Made employee schedules. Conducted employee reviews. Disciplined employees as needed. Handled purchasing and accounting functions for the restaurant. Made marketing decisions. Hired and trained new employees.

CUSTOMER SERVICE EXPERIENCE

Customer Service Representative – XYZ Warehouse, Warren, MI, Oct 2010 to Oct 2012: Worked in a call center handling customer complaints. Learned to deal effectively with angry customers. Worked with management to improve call center practices.

SPECIAL SKILLS

I have experience as a leader among my peers and with those with less experience. My experience in a call center environment taught me about the processes and situations that arise in that atmosphere. I have the confidence to be able to communicate effectively with an employee or a customer. I am excellent at seeing the big picture and figuring out what needs to be done to provide the best service to the customer. I am a great motivator and enjoy encouraging others to perform their job to the best of their ability.

REFERENCES

Available upon request

Jennifer Williams
1234 Merriwether Court, Jonesville, KY 39921
Phone: 345.555.6789, Email: jwolf@email.com

SUMMARY

After years of successful employment in the sales and insurance industries, I plan to change direction into the business of medical sales. My strong sales background, and medical knowledge gained from medical claim adjusting, have prepared me for this career. I am eager to put my skills to work.

EDUCATION

Kentucky College, Louisville, KY, Degree: Marketing GPA: 3.4/4.0, 2002.

MEDICAL EXPERIENCE

Claim Representative, American Insurance, Jonesville, Kentucky, 2012 to 2014
Transferred to Claims Department. Investigated complex medical claims. Received extensive training in medical claims management. Worked with physicians and other medical practitioners to assess claimant injuries and treatment plans. Analyzed medical reports.

SALES EXPERIENCE

Agent - American Insurance, Jonesville, Kentucky, 2010 to 2012:
Sold life and hospital indemnity insurance. Consistently met and exceeded sales quotas. Made cold calls. Visited customers' homes to conduct sales presentations. Analyzed customers' existing policies and recommended products to better fit their needs. Completed applications and health questionnaires. Worked independently. Recruited and trained new sales personnel.

Sales Representative, Jonesville Paper Products, Jonesville, Kentucky, 2008 to 2010:
Sold paper products to local businesses and governmental departments. Serviced existing customers and developed new business through networking and cold calls. Obtained several new high-volume customers for the company.

Independent Consultant, American Beauty (Cosmetics), 2006 to 2008:
Sold beauty and cosmetic products as a self-employed consultant. Conducted in-home demonstrations. Recruited new consultants. Top salesperson two consecutive years.

SPECIAL SKILLS

I am a people person who easily builds rapport with all types of individuals. I can easily conform to the situation and find ways to interject my message into natural conversation. I have experience dealing with busy medical professionals and know how to speak their language. I am a driven and self-motivated individual who has proven my ability to rise above goals that are set for me.

REFERENCES: Available upon request.

Appendix E: Sample Cover Letters

There are two cover letters in this appendix. Feel free to use these as models and adapt them for your own use.

426 Strawberry Hill
Tall Oaks, MI 48343
(555) 789-5432

August 30, 20xx

Mr. Willard White
Chief Financial Officer
MedRed, Inc.
3434 Medical Road
Ann Arbor, MI 48333

Dear Mr. White;

I am writing in response to your advertisement in the Detroit Times of August 29 for an Assistant Controller. I have had seven years experience as an Accounts Receivable and Payable Clerk for a medical supply company. I have learned a great deal and would like to advance my career in a growing and challenging medical device supplier.

In my current position as A/R and A/P Clerk, at DuraMed, I have responsibility for maintaining our accounts receivable and am proud to say that our "days paid" has averaged 22 days for the past three years. Our accounts payable is maintained at a precise 28 days and has remained so, for five consecutive years. I have also had the opportunity to acquire skills in all Microsoft Office programs and use those skills in analysis and reporting.

I would welcome the opportunity to meet with you to discuss in further detail my contributions at DuraMed and my value to you at MedRed. I have enclosed my resume for your review. I will contact you on Wednesday, Sept. 3 at 9:00 am, to arrange a meeting at a time that is convenient for you. If you would prefer to contact me, I can be reached at home at (555) 789-5432 or at work at (555) 468-1234.

Thank you for your consideration and I look forward to meeting with you soon.

Sincerely
Jacob Marley
Jacob Marley

Enc: Resume

Note: This style was done by setting a tab stop at ⅝, 3½, and 5½. It is a more "old-fashioned" and traditional style.

Cassandra Austin
456 Main Street
Sometown, MI 48999
(555) 342-7968

June 3, 20xx

Ms. Lucy Benson, President
Women's World
485 State Street
Super City Park, IL 60500

Dear Ms. Benson;

At the recent Women's Work World Convention, your production manager, Jean Carter suggested that Women's World is looking for a Sales Director to replace your departing director. I believe I am an ideal candidate for that role working for *you*.

My background as Production Manager for Girl's Time magazine has prepared me for the next advancement in my career. Our magazine quadrupled in size, sales and distribution over the past five years, in part because of my work in re-structuring our production capacity and distribution channels.

I have watched Women's World flourish under your leadership for the past seven years and admire the direction you have taken the organization. It would be an honor and I would be thrilled for an opportunity to assist you in furthering your goals.

I have enclosed my resume for your review. I will contact you on Thursday at 10:00 am so that we can arrange a meeting at your convenience. Feel free to contact me if that is not a good time for you. I can be reached at my cellphone number (555) 342-7968, anytime.

Thank you for your consideration. I look forward to meeting with you soon.

Sincerely

Cassandra Austin
Cassandra Austin

enc: Resume

Appendix F: Telephone Call Log

(For calls <u>from</u> employers, you may get the information in any order, so be prepared!)

Date: _____   Time: _____

Name of Person calling: _____

Phone Number: _____

Company: _____

Job Applied for: _____

Appointment Date: _____   Time: _____

Interview location: _____

Interviewers Name: _____

Phone Number: _____

Special Directions (to the location, who to contact upon building entry):

_____

_____

_____

_____

Where to Park?: _____

_____

Special Instructions (anything I need to bring with me?): _____

_____

_____

Telephone Call Log for Calls <u>to</u> Employers

Date: _____   Time: _____

Company: _____

Name of Person Called: _____

Phone Number: _____

Reason for Calling (Spell it out before you call. Were you calling to set up an Informational Interview, following up on a job application, heard about an opening, referred by someone, other?) :

_____
_____
_____
_____

Any key points you'd like to make to support your purpose, your reason for calling:

If the person you are trying to reach wasn't available, to whom did you speak?

Name: _____
Title: _____

Outcome:

_____
_____

If you have an appointment set-up as an outcome:

Appointment Date: _____   Time: _____
Interview location: _____
Special Directions (to the location, who to contact upon building entry):

_____
_____
_____

Where to Park?: _____

_____

Special Instructions (anything I need to bring with me?): _____

_____
_____

Appendix G: Pre-Interview Checklist

Double-check the following:

- Resume - extra copy to take with, reviewed to be ready to answer questions
- Appearance
  - Hair clean and in place.
  - Men facial hair trimmed or shaven?
  - Clothes clean, pressed, and job appropriate
  - Women avoid: too much cleavage, skirt too short, too much make-up?
  - Perfume or aftershave – none
  - Piercings removed, tattoo's covered?
  - Teeth, brushed, mouth rinsed
  - Smoke (cigar, cigarette, pipe, other) - don't, do not smell of smoke, period.
  - Gum chewing – don't.
  - Fidgety
  - Shoes shined.
- Travel Plans (plan to be a wee bit early, about 15 minutes)
- Name of interviewer
- Job title and duties reviewed.
- Expect to sell to get the job (USP, STAR).

Remember employers are looking for people who:
- want to do the job
- can do the job
- are willing to do the job
- will be here, on time, reliably and dependably.
- will show up ready to work
- get along with others
- are trustworthy
- are affordable
- are worth investing in
- will stay.

- On the way in
  - Be on time (15 minutes early)
  - Smile
  - Mind your manners
    - Don't sit until invited to
    - Don't remain seated when an interviewer enters the room if they weren't there when you were brought in
      - Greet everyone with a pleasant greeting
      - Say please and thank you
  - Turn off your cell phone before you enter the building (or at least silence it)
  - Calm yourself,
  - Remind yourself to listen and answer the question asked, and slow down.

The End

I would like to thank you for reading this book. I hope you learned something useful that you can apply to your life. I wish you well on your journey through life and that you not only figure out what work will be most rewarding for you but that you go out and get it!

- Charley

96166660R00151

Made in the USA
San Bernardino, CA
18 November 2018